# THE GREEN
## Southwest
## Cookbook

### Fresh ▸ Zesty ▸ Sustainable

Janet E. Taylor

RIO NUEVO
PUBLISHERS

*To all the local sustainable farmers and ranchers
and to those who support them by bringing healthy
sustainable foods to their tables.*

Rio Nuevo Publishers®

P.O. Box 5250, Tucson, Arizona 85703-0250

(520) 623-9558, www.rionuevo.com

Text copyright © 2012 by Janet Taylor.

Photos by Robin Stancliff copyright © 2012 by Rio Nuevo Publishers, except as noted below.

Other photo credits:

Victor Beer, pages 111, 118, 164

Canyon Ranch, page 18

Lodge on the Desert, page 19

Queen Creek Olive Mill, page 171

Agustin Taylor, page 188

Sally Thomson, page 107

Walking J Farm, page 127

Design: Jamison Spittler, Jamison Design.

Printed in China.

10 9 8 7 6 5 4 3 2 1

Library of Congress Cataloging-in-Publication Data

Taylor, Janet E.

  The green Southwest cookbook : fresh, zesty, sustainable / by Janet E. Taylor.

    p. cm.

  Includes index.

  ISBN 978-1-933855-52-3 (pbk. : alk. paper) -- ISBN 1-933855-52-5 (pbk. : alk. paper)

1.  Cooking, American--Southwestern style. 2.  Cooking (Natural foods) 3.  Cookbooks.  I. Title.

TX715.2.S69T375 2012

641.5973--dc23

2012005313

# CONTENTS

*Hibiscus Tea Margarita (recipe on page 34).*

# INTRODUCTION

In 1971 **Agustin and I** married and took off for Tucson. I taught at the Southwest Indian Youth Center on Mount Lemmon, where I met Henry, an instructional aide, who became my friend. We worked together and often ate food that was completely foreign to me, such as bean and nopalito burritos. I learned a lot from him about vegetarianism and the importance of eating whole grains, seeds, nuts, beans, fruits, and vegetables. He also influenced our decision to join the Food Conspiracy (a health-food-oriented and socially conscious food co-op offering locally grown, chemical-free, and organic foods). My duty as a member was typing and then printing the newsletter on a mimeograph machine.

Being involved at the Food Conspiracy helped me become a more conscious food consumer. It immersed me in an environment of healthy eating, surrounded by people who were also very mindful of what was environmentally friendly. I left behind the hamburger joints and Jack in the Box tacos from my days living in the Midwest.

Another change in our lives arrived in 1974 with the birth of our daughter Elicia, who was diagnosed with high cholesterol at birth. Since my husband's family has a history of cardiovascular disease, I was on a mission to find out what could be done to cut his and her risk of succumbing to the disease later in life. I dove deep into the vast sea of conflicting nutrition science.

In my search for a cardio-healthy diet, I came across the mid-twentieth-century Seven Countries Study, headed by Ancel Keys, in which he concluded that cholesterol levels could predict the risk of heart disease and that these levels have a direct relationship to the amount of saturated fat (from meat, poultry, and dairy) in the diet and that monounsaturated fat is heart-protective. However, most intriguing was learning about the culture and makeup of the traditional diet of isolated rural villagers in central and eastern Crete, Greece. Cretans had some of the lowest percentages of heart disease and various forms of cancer in the world and were among the longest living at that time. It made sense to take a serious look at their time-tested traditional diet and lifestyle. I had already reduced the amount of fat in our diet and was looking for what else they were doing that I wasn't.

This rural culture's way of the land and diet had common threads with that of their ancestors of the prior couple thousand years. They ate what their land produced—an abundance of a variety of plants and a little meat and dairy from sheep and goats, and meat and eggs from chickens that foraged on the land. From this bounty they were able to enjoy deliciously wholesome meals made with the freshest ingredients, and void of processed foods.

Their diet of the 1950s centered on plants—legumes and fresh beans, grains, vegetables, and wild greens. They generally served meat (predominantly lamb, goat, and chicken) once a week or reserved it for special occasions and festivals. They may have eaten fish a couple of times each week. Occasionally, they used meat or fish for flavoring stews, vegetable pies, soups, and casseroles. Also, they sparingly sprinkled goat cheese on food and ate yogurt in low-to-moderate amounts. Wild herbs, garlic, onions, and, of course, olive oil played a tasty role in adding wonderfully satisfying flavors to dishes.

Cretans were famous for pouring extra-virgin olive oil over salads and other dishes, and for dipping whole-grain bread such as the dark, dense rusk bread, which—along with olive oil—has been part of their diet for over 4,000 years. Grains made up a little over a third of their calories, as did olive oil, with a minute amount of fat coming from meat and dairy. (Their diet contained more fat than the US diet, but in the US, fat mostly came from meat, dairy, and trans fats.) The majority of the population were members of the Greek Orthodox Church and practiced its laws, one of which was fasting from meat more than half of the year and also fasting from olive oil about one-third of the year. This was not considered or mentioned in the Seven Countries Study; but does reveal more about their consumption of fat.

Their sweet tooth was satisfied with fruit (almost triple the amount as eaten in the U. S.) for both snacking and desserts. They also consumed wine on a daily basis. Ancel Keys commented that the Mediterranean people, in general, drank quite a bit of wine with meals, but drunkenness was uncommon.

Most of the men were sheepherders, farmers, or fishermen who walked or rode a bike to work, making hard physical exercise part of everyday living. Their caloric intake was not big in comparison to their physical exertion.

The Cretans' way of eating strongly influenced the Mediterranean diet that Ancel Keys made popular in the mid-1970s. He and his wife, Margaret, shared Americanized recipes from Crete, other parts of Greece, southern Italy, and southern France in their cookbook, *How to Eat Well and Stay Well the Mediterranean Way* (no longer in print). What is disturbing is that some of their recipes used oil of no specified type, as well as margarine, which is a trans fat. At that time trans fats had not been studied, and unfortunately the Keys pushed their use over that of lard and butter.

Fast forward to the turn of the twenty-first century: Dan Buettner and a team of scientists trekked through five areas of the world, visiting cultures that have an unusually high proportion of people in their 90s and 100s. Through his vivid account of their inspiring stories in his book, *The Blue Zones: Lessons for Living Longer from the People Who've Lived the Longest,* and on the Blue Zones web page, you're escorted into people's lives and environments, where you catch insightful glimpses of their health-promoting lifestyles and diets. The large majority of these people have able bodies and lucid minds up until the very end.

Culling through the experiences of the centenarians and other elderly people of the Blue Zones, Buettner came up with "the Power of 9," lifestyle habits common among the world's longest living people. From these commonalities, he winds up giving you nine lessons to create your own Blue Zone in our fast-paced industrialized world, and diet gets the most points.

Whether it is centenarians in the Blue Zones or the traditional people of Crete, their health-promoting way of eating is based on the same simple principles: a plant-based diet full of a variety of fruits and vegetables, with small amounts of animal protein (red meat, chicken, fish, dairy, and eggs) and no processed or fast food. Hearty whole grains and beans were the staples in these diets. Also, underlying their wholesome foodstuff was a culture that relied on local sustainable agriculture, which ensured a healthy environment.

Gardening was part of their lives, which helped keep them flexible and fit, in addition to providing a variety of fruits and vegetables. They also often gathered wild plants from the countryside, where natural biodiversity is inherent, allowing a variety of species to survive for future generations. By the nature of their non-industrialized lifestyles, it was free of chemical fertilizers and pesticides. The seasons dictated what was available and they made the best use of each season: they ate seasonal fresh fruits and vegetables when available, and canned, dried, or fermented foods during the off-season. Their livestock foraged for food among local natural pastures, which produced lean meats, milk, and milk products, as well as fertilizer for plants. It was common to have a few heritage chickens for eggs and for stewing. Most of these people were shepherds, farmers, or fishermen who followed the foodways of their ancestors. They learned the sustainable way of the land and eating habits from previous generations, who relied on locally available dietary resources. In modern vernacular, people of these traditional cultures are truly "locavores" and stewards of their land, who have acquired a keen knowledge of the foods they eat and how to put them together.

In our modern-day industrialized society, 99 percent of us are not going to choose the life of a shepherd who walks a good number of miles a day or a subsistence farmer or homesteader who manually tills the soil—and stays unbelievably fit in doing so. Instead, we will spend time doing our prescribed exercise just for the purpose of staying fit. We don't have to go so far as to have a goat or chickens in our backyard, although some of us may choose to do so. A garden, on the other hand, is a viable option for exercise and a healthy, inexpensive food source.

We can follow the wisdom of these healthy centenarians by translating their way of life into our modern-day lives by being "locavores." We can let the local farmers and ranchers do the work of raising non-GMO (genetically-modified organism) crops and chemical-free plants and animals that forage in open fields and ranges, and support their efforts by buying their harvest.

Follow me as we navigate through the local scene in southern Arizona, sharing stories of the hard-working farmers and distilling the information given by the farmers' market vendors and grocers who work with local farmers to bring us incredibly fresh foods. Subscribe to a Code of Healthy Sustainable Eating (see the next section) and ready your taste buds for deliciously healthy recipes based on the principles of food ethics. Then, grab your shopping totes and let's head on out to visit the farmers and ranchers at the local markets!

## Code of Healthy Sustainable Eating

A code is a set of principles that guides you in making ethical choices. I wanted to provide something more than "rules," because they are too often broken. And what is more ethical than being a conscious eater who thinks not only about his or her own health, but also that of the environment and all who live on this planet?

### Eat a Plant-based Diet

The Seven Countries Study of the mid-twentieth century connected saturated fat from meat and dairy consumption to cardiovascular disease. Since then, numerous research studies have been conducted to prove or disprove Key's conclusion. Let's assume that saturated fat from meat itself is not the culprit; but due to the over-indulgent amounts of these fat-laden foods eaten, fruits, vegetables, beans and whole grains are shoved off your plate, depriving you of plant foods' health-promoting and protective benefits. Take, for example, one of the American food icons, the hamburger. Four to eight ounces of ground beef are accented with a tomato slice, a few onion slices, pickles, and a piece of head lettuce between a processed fibreless white-flour bun. Add trans-fat French fries or chips, which have little nutritive value. Where are the healthy vegetables?

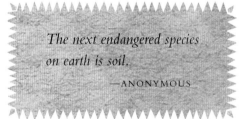

*The next endangered species on earth is soil.*
—ANONYMOUS

You don't have to go vegan or vegetarian to follow a plant-based diet. Simply eat the majority of foods from plant sources rather than animal sources. Vegetables, herbs, fruits, legumes (dried peas and beans), whole grains, nuts, and seeds provide protein, carbohydrates, fat, vitamins, minerals, and phytonutrients. Aside from tasting great and offering an unending variety of recipes (that may or may not be accented with meat), plant foods promote a healthy weight and good health. Also, consuming less meat, most of which is produced on factory farms, will reduce greenhouse gases.

Numerous laboratory studies exist that have tested the disease-fighting compounds empowered in plants, many of which are mentioned throughout this book. Scientists know that by combining two or more plants, the compounds within each plant work synergistically or as a team and become more powerful in protecting against diseases than when eaten alone.

### Eat Meat from Sustainably Raised Livestock

Sustainably raised cattle, hogs, sheep, and poultry are not raised in industrialized, large-scale confinement animal feeding operations (CAFOs); but are allowed to roam freely in an open environment, foraging on nutritious plants. In CAFOs, ruminants (cows and sheep) are finished on grain, which is not their natural diet. Nature intended that ruminants graze on plants that their digestive systems can handle; while poultry add bugs, slugs, worms, and grain to their diet; and hogs will till the soil while eating grass, roots, grains, bugs, and whatever else they find there. Eating a smorgasbord of natural foods and exercising in the great outdoors produces animals with less total fat. They have a healthy balance of omega-3 and omega-6 fats, and cattle have more than double the good fatty acid CLA compared to grain-fed animals. By choosing pastured livestock you reduce environmental damage and support local farmers while bringing to your plate hormone-and-antibiotic-free meat, eggs, and dairy that is safer, more nutritious, and holds more flavor than foods grown in factory farms.

### Consume Dairy Products Sourced from Sustainable Small Farms

For those of us who buy organic milk and other organic milk products, most of us do so because we believe it is healthier than conventional products. We also pay a premium price for that healthy edge. We may like the taste of one over another; but really never stop to think, "How organic is this?" Until I came across the Cornucopia Institute's Organic Dairy Report/Ratings, I tended to buy the least expensive organic milk. I shop differently today, because I learned that not all organic milk is created equal. The Cornucopia Institute bases its rating on facts surrounding how companies are producing or procuring their raw-milk supply. Small dairy farmers or companies that ethically abide by the most sustainable and humane organic practices—and co-ops that source milk from these kinds of small dairy farmers—come out on top.

The Cornucopia Institute is a nonprofit organic watchdog group whose Organic Integrity Project states that they will "act as a corporate and governmental watchdog, assuring that no compromises to the credibility of organic farming methods and the food it produces are made in the pursuit of profit. We will actively resist regulatory rollbacks and the weakening of organic standards to protect and maintain consumer confidence in the organic food label."

Unfortunately, the organic milk industry is not a picture-perfect industry, due to a few large players. In the beginning, all of the organic milk came from small ethical family farmers who naturally practiced sustainable agriculture and had small herds of dairy cows. The majority of these farmers were forced out of the conventional market by conglomerate dairies that were taking over the dairy industry and "killing off" the small sustainable dairy farmers with their low market prices. When the same large industrialized dairies realized that their profits were being eaten away by consumers switching to organic milk, they wanted to get in on the small farmers' game. So, they started organic factory farms similar to the large industrialized non-sustainable conventional ones they were running—with one farm having 7,200 milking cows.

These non-sustainable large factory farms have often taken full advantage of loopholes in the USDA Organic Certification guidelines, making their organic operations oftentimes debatable. Yet we see the USDA Certified Organic label and take it at face value, thinking that all organic dairy farmers practice sustainability, which means providing clean nutritious food while preserving and enhancing the environment, conserving natural resources for the present and future generations, providing a fair income to farmers, and encouraging rural communities to thrive.

These loopholes have allowed factory dairy farms to run at much less cost per cow than on the small farms, because they don't provide adequate pasture for grazing and don't graze cows throughout the year. Due to massive numbers of cows in confinement, more disease occurs, and cows are slaughtered and often replaced with conventionally raised calves—whereas the small farmers' herds are pastured year-round, and most of their calves are born on the farm and are raised as organic cattle their entire lives, although this is more costly. Hopefully, the FDA's revised pasture rule for organic dairy, which passed in February 2010, will close some of these loopholes.

### Choose Foods Grown without Chemicals

Many local farmers provide organically grown produce but are not certified organic growers due to the cost of USDA certification. However, their produce often exceeds organic standards and is usually grown sustainably, assuring productivity on the land for generations. Get to know your farmer and his or her farming practices to determine if the produce is organic. Large-scale industrial agriculture has stepped up to meet the demand for organic produce and profits nicely from it. Their farming methods, however, are not always sustainable.

There has been a long-standing debate and conflicting research about whether or not organic produce is more nutritious than conventional produce. Organic produce is generally grown in healthier soil than conventional produce. Plant tissues also contain antioxidants, which are generated to protect the plants from disease and pests. When we eat these plants, these antioxidants protect our bodies from disease as well. Studies have shown that higher levels of antioxidants exist in organic plants as compared to conventionally grown plants. One such study conducted by the University of California–Davis showed that organic tomatoes were on average 79 and 97 percent higher in antioxidants quercetin and kaempferol, respectively, than in conventional tomatoes. Scientists believe that while organic plants produce more antioxidants to ward off disease and pests, the chemicals poured on conventional plants not only eliminate pests, they also alter the development of antioxidants, since these are no longer needed to combat invaders.

Nutritional benefits aside, organic agriculture also generates less pollution than conventional agriculture. The negative impact of environmental pollution on our health has been known about for over 50 years. In 1962 ecologist Rachel Carson wrote *Silent Spring*, in which she confronted the chemical industry's disregard of the insidious effects of DDT and its freewheeling use of pesticides, which she cautioned would contaminate our food chain and cause genetic damage, cancer, and extinction of entire species. DDT has since been banned in the US, yet fifty years later, we are still struggling with the power of this industry and the damaging effects of its products on our health and the health of the environment through air, land, and water pollution.

The EPA points out that the major source of pesticide exposure is through eating. Consequently, by serving conventionally grown produce, you are more than likely serving up some toxins with your meals, which are especially harmful to infants and children. Due to their smaller size, children absorb larger levels of pesticides, and their immature internal organs and excretory systems are incapable of fully removing these substances from their bodies. The EPA points out that during this "critical period" of development, toxins could harm the nervous and immune systems. A study in *Pediatrics Journal* (May 2010) showed that exposure to organophosphate (a common pesticide) at levels most children would experience in the US, might contribute to the prevalence of attention-deficit/hyperactivity disorder (ADHD). In addition, pesticides block absorption of essential nutrients needed for normal, healthy growth.

Choosing organic produce limits our exposure to toxins. Unfortunately, availability of organic produce or budgetary restraints may restrict purchasing it. As an alternative, the Environmental Working Group (EWG) recommends avoiding the twelve or so (aka the "dirty dozen") most contaminated conventionally grown fruits and vegetables (currently peaches, strawberries, apples, domestic blueberries, nectarines, cherries, imported grapes, celery, sweet bell peppers, spinach, kale, collard greens, and potatoes—the list is periodically updated) by choosing instead the least contaminated conventionally grown produce (avocados, pineapples, mangos, kiwi, domestic cantaloupe, watermelon, grapefruit, honeydew, onions, sweet corn, sweet peas, asparagus, cabbage, eggplant, and sweet potatoes). By doing so, almost 80 percent of pesticides in your diet will be eliminated. However, many of these "dirty dozen" fruits and vegetables are high on the ORAC (Oxygen Radical Absorbance Capacity) list of powerful antioxidants and need to be a regular part of a healthy diet abundant in a variety of fruits and vegetables.

We also need to realize how our food choices impact other people, such as those living or working near conventional agriculture fields. They are at a higher risk for certain cancers and other diseases or conditions because they get a double whammy of harmful toxins just from their locale. Research studies indicate pregnant women who live near California farm fields sprayed with organochlorine pesticides may be more likely to give birth to children with autism. Furthermore, in the May 2010 issue of *Neurology,* a study suggests an association between pesticide exposure and increased risk of dementia later in life. Yet another study, published in the *American Journal of Epidemiology* in 2009, provides evidence that exposure to a combination of maneb and paraquat pesticides increase the risk of Parkinson's disease, particularly in younger subjects and/or when exposure occurs at younger ages. A follow-up study in 2011 by UCLA School of Public Health found that living or working near fields that used agricultural pesticides increased the risk for Parkinson's disease threefold.

We can make a difference by voting for synthetic-pesticide-free and fertilizer-free food with our food dollars, which will send a resounding message for support of environmentally healthy farming methods that encourage biodiversity of plants and animals, and conserve natural resources by eliminating petroleum-based herbicides and fertilizers.

*Eat Vegan or Vegetarian One or More Days a Week*

Studies have shown that being a vegetarian or vegan might do your body good, and it is a fact that an organic vegan diet is the least harmful to our planet. In the 2010 publication, *Assessing the Environmental*

*Impacts of Consumption and Production*, scientists from the United Nations Environment Programme concluded: "Impacts from agriculture are expected to increase substantially due to population growth, increasing consumption of animal products. Unlike fossil fuels, it is difficult to look for alternatives: people have to eat. A substantial reduction of impacts would only be possible with a substantial worldwide diet change, away from animal products."

As far as health is concerned, the benefits of a vegetarian diet can be seen among the Seventh-day Adventist community in Loma Linda, California, one of the Blue Zones—where a significant number of centenarians live who have able bodies and lucid minds—covered in Dan Buettner's book, *The Blue Zones: Lessons for Living Longer From the People Who've Lived the Longest*. The Seventh-day Adventist church encourages a vegetarian diet and abstinence from alcohol and tobacco.

Studies of Adventists show that practicing a vegetarian diet has definite health advantages. In The Adventist Mortality Study (1958–1966), results showed that compared to other Californians, Adventists experienced lower rates of death for: all cancers (60 percent [of non-Adventist rates] for Adventist men, 75 percent for Adventist women); coronary heart disease (66 percent for Adventist men, 98 percent for Adventist women). Another result showed that the risk of coronary heart disease was significantly lower in vegetarian compared to non-vegetarian Adventists.

The Adventist Health Study-1 (1974–1988) showed that vegetarians had a lower risk of obesity, hypertension, and diabetes. The risk of fatal heart disease in men was significantly related to beef intake; risk of colon cancer was increased by 88 percent in non-vegetarian compared to vegetarian Adventists.

The Adventist Health Study-2 (2002–present) is made up of US and Canadian Adventists ages 30 and over, which includes 26,000 black participants. Data show a progressive weight increase from a total vegetarian diet toward a non-vegetarian diet. Levels of cholesterol, diabetes, high blood pressure, and metabolic syndrome all had the same trend—the closer to being a vegetarian, the lower the risk in these areas. This was true for black as well as non-black participants.

Even though a vegetarian diet is the simplest, least expensive way to reduce the risk of debilitating diseases, most of us won't cut meat from our diet. Yet, eating a meatless meal based on whole foods or having a meatless day one or more times during the week might be feasible for some of us and would promote better health. As far as the planet's health: based on professors Eshel and Martin's research at the University of Chicago, the Environmental Defense Fund had stated that if every person in the US gave up red meat one day each week, the carbon dioxide savings (a cause of global warming) would be equivalent to eliminating 8 million cars off the road in one year. Similar research was done by the Environmental Working Group and published in *Meat Eaters Guide to Climate Change and Health*, July 2011. It's cheaper than buying a hybrid car!

## Choose Local and Eat within Seasons

Farmers' markets often offer more than food for purchase and are much more enjoyable than pondering the produce and spending too long reading labels in a supermarket. On Sunday mornings, my husband and I often take my mother, who is 95, to St. Philips Tucson Farmers' Market for walking exercise. We also all like to be entertained by our friendly rancher, Gregg Vinson, singing a tune with the bean soup lady, Martha Burgess (envision Minnie Pearl), singing and strumming her guitar. We enjoy taste-testing the various foods and socializing with friends and the farmers who have become friends. Even though the

Community Food Bank's Santa Cruz Farmers' Market is clear across town from us, we enjoy going there, too. Aside from the social aspect, all of the food at the Santa Cruz market must be grown or raised in Arizona and the vendors can only sell their own products. The Food Bank also stipulates that produce must be free of synthetic pesticides and fertilizers. At many markets not all food is locally produced or grown. Therefore, ask the vendor questions about the food he or she is selling; is it local and free of chemicals, grown in a greenhouse, are they the grower, etc.?

I have found that farmers who practice organic sustainable agriculture really enjoy sharing their methods of farming with me and welcome my visits. One late Saturday afternoon, I visited with Adam Valdivia of Sleeping Frog Farms while he was picking Swiss chard for the next day's farmers' market. I also spent a Sunday morning visiting Jim McManus, Tina Bartsch, and their children at their Walking J Farm. While Tina was working their farm stand, she took a few customers to their garden to gather some fresh vegetables for them—oh, yeah, that's as fresh as it gets. These are two of many small organic farmers, stewards of our land, who passionately believe in sustainable agriculture. This transparency (showing how things really are) regarding how our food is grown can give us confidence and trust in making the most informed buying decisions.

To sustainable farmers and us foragers of deliciously fresh organic food, it's all about the local harvest that assures pure, tasty vegetables at the height of freshness, with all the nutrition still locked in and not diminished by transportation time. It's about preserving diversity of crops through variety, such as heirloom Jimmy Nardello peppers and lemon cucumbers, and eighteen different species of apples all from the English family's orchard in Willcox. It's about farmers listening to what customers want and making it happen. It's about preserving rich, fertile soil that nourishes the plants. It's about supporting local farmers and in turn contributing to our local economy rather than sending our dollars to the corporate headquarters of some large supermarket and agricultural conglomerate a thousand or so miles away. It's about drastically reducing the food miles traveled and in turn reducing the carbon in the environment.

How close or how far away is local? Unlike certified organic, there is no legal definition of local. Locavores.com sets it within a 100-mile radius. Regardless of where you live, locally grown and raised products are available. There are a number of searchable databases on the Internet such as www.localharvest.org that list farmers, ranchers, and farmers' markets throughout the US. Additional resources are listed on page 186. Your newspaper may include farmers' markets in their list of weekly events. Also, you can join a CSA (Community Supported Agriculture). You purchase a share of the farm's harvest and reap the benefits of the peak of ripeness (usually once each week) of the harvest and share in the risks of growing food. It is the best way to support local farms, because the farm gets money up front.

Buying local doesn't mean that you have to sacrifice eating bananas (#1 selling and most packable fruit) or avocados (for our Southwest cuisine) grown in nearby California, but opt not to buy those from far-off Michoacán, Mexico, or from Florida (unless you live in the region), over 2,000 miles away. What's important is making the majority of your purchases through locally grown organic sources and not buying out of season.

## Look for Place-of-Origin Labels

Place-of-origin labels on foods makes us aware of where our food is grown or raised, which gives us the knowledge needed to choose foods that originate locally, within our state or a nearby state, making it easy to support local sources or choose to buy food with the least amount of food miles.

The Country of Origin Label (COOL) is mandated by the federal government. According to the USDA, the labeling law "includes muscle cuts and ground beef (including veal), pork, lamb, goat, and chicken; wild and farm-raised fish and shellfish; fresh and frozen fruits and vegetables; and peanuts, pecans, macadamia nuts, and ginseng sold by designated retailers." This law makes it possible for consumers to identify which crops and livestock are products of the United States, which is important to domestic farmers and ranchers. Agri-food conglomerates are expanding food production into the developing world, where labor and land are cheap and environmental protection and pesticide rules are lax. This could impact the health of our food supply and the environment.

*Eat from Your Garden*

Standing in our garden, biting down on a sweet 'n juicy Negro Azteca cherry tomato, triggered a memory of my brother and me barefoot in our family's garden, eating juicy all-over-the-face Brandywine tomatoes that my parents grew from seeds passed down from our grandmother. My sensory memories of perfumed fruits, juicy tomatoes, ultra-sweet sweet corn, sweet raspberries, firm, flavorful sugar-snap peas, and purple beans make it easy to bypass unappealing supermarket produce. This flashback to the 50s and 60s also makes me aware that our family's garden was a fundamental part of a healthy lifestyle. Aside from providing fresh, tasty, and nutritious food, gardening builds muscle, increases flexibility, and can provide an aerobic workout. Exercise combined with being outside can also be a stress buster.

Our Tucson garden is covered with a variety of organic vegetables, many of which are heirloom varieties that have adapted to their environment throughout the years and by open pollination have given to new varieties. These unique heirlooms often present us with some "fairytale" looking plants, whose genetic legacy empowers them with antioxidants to ward off pests and disease—and these health-promoting benefits are passed on to us when we eat them. They also encourage biodiversity in the plant kingdom.

Since we eat in season and grow a good bit of our organic produce, we save money over the long haul. Saving seeds, trading seeds with friends for the next season, and composting can curb gardening expenses. Composting makes a healthier, richer soil for plants to flourish and also reduces the need for water, fertilizers, and pesticides (healthier soil helps plants fight off disease and pests). According to the EPA, 26 percent of the US municipal solid waste in landfills comes from yard trimmings and food residuals, which could be turned into environmentally beneficial compost. Money is also saved by not buying compost, which again costs carbon dollars to package in plastic and ship.

Given that plants suck carbon out of the atmosphere, turn it into rich plant matter, and release oxygen back into the atmosphere, backyard gardens have a reverse greenhouse effect. One family's garden may seem insignificant; but thousands or millions of backyard gardens can make a big difference in sequestering carbon and storing it in the ground, which makes it a win-win hobby for all of us.

The Community Food Bank of Southern Arizona offers free plots and guidance in gardening at their community garden for people to grow vegetables for their family and to sell on consignment at the Community Food Bank's markets. They also have a demonstration garden where people can learn about gardening in the desert. A number of other community gardens have cropped up over the past few years in Tucson. All these projects foster healthy communities and food justice, where everyone has sufficient food, equal access to health-promoting food, and the right to grow or raise and distribute healthy food.

There is nothing more local than eating food grown in your yard or in a nearby community garden.

*Preserve the Harvest*

In southern Arizona, we are fortunate to have some fresh vegetables or fruits just about year-round. Late spring and early fall bring us an abundance of tomatoes, some of which we turn into canned tomato soup, salsa, enchilada sauce, and adobo sauce for those off-season months. Our lemons are ripe in the winter months, so we juice them and freeze the juice to enjoy lemonade in the summer. Whenever you can't eat or drink it all during season, preserve it! It is healthier than the commercial alternative and saves a bunch of money, too. It also eliminates the "carbon" miles that canned and frozen foods have to travel. Rather than go into the art of canning, which could be another book, an excellent source is the *USDA Complete Guide to Home Canning* (2009 revision), from the United States Department of Agriculture, National Center for Food Preservation. It will teach you everything you need to know about canning, pickling, fermenting, dehydrating, smoking, and curing foods.

*Eat Real Food—Eliminate or Limit Processed Foods*

Until the 1950s Americans ate food in its natural state and mostly from local sources. However, since the 1960s demand for fast food and processed food has been at full throttle, leaving wholesome foods, good health, sustainability, and many small farmers in the dust. Today, 90 percent of food dollars is spent on processed foods, causing a vast sprawl of highly processed, chemically enhanced, sugary, salty, fat-laden foods in the supermarket.

This food culture has sown the seeds for chronic disease and contributed to an ailing environment. For example: sugary foods and simple carbohydrates, void of fiber, immediately kick in and raise blood sugar (glucose) for a burst of energy, then soon fade into fatigue and hunger; so we eat some more. Many doctors believe that this repeated demand for insulin to regulate frequent spikes of glucose in the bloodstream can tax the pancreas too much over time, causing it to malfunction, resulting in type 2 diabetes.

In addition, Americans have created the perfect formula for weight gain by vastly reducing whole food consumption and replacing it with large portions of calorie-dense, nutrient-poor, refined, sugary, high-fat processed and fast foods, which produce a lot of excess sugar that is not used as energy, resulting in fat storage. Thus, it is no surprise that the Gallup–Healthways Well-Being Index shows that Americans have never been so overweight and obese—36.3 percent of adults are overweight and 26.6 percent are obese. And even sadder, according to the Center for Disease Control, childhood obesity has more than tripled since 1980.

Furthermore, the excess amounts of sugar from simple carbs can lead to increased cholesterol, decreased HDL, and increased triglycerides, which in turn increase our risk for cardiovascular disease. Factor in the heavy doses of salt and bad fats, and the risks go higher.

Aside from the health dangers of sweet or refined food, a study published in the June 2010 issue of *Circulation* showed that the consumption of processed meats (smoked, cured, or salted, or any meat containing chemical preservatives such as nitrates)—not red unprocessed meat—is associated with higher incidence of CHD and diabetes mellitus. One hot dog or two slices of deli meat—about 50 g—per day was associated with a 42 percent higher risk of CHD and a 19 percent increased risk of diabetes.

Can we escape dementia? It may be possible if we avoid eating foods that contain nitrates. Dr. Suzanne M. de la Monte and Rhode Island Hospital and Brown Medical research colleagues concluded from their research that there is reasonable evidence that nitrosamines (nitrates found in processed foods and chemical fertilizers) is the root cause of Alzheimer's and dementia, along with several other insulin-resistant diseases; and it only takes low doses over a period of years to cause Alzheimer's and these other diseases. Adding high fat to the diet makes the disease-causing effects of nitrosamines much worse. She suggests eating organic foods and limiting processed foods to protect yourself.

If you are trying to be healthier by eating some vegetarian or vegan meals, forget the processed fake meats and cheese or anything where food manufacturers are trying to simulate the taste of meat or chicken—organic or not. These are highly processed foods that may contain a lot of junk and are usually full of salt. Even though billed as a healthy alternative or health food, they usually are not. Instead, enjoy the vegan and vegetarian recipes in this book.

It must be noted that not all processed food is junk food or bad for you. Frozen organic fruits and vegetables without added sugar or salt are as nutritious and sometimes more so than fresh, because they are picked at the height of ripeness and frozen within a few hours—whereas, as time elapses in your kitchen, pantry, or fridge, fresh fruits and vegetables lose some vitamin C. Canned tomatoes are great for making tomato-based sauces, and since they are cooked, are higher in lycopene than fresh, which is an antioxidant that may reduce the risk of heart disease and some cancers. Another time-saver is canned beans, where the difference in the nutritional value of cooked and canned is minimal. While canned tomatoes and beans are often loaded with salt, low-salt and salt-free versions are available.

Unfortunately, convenience is often paired with some drawbacks, and canned food and drinks are no exception. The lining of nearly all cans contains BPA (Bisphenol A), which independent testing by the Environmental Working Group (EWG) found leaches from the can's lining into the food or drink. The FDA has gone from stating that it was safe in 2008 to expressing concern about its effects on fetuses, infants, and children in 2010—$30 million has been allotted to study its effects on health. The EWG points out that low doses may increase the risk of prostate and breast cancer, obesity, type 2 diabetes, miscarriage, and birth defects. In addition to directly ingesting this toxin from food, the industrial waste pollutes the land, rivers, and air.

Some food manufactures have started replacing BPA liners with a safer lining. Mike Potter, founder of Eden® Foods asked can supplier Ball® Corp. what lining was used prior to BPA. It was enamel from vegetable resins. In 1999 Potter started using it for his organic beans, but at an added cost. If you have a choice between food sold in glass or a can, choose glass.

Highly processed foods are cheap, in part due to processed ingredients made from government-subsidized crops that encourage an oversupply of corn, wheat, rice and soybeans—and 75 percent of these subsidies go to industrial agriculture that does not practice sustainable farming. This conflicts with the Department of Agriculture's "My Plate" food guide, which recommends plenty of fruits, vegetables, and whole grains, and limited fat and sugar. On the other hand, if everyone ate the recommended servings of fruits and vegetables, there might not be enough to go around, since land designated for subsidized crops cannot be planted with non-subsidized crops or farmers will be penalized.

Production and packaging of processed foods use large amounts of energy, water, and other raw materials and create air pollution, solid waste, and wastewater. Additional energy is consumed by the "food miles" traveled to ship these foods around the country. Packaging materials generate consumer garbage, which takes more energy to recycle or adds to landfills and sometimes takes hundreds if not thousands of years to decompose. So, vote with your food dollars for whole, unadulterated food—your demand for such food can tilt production away from processed foods and into the hands of local farmers, and in the process create a stronger local economy.

## Cap Your Sweet Tooth

A 2009 American Heart Association (AHA) scientific statement voiced concern regarding excess consumption of sugar in the setting of a worldwide pandemic of obesity and cardiovascular disease. When the statement was published, it was noted that from 2001–2004, the mean intake for all Americans was 22.2 teaspoons per day. Adolescents (14–18 yeas old) consumed the most at 34.3 teaspoons per day. Added sugar intake in American adolescents is believed to be linked to increased cardiovascular disease risk, according to the results of a cross-sectional study reported in *Circulation*. The AHA suggested that moderately active women should consume no more than 100 calories (about 25 grams or 6 teaspoons) of added sugar per day, while moderately active men no more than 150 calories (about 37 grams or 9 teaspoons). This bittersweet saga of overconsumption has had a rippling effect in our environment, as seen in an increase in non-sustainable production of sugar cane and high-fructose corn syrup, which devotes vast acreages of cropland to growing just one crop, reducing plant diversity and requiring reliance on petrochemical fertilizers.

The amount of sugar in packaged food is at the mercy of manufacturers, and it is virtually in all processed foods. Unfortunately, naturally occurring sugar is not separated from added sugar on the labels; so look at the ingredients in addition to the grams of sugar. If sugar is high up on the list, there's a lot of added sugar. Any ingredient ending in "ose" is a sugar.

Sugar is sugar, whether it is white or organic raw sugar, high-fructose corn syrup, honey, maple syrup, agave nectar, or any of the words ending in "ose," and none offer significant nutrients. Manufacturers pump sugar into foods because it is addictive, and what do addicts do? They crave more. Processed food manufactures also play to the idea that lowfat foods are healthier. (How about a "healthy" lowfat bran muffin?) Sugar has been added to compensate for the lack of flavor that fat provided. With that idea implanted in our minds, we may think, "Let's eat some more—it's not fattening!"

To feed the sugar addiction, high-fructose corn syrup is being used extensively and somewhat excessively in processed foods because it's sweeter and cheaper than cane sugar, and it enhances flavor and extends shelf life. It also costs considerably less to produce than cane sugar, due to US government subsidies to corn farmers and tariffs on imported sugar cane. Non-sustainable agriculture practices are used in growing the majority of corn in the US, and according to the USDA, 88 percent is now genetically engineered.

Research studies indicate that fructose (high-fructose corn-syrup is 55 percent fructose; 45 percent glucose) tricks your brain into thinking that you are still hungry; thus you keep eating. Also, results of a 2010 Princeton study indicate that high-fructose corn syrup may contribute to an increase in triglycerides, weight gain, and abdominal fat significantly more than table sugar (which is 50 percent fructose; 50 percent glucose).

"Pure" cane sugar is not so pure. The World Wildlife Fund's 2004 report, "Sugar and the Environment," has pegged sugar cane as possibly being responsible for more biodiversity loss than any other crop. Natural habitats are being destroyed to make way for sugar cane plantations. Its production uses massive amounts of irrigation water, chemical fertilizers, and pesticides, and polluted wastewater is discharged into the environment from sugar mills. We can combat these environmental maladies by eating less sugar-laden processed foods and by buying the least processed organic sugar from sustainably raised organic sugar cane.

Agave nectar is another sugar that has gained popularity in the past few years and is surrounded by controversy. In 2010 the Glycemic Research Institute found that during five years of human in vivo clinical trials, diabetic subjects experienced severe and dangerous side effects related to ingesting agave. They also warned people with metabolic syndrome, insulin resistance, and pre-diabetes of the possible dangers associated with agave. Most agave is highly processed, which is bad for the environment and for your health—an increase in processing also increases the amount of fructose. Unless the amount of fructose is listed on the label, it is difficult to ascertain. Depending on the amount of processing, there can be a range from 50 to over 90 percent fructose. At 55 percent, it would be equal to high-fructose corn syrup. Also, it costs way more than evaporated cane juice and is about the same cost as honey.

Honey, especially unheated honey, is the least processed sugar, and thus has little negative environmental impact. Buying honey also supports local beekeepers, whose bees are important pollinators that benefit local ecology. It is sweeter than sugar, so less is required. It has about the same amount of fructose as high-fructose corn syrup but again is minimally processed, especially raw honey. Children under one year old should not eat honey due to the chance of the honey containing botulism spores, which an infant's immature digestive system can't handle. Some experts recommend that baked goods and other cooked foods containing honey should not be given to infants because the cooking temperature and length of cooking may not be sufficient to pasteurize the honey.

## Steer Clear of GMO Foods

Since food products containing GMOs are not required by the FDA to be labeled as such, the best way to avoid them is to buy organic. The next best option is to buy products with the Non-GMO Project seal. According to the Project's website, they are the only organization offering independent (third party) verification of testing and GMO controls. They state: "the product has been produced according to rigorous best practices for GMO avoidance, including testing of risk ingredients." Ingredients must be less than 0.9 percent GMO to carry the label.

## Prevent Cancer with Anti-angiogenic Foods

In May 2010, a chill ran through my body and tears swelled in my eyes as my brother Paul, in his matter-of-fact manner, told me he had stage 4 colon cancer and liver metastases. Six months later, he was gone. The cancer could have more than likely been nipped in the bud by early-detection colonoscopy, which he didn't have. Who knows—perhaps it could have been avoided altogether by eating cancer-preventive foods.

During those six months, I did a lot of research about cancer, and the most intriguing to me was cancer-preventive work being done at the Angiogenesis Foundation. Dr. William Li, president and medical director of the foundation, says recent research indicates that all of us have microscopic cancer cells growing within us, calling them "cancer without disease." These cells are usually kept in check by our body's natural cancer-fighting system. He says a key component of this system is angiogenesis. What is angiogenesis? As described on the foundation's website:

It is the growth of new capillary blood vessels, a natural process of the body, which is necessary for healing and reproduction. Abnormal blood vessel growth, either excessive or insufficient, is considered the "common denominator" underlying many deadly and debilitating conditions, including cancer, skin diseases, age-related blindness, diabetic ulcers, cardiovascular disease, stroke, and many others.

When it comes to cancer, as long as those microscopic cells lack a blood supply that would bring oxygen and nourishment to the tumor, its growth will be halted. After learning that 30–35 percent of environmentally caused cancers are related to diet, Dr. Li was convinced that "we can eat to starve cancer." So, in pursuit of foods that are naturally anti-angiogenic—boosting the body's defense system to beat back blood vessels that are feeding cancers—he states that, "Our search has taken us to the market, the farm, and to the spice cabinet, because what we've discovered is that Mother Nature has laced a large number of foods and beverages and herbs with naturally occurring inhibitors of angiogenesis." In other words, those innocuous cells will never turn deadly. "This could help healthy people as well as people who've already beaten cancer once or twice and want to find a way to keep it from coming back."

Also, a combination of these foods is believed to maximize potency. The researchers in the foundation are creating a rating system that scores foods according to their anti-angiogenic cancer-preventive properties.

Dr. Li believes that "for many people around the world, dietary cancer prevention may be the only practical solution, because not everybody can afford expensive end-stage cancer treatments, but everybody could benefit from a healthy diet based on local, sustainable, anti-angiogenic crops." The majority of recipes in this book contain one or more of these disease-preventive foods, giving you tasty options to stay healthy. See page 185 for the listing of foods.

### Prepare Meals and Treats from Scratch

Meals made with garden-fresh ingredients and truly free-range meat or poultry are more flavorful, nutritious, and satisfying than meals made from packages. Unlike with packaged foods, you know what you are eating and are in control of the ingredients. Make enough that there will be leftovers to freeze and serve when there's no time to cook.

### Involve Children in Preparing Food

When children are involved in preparing a meal or baking, they will be more inclined to eat what they helped prepare, or at least give it a try. It can be a learning experience and an enjoyable activity for mom or dad to spend quality time with them. Healthy or not-so-healthy attitudes and food habits begin at home, with parents as role models. Our grandsons— Ty, age eight, and Aaron, age five—helped plant sugar snap peas in our garden, picked them, and assisted in cleaning and sautéing them. They enjoyed eating the peas—and even more, telling the diners what their part was in growing and cooking them. My children and our grandsons were each around age two when they started helping in the kitchen—sometimes it was a bit messy, but not any more than giving them water colors or silly putty to play with.

### Eat Until You Are 80 Percent Satisfied

Okinawa has one of the world's highest concentrations of centenarians. The majority of Okinawan elders enjoy a high quality of life marked by lucid minds and a low rate of lifestyle-related illnesses such as cardiovascular disease, cancer, diabetes, osteoporosis, dementia, and Alzheimer's disease. According to the ongoing Okinawa Centenarian Study, which started in 1976, Okinawan's diets are low in calories, with a low glycemic load; and they practice the dietary philosophy known as *hara hachi bu*—to stop eating when they are 80 percent satisfied.

## How-To Fire-roast, Toast, and Grill

*Vegetables and Portobello Mushrooms*

Fire-roasting vegetables brings out or develops their flavor while preserving nutrients and retaining the freshness and firmness of the flesh. Fire-roasted chiles and tomatoes, in particular, are essentials in creating bold flavors and fragrant Southwest cuisine. You can fire-roast vegetables under the broiler of your oven, on a gas or electric grill, or over charcoal. The open-flame method imparts a smoky flavor—especially if roasted over charcoal or wood chips. Broiling, however, is most efficient when you are pressed for time. Since grilling vegetables varies a little, each vegetable is listed here with specific details. Some vegetables require a little oil before and during roasting, while others are often not oiled until after cooking (this retains more of the health-promoting properties of the oil).

For most vegetables, the broiler or electric or gas grill will be set at high heat. Once it is hot, place the vegetables on a broiler pan and put it under the broiler as close to the heat as possible. If using a grill, place vegetables on the grill. If you are using a barbecue grill, place whole peppers or tomatoes or other prepared vegetables on the grill over hot coals, but not in direct contact with the flame. A slight browning and grill markings on the vegetables add visual appeal. Some vegetables are grilled over moderate heat, which is indicated in their grilling instructions. Be careful not to burn the flesh. To retain a firm texture, allow the skin to cook quickly so the meat of the vegetable is only slightly cooked. If you want shish kabobs, tomatoes, bell peppers, onions, and summer squash all take about the same time to grill and can be grilled together on skewers.

Charred vegetables do not have the same risk of containing cancer-promoting elements (such as heterocyclic amines, or HCAs, and polycyclic aromatic hydrocarbons, or PAHs) as charred meat, poultry, and fish. Both HCAs and PAHs are created from fat dripping into the coals, which then permeates the food through smoke and flare-ups of the fire. Therefore, it may be good practice to grill vegetables before the meat to prevent the vegetables from soaking up PAHs and HCAs.

CHILES, BELL PEPPERS, AND TOMATOES—Grilling peppers and tomatoes is slightly different from grilling other vegetables. If they are to be used in a recipe or stuffed, they are blistered and charred rather than slightly browned. Chiles and bell peppers should be roasted whole and peeled after roasting, as the tough peel often has a bitter flavor. I usually don't peel tomatoes, leaving the charred skins to add color to the sauces and add more of a roasted flavor. If used on skewers with other vegetables such as summer squash and onions, peppers and tomatoes are not charred and peeled but cooked following the squash-roasting instructions.

Using high heat, place the peppers and tomatoes on a broiler pan as close to the heat as possible, or if using a grill, place on the grill. Turn the peppers or tomatoes as they blister and blacken, being careful not to burn the flesh. To retain a firm texture, allow the skin to cook quickly so the meat of the vegetables is only slightly cooked.

Some people prefer to wear gloves while working with hot chiles, because the capsaicin burns their hands. Once the peppers are blistered and blackened, place them in a bowl and cover with a plate to allow the skin to release from each pepper. Since they will continue to cook, remove from the bowl as soon as the skins have released. Allow the peppers to cool. Don't place in water or run water over roasted peppers, or some of the oils and flavor will be lost. Peel the skins off the peppers and remove the seeds and veins. If you like hot peppers, leave some of the veins intact. If you are roasting peppers that are going to be stuffed, make only a small incision from the stem to about 1 inch from the tip of the chile. After peeling hot chiles, wash your hands thoroughly because the heat (capsaicin) will remain on your hands. I have more than once gotten chile in my eyes from my hands, and it does burn! If chiles are threaded on skewers with other vegetables, they are not blackened and peeled.

CORN—Corn is one of the easiest vegetables to grill or broil. As the corn cooks, some of the kernels will brown. As this occurs, turn the corn; continue to do so until some of the kernels are browned on all sides of the corn. The specks of brown on yellow or white kernels add aesthetic appeal to recipes. Remove from the heat and either serve whole or cut the kernels from the corn and add to salads, beans, etc. If eating corn on the cob, spray it with olive oil instead of smothering it in butter.

EGGPLANT—Slice the eggplant into scant ¼-inch slices and lay on a cookie sheet. Brush or spray both sides with olive oil and sprinkle lightly with salt. Allow to sit for 30 minutes before grilling or broiling. Grill or broil at a lower temperature or not as close to the broiler. If cooked at a high temperature, the pieces tend to burn before they are done. Remove from heat when the pieces are somewhat translucent and a little tender. Transfer to a bowl and cover. They will continue to cook slightly. If the eggplant is not going to be used in another recipe, add a little olive oil, minced garlic or garlic powder, and salt and pepper.

GARLIC—Set the unpeeled garlic bulb on the grill or under the broiler. The skin will turn brown and be somewhat burned. Turn the bulb to assure even cooking. Depending on the method of roasting, this may take anywhere from 8 to 15 minutes. If you are roasting only garlic, use the dry roast method, which imparts more of a nutty, full flavor. Separate the cloves from the bulb. Don't peel. Place them in a heavy skillet over low to medium-low heat. Roast for 20–30 minutes, turning every 5 minutes or so to assure even cooking and browning. Whichever method you use,

the cooked garlic will be soft. Peel and add to recipes. It can be sealed and refrigerated for a couple of days.

ONIONS—When onions are grilled, some of the strong flavor is toned down and the sweetness comes out. Peel and cut into ½-inch slices. Follow the basic grilling or broiling instructions, but don't blacken. They will appear slightly translucent and have a crisp, yet tender texture.

PORTOBELLO MUSHROOMS—Trim ½ inch from the tip of each stem. Slice the mushrooms ½ inch (or less) thick and spray or brush lightly with a little bit of olive oil. Sprinkle lightly with salt and pepper. Preheat broiler or grill to high heat. Arrange slices on broiler pan, not touching each other. Position broiler pan on top oven rack and broil for about 2 minutes or until the mushrooms are sizzling and turning a bit golden. Turn and repeat on the other side. They should be tender yet firm.

SWEET POTATOES OR GARNET YAMS—The deep, rich color of the garnet yams and their texture make them my favorite of the two. Cut the sweet potato or yam into ¼-inch slices. Since it is a very dense root vegetable, it needs to be steamed prior to grilling in order to prevent it from burning before it is fully cooked. In a vegetable steamer, steam the slices for about 5 minutes or until they start to lose their firmness. Brush or spray lightly with olive oil. Grill or broil at medium high heat for about 5 minutes or until they start to lose their firmness. Brush or spray lightly with olive oil. Grill or broil at medium high heat for about 5 minutes on each side or until they can be penetrated with a fork. The garnet yams will turn a deeper orange when cooked. Transfer to a bowl and cover. They will continue to cook a bit. They taste great without any added oil or seasoning. However, a few squirts of lime juice and a sprinkling of New Mexico red chile pepper powder adds some excitement—test one slice with chile pepper to determine the heat.

ZUCCHINI AND YELLOW SQUASH—Depending on the size of the squash, vertically cut it into fourths or eighths. Broil or grill until crisp yet tender according to the basic grilling instructions but don't blacken them. Transfer to a bowl and cover. They will continue to cook a bit. If the squash is not going to be added to a recipe, brush or spray with olive oil, and sprinkle lightly with salt and fresh, coarsely ground pepper.

### Fish and Chicken

When broiling or grilling fish or chicken, use a high temperature and cook very quickly to lock in the flavors. Bake fish and chicken at no more than 350 degrees F. Baking fish (or vegetables) in parchment paper retains all the juices and flavors and preserves most of the nutritional value. Aside from contributing to a healthy form of cooking, parchment paper also makes cleanup a lot easier.

### Toasting

DRIED CHILES—The purpose of toasting dried chiles is to release the perfume captured in the chile, creating a full, bold flavor. Be cautious while working with the chiles. You may choose to wear gloves, but don't touch your eyes or lips! Make sure to wash your hands thoroughly after working with chiles. Remove the stem and hard cap at the base of the stem. Open up the chile and shake out the seeds, removing the remaining seeds with your fingers. Separate or tear the chile apart to remove most of the seeds, for they are often hiding within little folds of the chile. If you can see the veins, you might want to carefully remove some of them, making sure that you're not throwing away a lot of the chile. There are varying degrees of drying especially with the chipotle; you might get a chipotle that is moist or one that is really dry. The dryer ones are an earthy brown and have a very fragrant, smoky aroma, whereas the softer ones are red in color and have the texture of a soft sun-dried tomato. Place a small heavy skillet over medium heat. Put the torn chile into the skillet. Be careful not to burn them, which can happen very quickly, or they will become bitter and will have to be discarded. When you start smelling the aroma of the chipotle, they are toasted. Remove from the burner and the skillet to prevent the chiles from burning.

TOASTING SEEDS AND NUTS—Place a small heavy skillet over medium heat. When the perfume of the seeds is released and the seeds become slightly darkened—not browned—remove from the skillet to prevent burning. Cumin and coriander seeds are often toasted and ground.

TOASTING DRIED HERB LEAVES—Place a small heavy skillet over medium heat. When the perfume of the herb is released and the leaves are darkening slightly around the edges—not browned—remove from the skillet to prevent burning.

DRYING CITRUS ZEST—Preheat the oven to 225 degrees F. Into an oven-safe dish or pan, grate the zest from the citrus, avoiding the white pulp just under the skin. Place the pan on the middle rack of the oven and dry the zest for 20–25 minutes or until dry but not brown. Allow to cool. It may be stored in an airtight container in the refrigerator for about three weeks.

### Working with Tortillas

Tortillas have to be pliable in order to be rolled without breaking. There are a number of methods to accomplish this. If you are using a gas stove, place the tortilla over the burner with a medium flame. Turn the tortilla a few times until it is heated and pliable—not hard. Remove from burner, fill, and roll or fold. If you are using an electric stove, place a griddle or heavy iron skillet over a large burner and turn to high heat. When hot, place the tortilla directly on the uncoated griddle or skillet. Turn a couple of times until the tortilla is heated and pliable—not hard. Remove from heat, fill, and roll or fold.

## Local Sustainable Chefs

These three featured chefs bring flavors of the Southwest foodshed to their diners and are mindful of sustainability and supporting local farmers and ranchers. I feel privileged to present their stories and a few deliciously healthy recipes they created for your health and enjoyment.

*Corporate Chef Scott Uehlein, Canyon Ranch*
Since its beginning in 1979 as a mom-and-pop health resort on the outskirts of Tucson, Canyon Ranch has been a leader in the development of "spa cuisine." This is somewhat ironic, since the Ranch has always fought that label—Canyon Ranch is immeasurably more than what most people think of as a spa and the food is deliciously nourishing cuisine that rivals dining experiences at leading hotels, restaurants, and resorts around the world. The ranch's food has been given top honors by *Condé Nast Traveler* and *Gourmet* magazine, which stated that Corporate Chef Scott Uehlein and his staff "have brought Canyon Ranch cuisine into a new dimension."

Unlike other top chefs, the Ranch's talented Chef Scott must not only meet the highest culinary standards but also adhere to an exacting set of nutritional standards, while satisfying some of the most discriminating palates. This has been accomplished through the collaborative efforts of Chef Scott and his culinary team working closely with a gifted nutritional staff. Whereby, a balanced approach to eating is presented, which includes a large variety of plants (vegetables, fruits, whole grains, beans, nuts, and seeds, and herbs and spices); leanest cuts of meat and chicken; and sustainable wild and organic fish.

*Chef Scott Uehlein.*

Chef Scott says, "I only half-laugh when people tell me how surprised they are at how flavorful our food is. It's all about flavor. Because our use of ingredients like butter and sodium are limited, we must carefully balance flavors and textures to create food that's deeply satisfying without excessive fat or sodium.

"When we begin to build a menu item, we build it from the ground up, so our dining guests do not have any preconceived notions as to what the dish will taste like. As the dish takes shape, we look for key elements. Those elements are: sweet, sour, bitter, and salty, and, of course, the 'fifth sense' of umami."

Sweet, sour, bitter, and salty can come from many sources, explains Chef Scott. Sweetness in a savory dish might be captured as a taste element through caramelization, the addition of a fruit element, or even a natural sweetener like honey, maple syrup, or evaporated cane juice. Sweet is easy to overdo; it's used in savory dishes as balance to sour. Sour is incorporated through the introduction of an acid, generally citrus or vinegar.

Bitter may be very subtle, like a slight bitter taste from marking fish on the grill, or more bold, in the form of bitter greens—the slight bitterness of the spinach in Spinach Salad with Strawberry Champagne Vinaigrette (recipe on page 135), for example, is played off against the other ingredients. Either way, without bitter, the balance of the dish will be off. Salty simply means a properly seasoned dish, not salty like potato chips are salty.

"All of these elements need to be present for the dish to be properly balanced. Throw too much of one element into the mix, and you will have a dish that is out of balance and fails to satisfy. Forget to incorporate everything, and you end up with a dish that is missing something. All the elements have to be there," says Chef Scott.

Chef Scott explains that umami, which is the sensation of "savoriness," is almost a mouth-feel as much as a taste, but is perceived by certain receptors on the tongue, and is found naturally in higher concentrations in foods such as soy sauce, mushrooms, and meats.

Since the Ranch's concept of health and well-being encompasses a healthy environment, the food served must be organic, seasonal, and local or regional, insofar as possible. This also assures incredibly fresh foods that are reflected in the flavorsome meals served. Thus, Chef Scott has developed a strong local and sustainable orientation with nearby ranchers and farmers who provide fresh produce and grass-fed organic meats and chicken. Scott also mentioned, "Incorporating native ingredients, such as prickly pear nectar, cholla buds, and mesquite flour, add variety and healthfulness to our cuisine, as well as improving the Ranch's 'green' profile."

Scott and the Ranch have graciously shared three recipes for you to try, on pages 93, 135, and 182. For more delicious and healthy recipes from Canyon Ranch, pick up a copy of *Canyon Ranch Nourish: Indulgently Healthy Cuisine,* by Scott Uehlein and Canyon Ranch. You will enjoy more than 200 of their most popular, easy-to-make recipes with complete nutritional information, guidelines for selecting and cooking the healthiest and most delicious food, plus Canyon Ranch nutrition philosophy and indices to gluten-free and dairy-free recipes.

*Chef Ryan Clark.*

## Executive Chef Ryan Clark, Lodge on the Desert

For the past couple of years, Chef Ryan Clark has been dazzling the local culinary scene and those who dine at historic Lodge on the Desert in Tucson, Arizona, where he is the executive chef. He has been awarded a number of accolades for his creative and delicious cuisine by his fellow chefs in the community through various chef-judged competitions.

Chef Ryan was classically trained at the legendary Culinary Institute of America, Hyde Park. Upon graduating, he continued developing his natural culinary talents for a while in New York, and then returned to Arizona and interned under Iron Chef America Beau MacMillan at Elements Restaurant at Sanctuary Resort in Paradise Valley. He then moved on to his hometown of Tucson and worked in the kitchen of Chef Scott Uehlein at the world renowned Canyon Ranch, where food not only had to be delicious, but also healthy.

Chef Ryan's "slow food" culinary philosophy of "farm to table," which is supported by Lodge on the Desert's commitment to environmental sustainability, has led him on many quests for clean, in-season, locally grown organic or chemical-free foods. He has gotten to know and buys from quite a few local farmers and ranchers, such as the folks from nearby Double Check Ranch, who provide complete food transparency by owning the entire beef cycle—from the pasture, to processing, and to handing over the beef to the consumer.

He also procures dewy fresh produce from Sleeping Frog Farms through a community-supported agriculture share that the Lodge purchased. By doing so, Chef Ryan is not only assured of fresh produce delivered on a regular basis, but he is also supporting Sleeping Frog Farms by sharing the risks of farming and providing them with important up-front money and a guaranteed market for their produce (the true stamp of a sustainable chef). It also gives Chef Ryan greater access to their high-demand organic heirloom vegetables.

In addition to buying from local farmers and ranchers, he also harvests a variety of citrus from the citrus trees at the Lodge, and a variety of herbs and an array of heirloom vegetables from the Lodge's seasonal organic garden, which he oversees. And in the name of sustainability, and to have a great natural fertilizer for his garden, he composts plant scraps from the kitchen in a huge compost bin.

Following the principles of food transparency—from production to plate—Chef Ryan takes a made-to-order stance on charcuterie items that may otherwise be cured with harmful nitrates and chemicals. He naturally cures bacon, prosciutto, pastrami, tasso, and chorizo in house. He also turns local organic milk into cheese and crème fraiche. Additionally, guests will never find a bottle of steak sauce or breakfast preserves on the table because he makes his own.

When it comes to seafood, Lodge on the Desert's culinary team follows Seafood Watch principles that help keep the world's oceans clean and healthy. Seafood Watch educates all interested parties to help the ecosystem by not overfishing and damaging their future.

Chef Ryan's "New American" culinary style and his commitment to celebrating local foods are reflected in a menu, which changes monthly and with the seasons. It is sparked with imaginative dishes and drinks that hold a strong presence of many traditional local flavors and ingredients. (Some of the regional nuances include mesquite sweet potato pancakes, blue corn tamales with calabacitas filling, grilled prickly pear cactus, lodge chorizo, tamarindo pod sangria, prickly pear mojito, and black rice horchata.) With Chef Ryan's belief that people should know where their food comes from and how it is prepared, this information is often provided on the menu. He also enjoys talking with the clientele and giving them insight into where their food is grown or raised.

One of the attributes that I find so endearing about Ryan is that he takes the time from a demanding schedule to share his culinary knowledge with young children and aspiring local high school and Pima Community College culinary students. I remember at the end of a week-long Chef & Child Foundation's "That's Fresh Cooking Teams," it was Chef Ryan who the children honored with a personalized apron.

When I asked him for a few recipes, with a smile and enthusiasm on his face, he quickly responded, "I'll make up a few recipes for your book." I had to hold him back or he would have supplied recipes for half the book; and I told him that he needed to reserve those for his book, which I am sure will become a reality. During the mean time, take time to savor the flavors of the drinks and dishes he is sharing with us, which can be found on pages 33, 34, 99, and 108.

*Chef Elizabeth Mikesell, Pima Community College*
After graduating with a BFA degree from the University of Arizona in 1969, Chef Elizabeth Mikesell, as she puts it, "on a wing and a song," went to Europe and for four years trained in the culinary industry. She says, "I grew my talent from an interesting cross-food profile." On her return to the United States she co-owned and was chef at a restaurant in Lenox, MA. She commented that the *Saturday Night Live* cast frequented it and *Gourmet* was asking for their recipes—"It was a real boost for our egos!" She eventually moved back to Tucson, married Robert, worked in a number of

restaurants, and was executive chef at a local country club for 13 years. She then turned her attention to being a culinary educator at Pima Community College, where she has worked since 2001.

Chef Elizabeth commented, "I have been concerned about and working to alter the nutrition and obesity issues evident in America's youth for several years." Part of her advocacy is through serving on the board of the national Culinary Federation Education Foundation (ACFEF) Chef & Child Foundation (CCF), which she has done since 1992 and was its chairperson from 2005-2011. Currently she is working closely with Hattie Mae and Pals, the first large scale children's wellness center in the country being constructed on the gulf coast of Mississippi where childhood obesity is among the worst in the country, to establish Chef and Child training programs for the children.

Recently she was invited to the White House with 99 other chefs for the kickoff of Michelle Obama's "Chefs Move to Schools" campaign. In the program, chefs will work with schools in their communities to help solve the childhood obesity epidemic. Elizabeth declared, "It is extremely fulfilling to at long last witness a tide that may turn around the toxic eating trends in America from the past several years. I am even more delighted to know that chefs will play such a key role in that process."

The program will pair chefs with interested schools in their communities to adopt the school and work with teachers, parents, and school nutrition professionals to help educate kids about food and nutrition. At Sam Hughes Elementary School, Chef

*Chef Elizabeth Mikesell.*

Elizabeth gives cooking lessons on healthy foods and integrates produce from the students' organic garden.

Also for the past two years, she, the Chef & Child Foundation, and the American Culinary Federation have been presenting a "That's Fresh Cooking Teams" program for one week during the summer at the House of Neighborly Service in Tucson. A number of other chefs have willingly answered her call of volunteerism for this program. The mission statement for Kids Cooking Teams is "to facilitate a youth cooking team that emphasizes nutrition awareness, food safety, cultural diversity, team building, basic culinary skills, and self-esteem. These children will have the opportunity to experience themselves as special, creative human beings capable of nurturing themselves and others through food and making wise food choices for lifetime good health."

Since 2008, Chef Elizabeth has been involved with the Tucson Meet Yourself October festival, organizing the healthy ethnic Iron Chef competition for local high school and college culinary students. In addition, since 2008, she has organized the healthy ethnic recipe contest for elementary and middle school students.

I feel very fortunate to call Elizabeth my friend and have seen firsthand what hard work she puts in to help children and their families move to a healthier lifestyle. Chef Elizabeth has provided us with a few recipes (on pages 159 and 182) that she has developed and used in her cooking programs with children. Take the time to enjoy making them with your children, grandchildren, or a special child in your life. ▶

# BEVERAGES

Take stock of what you drink! Many Americans often choose a soft drink, soda, or packaged fruit juice over water and rack up the calories during the process.

As mentioned in the Introduction, the average American consumes about 22 teaspoons of added sugar a day, with teenagers ingesting even more. Sugar-sweetened beverages are the main source of these added sugars in the American diet. A single 12-ounce can of Coca-Cola Classic soda contains about 9 teaspoons of added sugar! That pretty much covers the sugar allowance for an entire day, according to the American Heart Association's guidelines.

Excess sugar carries with it adverse health risks, including obesity, high blood sugar, high blood pressure, and other risk factors for stroke and heart disease, according to the AHA. Barry Popkin, a renowned obesity and nutrition expert, states that 450 calories in beverages—40 percent from fruit juice and soft drinks and 20 percent from alcohol—are consumed each day by the average American. Juice—whether sweetened or un-sweetened—has just as many calories as soda, with little benefit. He suggests eating the whole fruit, which has much less sugar and contains fiber, which keeps you feeling full longer.

Unfortunately, parents don't usually stop to calculate the amount of sugar in conveniently packaged small disposable juice boxes. Drinks marketed as health-promoting, such as acai berry juice or acai blended health drinks; vitamin waters; energy drinks; sweetened soy, rice, almond, and hemp beverages; smoothies; coffee drinks; and chocolate milk all contain a lot of sugar—naturally occurring or not, it's still sugar.

By making your own deliciously satisfying drinks, you will be in control of the ingredients. Package them in reusable containers for school, work, or an on-the-go drink. It will be beneficial to your health and the planet's. However, there is one important note. Flavored drinks—pure fruit juice included—have increasingly taken the place of drinking water. It's important to drink fresh water as your main drink, and consume other drinks infrequently. ▶

*Prickly Pear Margarita (recipe on page 33).*

## Prickly Pear or Pomegranate Green Tea Cooler

1 cup steeped green tea

1–2 tablespoons fresh unsweetened pomegranate or prickly pear juice

**I serving**

Calories per serving: 10
Total fat: 0g
Saturated fat: 0g
Calories from fat: 0
Protein: 0g
Carbohydrates: 3g
Dietary fiber: 0g
Sugars: 2g

*The beautifully colored prickly pear has strong antioxidant properties. A few research studies indicate that prickly pear juice could have anti-cancer effects and may lower blood sugar in people with type 2 diabetes.*

▼ ▼ ▼

For a satisfying green tea cooler, combine the green tea with the pomegranate or prickly pear juice. Mix and pour over ice.

## Infused Strawberry Green Tea Cooler

4 cups water

4 green tea bags

8–10 sweet strawberries, sliced

Mint leaves, for garnish

**Serves 4**

Calories per serving: 11
Total fat: 0g
Saturated fat: 0g
Calories from fat: 1
Protein: 0g
Carbohydrates: 3g
Dietary fiber: 1g
Sugars: 1g

*Strawberries turn tea into a satisfying fruity drink with a lingering hint of strawberry in your mouth. Make sure the strawberries are sweet and full of flavor. Other fruits and berries make refreshing infused drinks, too.*

▼ ▼ ▼

In a pitcher, add water, tea bags, and strawberries. Refrigerate for at least 6 hours to steep. Then pour the mix over ice into a tall glass, and garnish with bruised (lightly press leaves with muddler or wooden spoon to release oil) mint leaves. As an alternative method, pour 2 cups of hot (not boiling) water over tea and steep for 5 minutes; then add the remaining water and strawberries. Refrigerate for about 2 hours before serving on ice with bruised mint leaves for garnish.

**Variation** Substitute chopped mangos or sliced peaches for the strawberries.

## Mesquite Bean Tea

40 mesquite bean pods, broken into pieces (bite down on a pod to test for sweetness before harvesting)

6 cups water for boiling

**Serves 4**

*I would choose a steaming cup of soothing mesquite bean tea over most teas. It has a pleasingly mild flavor with not only a distinct scent of honey, but also a sweet honey flavor. Maybe that's why one species is named honey mesquite. It is a traditional drink for Native Americans of the Southwest.*

▼ ▼ ▼

Rinse the pods with water; then in a saucepan, bring water and pods to a boil. Reduce heat, cover, and continue to boil for 30 or 40 minutes or until pods and pulp are softened. Turn off heat, keep covered, and allow to cool. Position a fine-mesh strainer over a one-quart pitcher and strain the liquid, while pressing against the broken-up mesquite pods with the back of a large spoon. (The sweetness is in the pulp and beans.) Serve over ice or reheat to serve hot. You can store the juice in refrigerator for a day or two.

## Green Tea

Green, oolong, and black teas come from the same plant. Green tea leaves are steamed, while black and oolong are fermented, resulting in green tea retaining more antioxidants called polyphones. Antioxidants scavenge in the body for free radicals, which are known to cause damage to the cells. Population-based clinical studies indicate that green tea may prevent coronary artery disease, lower total cholesterol and raise HDL, and help protect against some cancers. However, green tea alone is not a miracle tonic for good health. Total diet and exercise also play huge roles in preventing disease, as shown in the lifestyle of Okinawans. They get exercise from lifestyle, not planned exercise. They drink green tea and follow a plant-based diet, including fresh vegetables, whole grains, fish, small amounts of pork, and soy.

## Kumquat-Ginger Infused Water

1 inch piece of fresh ginger, peeled

About ½ gallon fresh water

3 fresh mint vines or stems, 8–10 inches each

2 cups kumquats, quartered and seeded

Ice

1 small sprig of mint per serving, for garnish

A few kumquat slices, for garnish

**Serves 8**

Calories per serving: 0
Total fat: 0g
Saturated fat: 0g
Calories from fat: 0
Protein: 0g
Carbohydrates: 0g
Dietary fiber: 0g
Sugars: 0g

*This drink is refreshingly colorful with a few stems of just-clipped mint suspended beneath floating sweet kumquat slices. Pressed ginger imparts a hint of mildly spicy flavor that plays against sweet-tart kumquat slices and pleasant notes of mint, delivering a pleasingly satisfying thirst quencher. Note that young spring ginger doesn't need peeling.*

▼ ▼ ▼

In a pitcher, press the ginger with a wooden spoon handle to release its juice. Squeeze or pierce a number of the mint leaves to release the flavor, add them to the pitcher, and then fill half full with water. Add kumquat slices and top off with more water. If necessary, stir to attractively suspend the mint. Allow it to infuse for about ½ hour in the refrigerator. Pour over ice in a tall glass and add a sprig of mint and a few kumquat slices for pizzazz. If serving a large group, use a two- or three-gallon glass beverage dispenser and double or triple the recipe, then fill with ice cubes. Citrus rind will gradually cause the drink to become slightly bitter, so serve within 4 to 6 hours.

### Variations

▸ Instead of kumquat, place slices from 2 oranges, 1 lime, and 1 lemon into a ½–gallon pitcher with about 20 mint leaves; add water and stir. Allow to steep in the refrigerator for 2 hours.

▸ Aromatic rosemary is full of antioxidants and can aid digestion. Instead of using kumquat and mint, add 3 or 4 rosemary sprigs—twist the leaves a few times to release the perfume—and drop into the water along with peeled grapefruit sections (the rind tends to be bitter). Let it steep in the refrigerator for about 1 hour.

## Fruit or Vegetable infused Waters

Infused waters with a hint of fresh fruit offer a tasty alternative to refresh and hydrate with almost zero calories. You can choose your favorite fruit (or vegetable or herb) and use more or less water. I've given you a few ideas to get you started.

## Agua Fresca de Melón (Watermelon Version)

4 cups cubed watermelon

¼ cup Key lime juice

1 tablespoon evaporated cane juice

4 cups water, divided

Lime slices

Ice

**Serves 4**

Calories per serving: 63
Total fat: 0g
Saturated fat: 0g
Calories from fat: 2
Protein: 1g
Carbohydrates: 16g
Dietary fiber: 1g
Sugars: 13g

*Sometimes, along with the flesh of some type of melon, the seeds and fibrous material are tossed into the drink, which adds a nutty flavor and more protein, nutrients, and phytochemicals. Gloria, my sister-in-law, makes a cantaloupe version using only the seeds and stringy fibers from the cantaloupe and adding a little evaporated cane juice to the water.*

▼ ▼ ▼

Blend the watermelon pieces, lime juice, evaporated cane juice, and ½ cup of the water. Pour over a coarse strainer into a pitcher; then stir in the remaining water. Serve over ice in a tall glass and garnish with a lime slice. For a thicker drink with more fiber, don't strain.

### Variations

▸ For a fizzy watermelon drink, blend melon as above, then substitute naturally carbonated mineral water for the 3½ cups of water poured into the pitcher, and serve immediately.

▸ Replace the watermelon with cantaloupe or honeydew, without the rind.

## Agua Fresca de Tamarindo

8–12 cups water, divided

6–8 tamarind pods

1 cinnamon stick

1 teaspoon pure vanilla extract

1–2 tablespoons honey

**Serves 6–8**

*Boiled tamarind pods are tart, somewhat sour, and carry an earthy or woody undertone; thus this drink is often made extremely sweet. Vanilla, a cinnamon stick, and a little sweetener create a tasty, cola-like balance of flavors. Also, it loses some of its sourness after it sits in the refrigerator for a couple of hours. Here's my slightly sweetened version.*

▼ ▼ ▼

In a small saucepan, bring 2 cups of the water, the pods, and the cinnamon stick to a boil. Reduce heat and simmer for about 20 minutes; then turn off heat and steep for about two hours or until pulp softens. When cooled, remove the hard shell and root-looking pieces, and discard them. Press the seeds and pulp against a fine sieve, forcing the juice through and into a half-gallon pitcher. Add vanilla, honey, and the remaining 6–8 cups of water (use the amount of water needed to achieve the desired strength). Serve over ice. This drink may be stored in refrigerator for a day or two.

**Variation** Skip the second addition of water, and in individual glasses mix a couple teaspoons of the brew with the desired amount of naturally carbonated mineral water, for a soda served over ice.

## Agua Fresca de Jamaica (Hibiscus Flower Tea)

1-inch piece of peeled ginger, sliced

4–6 cups water, divided

2 six-inch cinnamon sticks

¼ cup dried hibiscus flower

1 tablespoon evaporated cane juice, optional

1 unpeeled orange, sliced

**Serves 4–8**

Calories per serving: 19
Total fat: 0g
Saturated fat: 0g
Calories from fat: 0
Protein: 0g
Carbohydrates: 5g
Dietary fiber: 0g
Sugars: 4g

*A tall iced glass of vibrantly colored hibiscus tea has a crisp, refreshing character punctuated with a pleasing tartness, making it a refreshing caffeine-free summertime drink. For us, it is more refreshing without sugar. If a little sweetness is desired, a squeeze of fresh orange juice or a tablespoon of unsweetened pomegranate juice will probably give enough sweetness for most. Drink it plain or spice it up with the recipe below. It is also quite soothing served hot.*

*Note: Various research studies have shown hibiscus to lower blood pressure, and the deep red color is not only beautiful but an indication of its antioxidant power. It is also a good source of vitamin C.*

▼ ▼ ▼

In a small saucepan, press the ginger with a wooden spoon to release its juice. Add 2 cups of water and cinnamon sticks, and bring to a boil. Turn off heat, add hibiscus, cover, and steep for 20 minutes. If hibiscus is steeped for too long, it may become somewhat bitter. Strain into a pitcher, while pressing the liquid from the flowers. Add remaining water, evaporated cane juice (or add sweetener to each individual glass, to taste), and orange slices. Store in fridge for ½ hour to bring out the orange flavor. For a weaker tea, add more water. Serve over ice or serve warm. The orange rind will gradually cause the drink to become bitter. Therefore, serve within 4 to 6 hours.

### Variations

▸ Add a twist of lime and a few twisted mint leaves.

▸ Mix together 1 cup brewed green tea, ¼ cup hibiscus tea, and ¼ cup fresh unsweetened pomegranate juice or prickly pear juice.

## Aguas Frescas

For generations, street vendors throughout Mexico have enticed passersby with an array of large, glistening barrel-shaped glass jugs filled with colorful iced *aguas frescas* ("fresh waters"). My husband said when he was growing up in San Felipe de Jalisco, the maids would turn fresh fruit from the ranch or the local market into a refreshing agua fresca every day. He and his sister Gloria refer to today's aguas frescas as syrupy waters with a little fruit and don't believe they are much better for you than a soda. The drinks on these pages rely on the sweetness of the fruit rather than the overpowering sweetness of the sugar. Some of the more traditional favorites are presented, but flavors are pretty much limitless. Get creative and make your own signature aguas frescas.

## Horchata

1 cup brown rice

4–6 cups water

2 three-inch cinnamon sticks (preferred), or 1 teaspoon ground cinnamon

2–3 inches of lime peel with no white pith (use groove on zester or vegetable peeler)

1 vanilla bean (preferred), or 1½ teaspoons pure vanilla extract

1–2 tablespoons evaporated cane juice or honey

**Serves 4**

Calories per serving: 127
Total fat: 1g
Saturated fat: 0g
Calories from fat: 7
Protein: 2g
Carbohydrates: 25g
Dietary fiber: 1g
Sugars: 4g

*Horchata (a rice drink) is one of the most popular iced aguas frescas. My sister-in-law Gloria recalled watching the maids make horchata during the 1950s on her family's hacienda in southern Mexico. "They would grind the rice for the horchata on a metate y mano (rolling a rough cylinder-shape stone over grain placed on a rough stone concave slab)." She also remembers her grandmother dispensing it as a tonic for an upset stomach. Today, a food processor or blender is usually used. The drink can be light and very refreshing or sickeningly sweet. Most horchata in the US is extremely sweet (usually made from a mix) and not refreshing. Traditionally, it is made from uncooked white long-grain rice and mixed with sugar, cinnamon, and vanilla. This recipe uses basmati brown rice, which imparts a nuttier flavor and is sweetened with a tiny bit of sugar. I discovered the inclusion of lime zest makes an amazingly refreshing difference. It's a simple drink but does require advance planning.*

▼ ▼ ▼

Rinse the rice in cold water until the water runs clear. Place the rice and 2 cups of the water in a container, along with the cinnamon and lime peel. Cut the vanilla bean in half and slit open each half. Scrape the soft center of the bean into the rice water and drop each half of the bean shell into the water. Let this mixture sit at room temperature for a couple of hours and then place in the refrigerator for 12 hours.

Remove the vanilla bean halves and 1 cinnamon stick. Cut these into pieces, and place in a blender jar with 1 cup of fresh water; blend until the cinnamon and bean are finely ground; then strain the mixture into a pitcher using an ultra-fine strainer. Transfer the rice with the water into the blender and blend until the rice is processed into a fine grind (but not as fine as flour or powder); then strain through an ultra-fine sieve into the pitcher with the vanilla-cinnamon water. To eliminate most of the grit that typically settles at the bottom of the pitcher, you can place a flour-sack towel over the strainer. Scrape and rub the rice with a spoon to press more liquid through the towel; then make a pouch out of the towel and keep twisting to squeeze out any additional liquid. Add the remaining water.

Taste and, if desired, add more water, cinnamon, or vanilla. Serve over ice in tall glasses. Add more lime peel to the remaining mix; you can store horchata in the refrigerator for up to 3 days. Residue will continue to settle at the bottom of the pitcher. Simply stir and serve.

### Variations

▸ Substitute 2 cups of water with 2 cups nonfat milk.

▸ Add 1 cup of raw whole almonds or blanched almonds and an additional cup of water to the rice and soak them with the rice. If using whole almonds, after soaking, remove the skins from the almonds and discard the skins. Add 1 additional cup of fresh water and grind the almonds with the rice.

## Muddled Gingered Limeade

2 Key limes or 1 large lime, halved and then quartered, seeds removed

2 inches of fresh ginger, peeled and cut into slices

40 fresh mint leaves (I use chocolate mint from my garden)

1–2 tablespoons evaporated cane juice or honey

¼ cup lime juice

4 cups water

Crushed ice

**Serves 4**

Calories per serving: 30
Total fat: 0g
Saturated fat: 0g
Calories from fat: 1
Protein: 0g
Carbohydrates: 8g
Dietary fiber: 1g
Sugars: 5g

*Instead of blending, ingredients are muddled by slightly pressing and grinding the fruit with a muddler or wooden spoon (I use the spoon's handle), which releases the juices and healthy essential oils from the lime rind and mint leaves. These oils impart an enjoyably distinct flavor and aroma. This drink is like a mojito without the punch. If you wish, you could also add the punch! It's tangy and minty, with a bit of spicy ginger and just a tad of sweetness. Since bruised lime rind may impart bitterness after a couple hours, serve immediately after making.*

▼ ▼ ▼

Place lime pieces, ginger, mint, and evaporated cane juice or honey in a pitcher and muddle by pressing on the ingredients while twisting the muddler or wooden spoon handle. Make sure that each piece of ginger is mashed and that the juice is expelled from the lime. When the air is filled with the scent of lime and mint, stop muddling. Your objective is to achieve great flavors through bruising the lime rind and mint, not turning them to mush. Stir in the water and lime juice; then pour the mixture over crushed ice while holding back the ginger pieces with a spoon. If you want a clean drink, strain while pouring into glasses.

Variation   Substitute naturally carbonated mineral water for the water.

## Agua Fresca de Chia

1 cup fresh lemon or lime juice

¼ cup chia seeds

8 cups water

¼ cup evaporated cane juice or 2 tablespoons honey

**Serves 8–10**

Calories per serving: 44
Total fat: 1g
Saturated fat: 0g
Calories from fat: 12
Protein: 1g
Carbohydrates: 8g
Dietary fiber: 2g
Sugars: 4g

*When chia is mentioned, anyone who grew up in Mexico brings up agua fresca de chia. My husband remembers a pitcher of slightly sweetened, weak lemonade with a little chia floating atop and some settled at the bottom. He says skip the sugar and it is the best thirst quencher of all aguas frescas. The seeds aid in hydration and are also filling. They are full of protein and have an excellent balance of omega-3 to omega-6.*

▼ ▼ ▼

Combine all ingredients and stir vigorously. To keep the chia from clumping together, let the mixture sit for about 5 minutes and stir again, then stir again in another 5 minutes. Refrigerate for a couple hours to allow the chia to gel. Just prior to serving, give the drink a swirl to mix the chia. We usually cut the lemon juice in half and don't add any sweetener for a more refreshing drink.

## Pink Lemonade

1 cup fresh lemon juice,
or frozen juice preserved from fresh lemons

3 thin slices of beet bulb

4–5 cups water

1–2 tablespoons evaporated cane juice or honey

**Serves 4–5 (8 ounces each)**

Calories per serving: 31
Total fat: 0g
Saturated fat: 0g
Calories from fat: 0
Protein: 0g
Carbohydrates: 10g
Dietary fiber: 0g
Sugars: 6g

*Even though color does not affect its flavor, pastel pink lemonade has aesthetic appeal. A slice or two of raw beet dropped into the lemonade will make it an inviting shade of pink without affecting the taste. Making lemonade with fresh-from-the-tree lemons is so easy, and freezing juice from in-season lemons enables us to enjoy lemonade during the summer. Frozen pink lemonade concentrate brands are usually colored with grape juice and sweetened with both sugar and high-fructose corn syrup. Canned or bottled may be colored with beta-carotene, fruit, or an artificial dye.*

▼ ▼ ▼

Mix ingredients together and stir; test for sweetness and let sit for 5 minutes to allow the beets to bleed, creating pink lemonade. Serve over ice, holding back the beets as you pour into individual glasses.

### Variations

▸ Replace the beet slices with 4 or 5 large strawberries to add color. Remove the stems and slice the strawberries. Release the colored strawberry juice into the lemonade by pressing the slices against a fine sieve with the back of a spoon. Stir and serve over ice.

▸ Prickly Pear Lemonade: Prickly pear makes beautiful fuchsia lemonade with a hint of prickly pear flavor. Stir ½ cup of prickly pear juice into the lemonade. For those who don't have the fruit in the backyard, buy Cheri's Desert Harvest Cactus Syrup. She's already added the sugar; so, use 1 tablespoon of the syrup in place of the sugar. Arizona Cactus Ranch also offers a non-sweetened prickly pear juice concentrate. Add 2 tablespoons juice plus 1 tablespoon sugar.

## Prickly Pear Margarita, Chef Ryan Clark

1 ounce blanco tequila

1 ounce lime juice

1 ounce orange juice

1 dash bitters

¼ ounce honey

2 teaspoons prickly pear juice, frozen

_____

**Serves 1**

Calories per serving: 117
Total fat: 0g
Saturated fat: 0g
Calories from fat: 1
Protein: 0g
Carbohydrates: 24g
Dietary fiber: 0g
Sugars: 10g

*A delicious and colorful adult margarita shared by Ryan Clark, Executive Chef of Lodge on the Desert in Tucson, Arizona.*

▼ ▼ ▼

Add tequila, lime juice, orange juice, bitters and honey to a mixing glass. Add ice and shake until chilled. Pour out into a margarita glass and fill with ice if needed. Crush up frozen prickly pear juice so that it resembles a granita or sorbet. Top margarita with a small scoop and garnish with a lime wedge.

### Preparing Fresh Prickly Pear Juice

Most people cook the pears and make juice; but I prefer the flavor of fresh juice. To harvest pears, I hold the fruit with tongs and then twist them off the plant, and drop them in a bucket. Never pick up the fruit with your fingers or you will have tiny little stickers embedded in your skin. Then don a pair of heavy kitchen gloves, fill the sink with water, and rinse the fruit by swishing the pears around with a long handled spoon. Drain, and repeat a couple times. Then holding with tongs, scrub each one with a kitchen brush. Using a sieve with small holes or a colander, push the juice through the holes. Using a clean colander, place over a large bowl, line it with a flour sack towel, pour in a couple cups of juice and allow the juice to seep through the towel. The towel will become coated with pulp and some stickers; so frequently rinse off the film with water. Repeat until all of the juice has been filtered. Throw away the towel. With a clean towel, using a clean colander, filter the juice again. Freeze in batches for later use. The fruit is a rich source of magnesium and the amino acid taurine, which are believed to be good for the heart and brain. The brilliant fuchsia color is from betalain, the same pigment that colors beets. It's a potent class of antioxidant power that is believed to help detoxify the body and reduce inflammation. However, it may be somewhat destroyed from prolonged cooking—another reason for fresh juice!

## Hibiscus Tea Margarita, Chef Ryan Clark

1 ounce blanco tequila

¾ ounce lime juice

½ ounce honey

4 ounces strong-brewed hibiscus tea

**Serves 1**

Calories per serving: 118
Total fat: 0g
Saturated fat: 0g
Calories from fat: 0
Protein: 0g
Carbohydrates: 25g
Dietary fiber: 0g
Sugars: 12g

*A delicious and colorful adult margarita shared by Ryan Clark, Executive Chef of Lodge on the Desert in Tucson, Arizona.*

▼ ▼ ▼

Add tequila, lime juice, and honey to a mixing glass. Add ice and shake until chilled. Pour out into a margarita glass and fill with ice if needed. Top off with hibiscus tea.

## Basil Gimlet with Watermelon Ice Cubes, Chef Ryan Clark

2 ounces vodka

½ ounce lime juice

4 leaves fresh basil

2 lime wedges

¼ ounce honey

3 watermelon cubes, frozen

**Serves 1**

Calories per serving: 165
Total fat: 0g
Saturated fat: 0g
Calories from fat: 1
Protein: 0g
Carbohydrates: 10g
Dietary fiber: 0g
Sugars: 8g

*A refreshing adult gimlet shared by Ryan Clark, Executive Chef of Lodge on the Desert in Tucson, Arizona.*

▼ ▼ ▼

Muddle limes and basil for a few minutes. Add vodka, lime juice, and honey into a mixing glass and cover with ice. Shake well until chilled and strain into a martini glass. Garnish with fresh basil and watermelon ice cubes.

*Basil Gimlet with Watermelon Ice Cubes.*

# APPETIZERS, DIPS & SAUCES

**Have you ever noticed** most appetizers served at parties are high-fat dips, cheeses, tiny fatty sausages, fried chicken wings, and so on? By dinnertime, you have consumed enough fat and calories to fill your quota for a week. Why eat any more? Over-indulging during the holidays and at parties throughout the year can lead to permanent weight gain. Many people believe that they can take it off after their eating spree is over. Unfortunately, this is not the case. Weight gain accumulates over the years with an end result of becoming overweight or obese, which may contribute to serious health problems such as heart disease and diabetes.

A research study published in the March 2000 issue of *The New England Journal of Medicine* found that adult participants gained about one pound between Thanksgiving and New Years, and those who were obese gained five or more pounds. It was also noted by Dr. Yanovski, the study's principal investigator, that a year after the study began, the participants had not lost the extra weight gained and were 1.4 pounds heavier. Another study, published in the November 2006 *Nutrition Journal*, reported that during Thanksgiving, college students gained from 1.05 pounds to more than five pounds. On the average, undergraduate males gained 1.3 pounds, undergraduate females 0.9 pounds, graduate students 1.8 pounds, and obese students 5 or more pounds. This doesn't sound like a lot of weight gain; but when you think of the accumulative affect of pounds adding on over the years, before you know it, you are ten pounds heavier, and it's tough to lose it.

To keep the needle or the digital mark on your scales stuck at a healthy weight, include some of the following nourishing appetizers. They are deliciously healthy alternatives to the salty, fat-laden appetizers usually served at parties.

Some of these recipes include a non-dairy vegan cheese, from which you can dream up a variety of different textures and flavors. It can replace cream cheese in appetizers, be spread on whole-grain muffins or toast, stuffed in pasta shells, or replace ricotta in eggplant Parmesan. It is a flavorful alternative to dairy cheese, with a number of health benefits. The secret ingredient in vegan cheese is cashews. Aside from being high in dietary fiber and a good source of heart-healthy magnesium, cashews also contain tocopherols, squalene, and phytosterols, which are also heart-protective. One-fourth cup of soaked cashews contains about 6 grams of fat, with a "good" fat ratio of 1:2:1 for saturated, monounsaturated, and polyunsaturated, with no cholesterol. Since cashews are high in fat and have a high energy density, they should be eaten in moderation, exchanging one fat for another, thus, not adding more fat to your diet. Every once in a while, give the cows a break and lessen your carbon footprint by enjoying some vegan cheese. ▶

*Appetizers with vegan cheese (recipes on pages 38–40).*

## Vegan Cheese with Herbs

1 ¾ cups raw cashew pieces

½ cup lemon juice

1 teaspoon oregano, crushed to release flavor

1 medium garlic clove, cut into 2 or 3 pieces

1 teaspoon sea salt

1 cup (loosely packed) torn fresh basil leaves or cilantro leaves

**Makes 2–2 ½ cups**

Calories per serving (1 tablespoon): 45

Total fat: 3g

Saturated fat: 1g

Calories from fat: 29

Protein: 1g

Carbohydrates: 0g

Dietary fiber: 0g

Sugars: 0g

*Since the cashews need to be soaked, plan ahead at least eight hours. Aside from the time needed for soaking the cashews, it takes about five minutes to make vegan "cheese." Soaking produces a smoother consistency and reduces the cashew flavor, along with the fat and calories by volume. Texture-wise, it resembles ricotta, and has an amazingly pleasing flavor for a creamy cheese replacement.*

▼ ▼ ▼

Soak the raw cashews in filtered water for 8 to 12 hours. They will almost double in size. Drain and rinse in a colander. Depending on the cashew and the length of time soaked, there may be more than 2 cups of soaked cashews, but you will use only 2 cups to make the cheese. Place the two cups of soaked cashews in a food processor and thoroughly blend with the other ingredients, except the basil, until creamy. Add the basil leaves and pulse until the basil is chopped and mixed into the "cheese." If using a food processor that has greater than a 9-cup capacity, it is not recommended to make less than a 2-cup batch, in order to achieve a smooth cheese consistency. The following appetizers call for 1 cup of vegan cheese. If you don't use it all for appetizers, it's great on whole-grain toast for lunch.

Variation: **Vegan Chipotle Cheese** Substitute Key lime juice for the lemon juice, add ½–2 chipotle chiles in adobo sauce, chopped, and 1 teaspoon adobo sauce (page 50, or use canned), and substitute fresh cilantro leaves for the basil. Follow the directions for Vegan Cheese with Herbs. Taste for spiciness; if desired, add more chipotle according to your and your guests' heat tolerances.

Variation: **Vegan Sweet Chipotle Cheese** Substitute Key lime juice for the lemon juice, add ½–2 chipotle chiles in adobo sauce, chopped, and 1 teaspoon adobo sauce (page 50, or use canned), add 1 additional garlic clove, ⅔ cup pitted dates, ½ teaspoon ground cumin, 2 teaspoons lime zest, and 1 teaspoon orange zest. Follow the directions for Vegan Cheese with Herbs. Taste and add more salt if necessary, and check for chile spiciness. Add the zests at the same time as the basil.

## Cucumber with Vegan Cheese

1 cup Vegan Cheese with Herbs (page 38)

2 cucumbers (7 inches each)

2 tablespoons chopped fresh dill weed

**Makes 48 pieces**

Calories per serving (1 piece): 15
Total fat: 1g
Saturated fat: 0g
Calories from fat: 10
Protein: 0g
Carbohydrates: 1g
Dietary fiber: 0g
Sugars: 0g

*It's a blessing to go to a party and enjoy a crisp and refreshing appetizer. Cucumbers fit the bill!*

▼ ▼ ▼

With fork tines, score the cucumbers from end to end; then slice into scant ¼-inch rounds. Top each slice with 1 teaspoon of vegan cheese and accent with specks of dill frond.

## Cucumber with Wild Alaskan Nova Lox and Vegan Cheese

1 cup Vegan Cheese with Herbs (page 38)

2 cucumbers (7 inches each)

4 ounces wild Alaskan Nova lox

2 tablespoons chopped dill weed

**Makes 48 pieces**

Calories per serving (1 piece): 25
Total fat: 2g
Saturated fat: 0g
Calories from fat: 16
Protein: 1g
Carbohydrates: 1g
Dietary fiber: 0g
Sugars: 0g

*Always choose wild Alaskan salmon over Atlantic-farmed salmon. The taste and texture of wild salmon is remarkably better than farmed. Aside from their culinary superiority, Alaskan salmon are also the most eco-friendly of all salmon, are healthier than farmed, and are low in contaminants.*

▼ ▼ ▼

With fork tines, score the cucumbers from end to end; then slice into scant ¼-inch rounds. On top of each cucumber ring, place a small, thin piece of salmon lox, followed by 1 teaspoon of vegan "cheese," and accent with specs of dill frond.

## Stuffed Salmon–Basil Rolls

1 cup Vegan Cheese with Herbs (page 38)

12–16 ounces wild Alaskan Nova lox

48 medium–large basil leaves

1 large red bell pepper, roasted and cut into 1/2 x 1/2-inch pieces (see Fire-roasting, page 15)

48 toothpicks

**Makes 48 pieces**

Calories per serving: 51
Total fat: 4g
Saturated fat: 1g
Calories from fat: 32
Protein: 4g
Carbohydrates: 1g
Dietary fiber: 0g
Sugars: 0g

*These are as tasty as they are attractive and wear the perfect colors for a festive Christmas cocktail party.*

▼ ▼ ▼

Place a 3½- to 4-inch piece of the salmon lox on the dull side of a basil leaf, then spread ½ teaspoon of vegan cheese over the salmon lox. Roll up the leaf; dot it with a piece of bell pepper, and cinch the pepper and basil with a toothpick.

Variation: **Chipotle-stuffed Salmon**
For a spicy kick, try using Vegan Chipotle Cheese (page 38).

Variation: **Sweet Chipotle-stuffed Salmon Wrapped in Basil**
For a spicy, sweet, and savory flavor, use Vegan Chipotle Sweet Cheese (page 38) prepared with cilantro, not basil.

Variation: **Sweet Chipotle-stuffed Salmon**
For a simpler dish, use Vegan Sweet Chipotle Cheese (page 38), and roll cheese and salmon together, skipping the basil and bell pepper.

## Basic Hummus

1 can (15 ounces) garbanzo beans, drained (reserve broth)

2 tablespoons organic raw tahini (sesame seed paste)

3 tablespoons lemon juice, adjust to taste

1–2 large garlic cloves, adjust to taste

1/4 teaspoon ground cumin

Salt

**Makes 1 3/4 cups**

Calories per serving (1 tablespoon): 19
Total fat: 1g
Saturated fat: 0g
Calories from fat: 2
Protein: 1g
Carbohydrates: 2g
Dietary fiber: 1g
Sugars: 0g

*Hummus is a traditional dish in Greece, many other Mediterranean countries, parts of the Middle East, and India. Since not all garlic has the same strength, taste the hummus as you make it. Individual tastes also vary in the degree of tahini and lemon flavors preferred. Therefore, keep adding lemon and tahini until you have achieved the desired blend. Garbanzo beans are a good source of folate (folic acid) and contain a good amount of fiber—both are heart healthy. The sesamin in sesame seeds has been found to lower inflammation and cholesterol. Serve with a tray of colorful raw vegetables, such as broccoli, summer squash, peppers, cauliflower, carrots, or cherry tomatoes.*

▼ ▼ ▼

Place all the ingredients in a blender and blend. Thin with reserved bean broth until the desired consistency is achieved. Adjust tahini, lemon juice, and garlic to taste. Blend for 3 minutes to achieve a smooth consistency.

Variation: **Spicy Cilantro Tepary Bean Hummus** After preparing the Basic Hummus recipe with tepary beans, add ½–1 teaspoon ground toasted chipotle pepper (rub whole toasted chipotle against a fine microplane grater) and process to thoroughly blend. Add ½–1 cup loosely packed, coarsely chopped fresh cilantro. Pulse a few times to finely chop the cilantro. Taste and adjust flavors by adding more cilantro, salt, or lemon.

## Tomato Bruschetta

1 grilled or broiled red bell pepper, diced to yield 1½ cups

1–2 thick slices of red onion, grilled or broiled, then diced to yield ⅓ cup

½ cup finely chopped fresh basil

1 tablespoon finely chopped parsley

1 cup diced and drained fresh unpeeled tomato

1 tablespoon minced fresh oregano, or 1 teaspoon dry oregano, crushed to release flavor

⅓ cup crumbled goat feta

1 tablespoon chopped Kalamata olives

1 teaspoon balsamic vinegar

1 tablespoon extra-virgin olive oil

¼–½ teaspoon sea salt

Freshly ground black pepper

Whole-grain or sourdough baguette, cut into about ¼-inch slices

Extra-virgin olive oil spray

**Makes 36 servings**

Calories per serving: 31
Total fat: 1g
Saturated fat: 0g
Calories from fat: 6
Protein: 1g
Carbohydrates: 5g
Dietary fiber: 0g
Sugars: 1g

*Fresh flavorful tomatoes, peppers, and basil are usually in abundance in our summer garden and are so much tastier than store-bought. One way to take advantage of this gorgeous harvest is by combining their wonderful flavors into a bruschetta topping.*

▼ ▼ ▼

Mix together the first 12 ingredients (bell pepper through black pepper) and allow to sit for about 30 minutes; toss with fork. Taste, season with a little salt and pepper if needed, then toss and taste again.

Lightly toast the bread slices and spray one side with olive oil. Top each slice with one tablespoon of topping and serve.

## Chipotle Herbed Shrimp on Rosemary Skewers

**Marinade**

2 teaspoons lime zest

1/3 cup fresh lime juice

3 tablespoons extra-virgin olive oil

2–3 medium garlic cloves, run through garlic press (yields 2 teaspoons)

1 teaspoon Mexican oregano, crushed to release flavor

1/2 teaspoon ground cumin

1/2 teaspoon ground chipotle chile

1 teaspoon smoked sweet paprika

1/4 cup minced fresh cilantro or basil (lemon basil has the best flavor)

2 teaspoons minced fresh rosemary

1/2 teaspoon sea salt

**Sauce**

3 tablespoons of marinade

1 tablespoon lime juice

1 teaspoon honey

**For the Skewers**

1 pound shrimp (16–20 count)

1–2 peaches (summer season) quartered, then halved

1 red onion, quartered

1/4 cup tequila

16–20 rosemary stems (6–8 inches long), for skewers

Sprinkling of evaporated cane juice

**Serves 8, as an appetizer**

Calories per serving: 75
Total fat: 4g
Saturated fat: 1g
Calories from fat: 34
Protein: 2g
Carbohydrates: 7g
Dietary fiber: 1g
Sugars: 3g

*Want to throw a party where everyone is happy and engaged in captivating conversations? Rosemary skewered appetizers should do the trick, since inhaling aromatic rosemary is known to instill a clear mind and lift spirits. Besides, these appetizers taste great, having a balance of sweetness from tequila-soaked peaches against the spiciness of the chipotle-herb marinade. (Serve with a quinoa or tossed salad and you'll have a meal that will serve four for lunch or dinner.)*

▼ ▼ ▼

Combine all the marinade ingredients in a bowl that will also be large enough to hold all the shrimp.

To make the sauce, transfer 3 tablespoons of marinade to a cup and add the tablespoon of lime juice and the honey. Set aside. When ready to serve shrimp, warm in a microwave until the honey dissolves—sauce should be warm, not hot.

Wash, shell, and devein the shrimp, gently toss it in the bowl with the marinade, and marinate for 30–60 minutes in the refrigerator. Toss the peaches in the tequila; set aside. While the shrimp and peaches are marinating, clip the stems of rosemary from the bush, if you have rosemary in your garden. Strip the leaves from the stem, top down, leaving a spray of leaves at the top of the stem. Sprinkle the peaches with a small amount of evaporated cane juice, then thread a piece of peach onto a rosemary skewer, followed by a shrimp and a piece of onion, and if room, another piece of onion and a piece of peach. Repeat until all the shrimp, peaches, and onions are used.

Shrimp will cook in 2–4 minutes on each side on a grill or under a broiler. Don't overcook. Arrange attractively on a platter and drizzle with the sauce.

### Variations

▸ Instead of peaches, use 1-inch square pieces of watermelon or fresh black mission figs cut in half.

▸ Substitute fruit with cherry tomato, zucchini, yellow crookneck squash, onion, or fennel bulb pieces for appetizing accents with the shrimp.

▸ This recipe is also ideal for lunch or dinner. Use eight 8–10-inch rosemary stems for the skewers, increase to 1½ pounds of shrimp, and add more fruit. Divide the shrimp and fruit among the skewers. Serve with Cilantro Lime Quinoa Pilaf (page 154) and a tossed salad.

## Herbed Cannellini Bruschetta

1¾ cups cooked cannellini beans (see page 155), or canned, drained, juice reserved

2 teaspoons lemon juice

1 cup medium-chopped heirloom tomato

2 tablespoons finely chopped fresh basil leaves

1 teaspoon finely chopped fresh oregano leaves

1 teaspoon finely chopped fresh rosemary leaves

1 teaspoon extra-virgin olive oil

1 baguette (12 inches), cut into ⅓-inch slices

2 garlic cloves, crushed

Extra-virgin olive oil to brush or spray on bread

### Makes 36 bruschettas

Calories per serving: 20
Total fat: 0.2g
Saturated fat: 0g
Calories from fat: 2
Protein: 1g
Carbohydrates: 3g
Dietary fiber: 1g
Sugars: 0.2g

*Bean appetizers are a tasty and filling alternative to cheese appetizers and are also less expensive. Once the beans are cooked, the bruschetta takes little time to put together. Great northern or navy beans are interchangeable with cannellini beans in this recipe. I believe the cannellini has a slightly better flavor than the other two, but it is two to three times more expensive. With its superior nutritional content, the drought-tolerant, wonderful-tasting tepary bean of the Sonoran Desert is also a great substitute.*

▼ ▼ ▼

To make the bruschetta topping, mash ¾ cup of the drained beans and then mix with the remaining 1 cup of whole beans. Combine the cooked beans with the next 6 ingredients (lemon juice through olive oil); then taste and adjust seasonings. Allow the bean mixture to sit for about 1 hour.

Toast the bread slices, rub one side of each toasted slice with garlic, and then spray or brush with olive oil. Top with about 1 tablespoon of the bean mixture and serve.

## Fresh Salsa

1 cup finely chopped salad tomatoes

1 medium-size jalapeño, finely chopped

2–3 tablespoons minced onion

1–2 teaspoons minced garlic

½ cup minced cilantro or basil

1 tablespoon olive oil

Pinch of sea salt

Freshly ground pepper

2 tablespoons Key lime juice

### Makes 1¾ cups

Calories per serving (¼ cup): 24
Total fat: 2g
Saturated fat: 0g
Calories from fat: 18
Protein: 0g
Carbohydrates: 2g
Dietary fiber: 1g
Sugars: 1g

*Fresh salsa adds enjoyable spicy flavor and a touch of color to fish, beans, poultry, and meats. Also, where there is color, you have phytonutrients. For the best flavor and texture, eat within a few hours; it can, however, be stored covered in the refrigerator for 1–2 days.*

▼ ▼ ▼

Toss all ingredients together and serve.

## Fig Salsa

1 ½ cups freshly picked chopped Mission figs

2 or more teaspoons minced organic serrano pepper

2 teaspoons minced organic red or sweet yellow onion

1 clove organic garlic run through garlic press

2 pinches organic lavender blossoms crushed between fingertips, optional but adds a subtle note

½ teaspoon dried organic thyme leaves crushed between fingertips or 1 tablespoon fresh

1 teaspoon key lime juice

Zest from 1 key lime

2 tablespoons garden-fresh minced lemon or sweet basil leaves or minced cilantro, include stems

Pinch of sea salt (optional)

1 teaspoon honey (only if needed)

### Serves 4

Calories per serving: 109
Total fat: 0g
Saturated fat: 0g
Calories from fat: 4
Protein: 1g
Carbohydrates: 28g
Dietary fiber: 4g
Sugars: 24g

*Ripe figs plucked from our tree immediately tantalize our senses with a fragrantly sweet scent and our memory assures us of a honeyed fruit that will dissolve in our mouths. (Figs are actually a flower.) Their sweetness calms and balances the flavors of the chiles, onions and garlic. Not only are they incredibly delicious but compared to most other fruits and vegetables, contain more soluble and insoluble fiber and calcium. They are also loaded with antioxidants reputed for fighting disease. Serve over fish or organic chicken or top off a fish taco, or add a bit of cinnamon and serve over pastured pork.*

▼ ▼ ▼

Gently toss together all the ingredients. Store-bought figs may not be sweet enough. Taste and if necessary, add the honey. Allow the flavors to meld for about 30 minutes.

## Roasted Butternut Squash Salsa

1 tablespoon extra virgin olive oil
or olive oil sprayed from pump

1 butternut squash (6 inches long)

1 teaspoon extra virgin olive oil

Pinch or two of sea salt

1 cup finely chopped organic sweet yellow onion

4 medium cloves organic garlic, run through garlic press

1 small organic red bell pepper, coarsely chopped

1 cup finely cut organic cilantro leaves
with some minced stems
or basil leaves with stems removed

1/2 cup fresh pomegranate fruit

1/2–1 minced jalapeño or Serrano chile pepper, seeded
and deveined

1 tablespoon organic lime juice

Zest from 1 lime

**Serves 4**

Calories per serving: 122
Total fat: 4g
Saturated fat: 1g
Calories from fat: 34
Protein: 2g
Carbohydrates: 22g
Dietary fiber: 4g
Sugars: 10g

*Carmelized butternut squash punctuated with a little spicy chile brings a wonderful combination of flavors and festive colors to the table. Serve over Lentil Stew (page 70), roasted chicken, or pork.*

▼ ▼ ▼

Preheat oven to 400 degrees F. With a vegetable peeler, peel the squash, cut it in half vertically, and then into ½-inch cubes. Coat a large roasting pan or the bottom of a broiler pan with a small amount of the oil; then add squash and toss with the remaining oil to coat, salt lightly, and then toss again. Roast the squash uncovered in the oven for 10–15 minutes or until lightly browned, occasionally tossing with a spatula. Remove squash from the oven; mix in onion, garlic, and red bell pepper; return squash mixture to the oven for 5 minutes or until onions are crunchy-tender and a little browned; but don't burn. Remove from oven and cool for 5 minutes; then, mix with cilantro, pomegranate, chiles, lime juice, and zest.

## Grapefruit Sauce

2 ¹/₂–3 grapefruit to yield about 1 cup of grapefruit sections without the membrane, hold over bowl while sectioning to reserve juice

1 cup fresh organic grapefruit juice, use leftover juice from sectioned grapefruit

8–12 soft dates, about ³/₄ cup, pit removed, loosely packed

¹/₂ chipotle chile in adobo sauce, canned or page 50

1 medium garlic clove, cut into thirds

¹/₃ cup fresh mint leaves

¹/₃ cup pomegranate seeds

**Serves about 6**

Calories per serving: 71
Total fat: 0g
Saturated fat: 0g
Calories from fat: 3
Protein: 1g
Carbohydrates: 18g
Dietary fiber: 3g
Sugars: 14g

*This is a wonderful sweet and spicy sauce that will add a little zip to fish and poultry. Instead of sugar, I've used local fiber-rich dates that are full of essential nutrients, vitamins, minerals, and phytonutrients.*

▼ ▼ ▼

In food processor workbowl with "S" blade in place or the jar of a blender, blend dates, juice, and chipotle until dates are chopped and dispersed in juice; then add the mint leaves and pulse to chop the leaves. Scrape sauce into microwave-safe serving bowl or sauce pan and mix with grapefruit sections and set aside. When ready to serve, serve at room temperature or slightly warm sauce in saucepan or in microwave. Just before serving, toss in pomegranate seeds; then spoon over fish or chicken.

## Southwest Enchilada Sauce Concentrate

8 large grilled organic red bell peppers

2 large grilled organic poblano chiles, optional

8 grilled organic tomatoes, about 3 cups cooked

2 grilled golf-ball-size garlic heads

1 tablespoon extra virgin olive oil

2 large organic onions

1 cup dry white wine or vermouth

1 cup tightly packed cilantro or parsley

8 chipotle chiles for medium-hot sauce (10–12 for hot), stems removed

2 chiles negro (black), stems removed

1 teaspoon sea salt

1 tablespoon honey

2 teaspoons sweet smoked paprika

2 teaspoons whole cumin seed, toasted and ground

2 teaspoons whole coriander seed, toasted and ground

2 tablespoons dried organic oregano leaves, toasted

⅓ cup organic lime juice

**Makes approximately 5 cups of concentrate or enough sauce for about 40 mild enchiladas**

Calories per serving: 31
Total fat: 0g
Saturated fat: 0g
Calories from fat: 4
Protein: 1g
Carbohydrates: 5g
Dietary fiber: 1g
Sugars: 3g

*Whenever I make enchilada sauce, I make this concentrate and usually use a little right away and freeze the remaining batch. Granted, it takes time to roast, toast, caramelize, and stew; but, the deep full flavors are well worth the time. Besides, preparing large batches saves time in the long run. So, I usually quadruple this recipe—a few simple enchiladas using leftovers can be tossed together in less than 15 minutes. Taste and health worthiness far surpass the popular "natural" enchilada sauces available in grocery stores. You are in control as to how much fat and what type of fat is used, organic ingredients, salt and sugar. Real food ingredients in homemade sauce develop the wonderfully satisfying flavors and don't rely on obscure taste enhancers that are "hydrolyzed" or "autolyzed."*

*Enchilada sauce is a healthy choice because the body absorbs more of the antioxidant lycopene from cooked than raw tomatoes and red peppers. Studies have shown that lycopene may lower cholesterol levels and provide protection against prostate cancer. Add a little oil and it becomes more bioavailable. This may explain why men living in Mediterranean countries, where large amounts of cooked tomatoes are consumed along with olive oil, have low rates of prostate cancer.*

*Note: Chipotle chiles are brown in color resembling a smashed cigar butt. Chile morita is smaller, plumper, moister and reddish. The chipotle has a smokier, woodier flavor than the morita. Either can be used, in the same quantity. Since the morita is smaller than the chipotle, my daughter Amanda doubled the morita in the recipe and had one extremely hot batch of sauce! See How to Fire-Roast, Toast, and Grill (page 15) for directions on how to grill the vegetables and toast the spices.*

▼ ▼ ▼

Grill red bell peppers, poblano chiles, tomatoes, and garlic. For the chipotle sauce, the red bell peppers and poblano chiles are not peeled as directed in the grilling instructions. Place bell peppers, poblanos, and tomatoes in a bowl, cover with plate and steam for 15 minutes to release skins; then, transfer to a plate to cool, retain the juices. Peel garlic, set aside. Charred (not burned) sweet red pepper, poblano, and tomato skins add a smoky flavor and color to the sauce. Therefore, only remove the extremely burned peels and discard. While holding over a bowl to catch the juices, remove seeds from the peppers and stems from peppers and tomatoes and set aside. (Don't run under cold water; flavorful oils will be lost.)

In a food processor, puree bell peppers, tomatoes, their juices, and garlic until smooth. Pour puree in bowl, set aside.

Coarsely chop onions in food processor work bowl. Heat the oil in a large skillet over medium-high heat and sauté onions until caramelized, 8–10 minutes. To speed up caramelizing, turn up heat for a short period of time. While onions are cooking, mince cilantro in food processor by pressing pulse a few times. When onions start sticking to the pan, deglaze with wine, stir in cilantro, and then the pureed pepper mix. Reduce heat to simmer.

Mix with the sauté, the pepper-tomato puree, salt, honey, and paprika. Cover and simmer over low heat while toasting the chiles and spices.

To release their perfume and develop a full bold flavor, toast spices, chipotles, and chiles negro. Break apart the chile and remove as many seeds as possible from the chipotle and chile negro; then add chile pieces to the sauté and simmer on low until chile pieces are soft and pliable, 1–2 hours. When sauce is done, remove from heat and allow to fully cool. Using a food processor or blender, blend the sauce in batches until a smooth puree is achieved.

Sauce can be stored in refrigerator for 2 or 3 days or frozen. Depending on the amount of enchiladas that will be made at a time, freeze according to your needs. ½–⅔ cup of concentrate will yield enough sauce for 4 to 5 enchiladas.

## Enchilada Sauce from Concentrate

½–⅔ cups enchilada sauce concentrate

2 cups mushroom, vegetable, or chicken broth

Zest from 1 key lime

1 teaspoon cornstarch or flour, optional

----

### Makes sauce for 8 enchiladas

Calories per serving: 71
Total fat: 1g
Saturated fat: 0g
Calories from fat: 9g
Protein: 2g
Carbohydrates: 13g
Dietary fiber: 2g
Sugars: 7g

*Adjust spiciness by using more or less concentrate.*

▼ ▼ ▼

When making enchilada sauce from concentrate, combine the first three ingredients and simmer over low heat for at least 5 minutes to combine flavors. For thicker sauce, add a thin cornstarch paste (cornstarch mixed with a little water). Use in the Shiitake Mushroom Enchiladas (page 80) or with any other enchilada recipe.

## Chipotles in Adobo Sauce

10 chile guajillo

2 chile pasilla-ancho

10 chipotles

4 cups water

1 teaspoon olive oil

1 cup minced onion

4 cloves garlic, minced

4 cups coarsely chopped ripe tomatoes

1 tablespoon dried leaf oregano, toasted and rubbed between palms

1 teaspoon dried leaf thyme, toasted and rubbed between palms

2 teaspoons honey

1 teaspoon smoky bitter sweet paprika

1 broken bay leaf

1 teaspoon salt

3 tablespoons vinegar

**Makes 10 whole chipotles in sauce**

Calories per serving (1 chipotle with 1 tablespoon sauce): 60
Total fat: 1g
Saturated fat: 0g
Calories from fat: 7
Protein: 2g
Carbohydrates: 13g
Dietary fiber: 2g
Sugars: 8g

*Adobo sauce is hot and full of chile flavor. A little will go a long way in recipes. This recipe is for a large batch and is meant to be frozen. Use ½–2 whole chipotles in your dish, depending on your heat tolerance.*

▼ ▼ ▼

Roast the chiles in an iron or heavy skillet or on grill over low heat until fragrant and somewhat soft, keep a watchful eye to avoid burning. Remove seeds from chile guajillo and chile pasilla-ancho. Then, boil all of the chiles in water until soft, about 30 minues. Remove the chipotles from the water and reserve. Allow the water and other chiles to cool. Place water and chiles (not chipotles) in blender and blend until pureed (This may need to be done in two batches.) Saute onion and garlic in oil until garlic starts to stick, and then add tomatoes, oregano, thyme, and bay leaf. Simmer over low heat for about 15 minutes. Add chile puree, honey, and salt; cook for a half hour. Then add whole chipotles and vinegar, cook for 5 minutes. Cool and store in the refrigerator for a couple days to allow the vinegar to pickle a bit. Divide sauce into 4 portions and add 2 or 3 whole chipotles to each portion. Freeze in plastic freezer bags or small glass containers with tight-fitting lids.

## Chipotle-Lime Rub

2 tablespoons Key lime zest

2–3 dried chipotles

3/4 teaspoon whole cumin seeds

1/2 teaspoon whole coriander seeds

1 1/2 teaspoons oregano leaves

12 black peppercorns

1 teaspoon onion flakes

2 sun-dried tomatoes (not the moist variety)

1/2 teaspoon mustard powder

2 teaspoons evaporated cane juice

1 teaspoon garlic powder

2 teaspoons salt

**Makes approximately 1/3 cup**

*There is no other chile like the wonderfully fragrant chipotle, with its distinctive woody flavor. It is a smoked, dried, red jalapeño, but oh how the drying and smoking change its character. This rub can be used not only on chicken, fish, and meats, but also in sauces, marinades, and salad dressings. A little goes a long way. Since I use it extensively, I usually triple this recipe whenever I make it. Be cautious while working with the chiles. You may choose to wear gloves, but don't touch your eyes or lips! Make sure to wash your hands thoroughly after working with chiles.*

▼ ▼ ▼

Dry the lime zest according to the directions on page 17. Toast the chipotles, cumin, coriander, and oregano, according to the directions on page 17, to release their flavors. Place zest, chipotles, cumin, coriander, oregano, peppercorns, onion flakes, and sun-dried tomatoes in a coffee or spice grinder. Grind until the consistency resembles that of a fine powder. Transfer the mix to a cup or small bowl. Add the mustard powder, sugar, garlic powder, and salt, and thoroughly mix. Store the rub in an airtight container in the refrigerator or freezer. It will keep for up to a month.

# BREAKFAST

**Upon rising in the morning,** you're running on empty and your brain is craving glucose—brain fuel. Research studies indicate that refueling with a mix of whole foods containing unrefined carbohydrates, protein, and a little good fat is beneficial for concentration, memory, problem-solving skills, productivity, energy level, weight control, and long-term health. The breakfast suggestions and recipes in this chapter are deliciously healthy whole-food options to start your day and keep you moving.

Alternatively, starting the day with processed, starchy carbohydrate treats such as refined sugary cereal, toaster pastries, doughnuts, or most bagels (all of which are real blood sugar spikers), causes hunger and carbohydrate cravings within a few hours. Such processed, counterfeit foods are stripped of fiber and nutrients, then replenished with synthetic vitamins and minerals, but remain void of health-promoting phytonutrient compounds.

Food engineers cannot artificially replicate the miraculous complexities inherent in whole grains. Researchers believe these compounds and nutrients work collectively in processing the nutrition in your body where it's needed. Rui Hai Liu, in the *American Journal of Clinical Nutrition*, September 2003, states that the evidence suggests antioxidants are best acquired through whole-food consumption, not as a pill or an extract.

So, what are phytonutrients? They could be compared to a superior army with an arsenal of weaponry and manpower actively protecting the plant from environmental dangers. These protective compounds ward off environmental elements that are damaging to the plant, such as ultraviolet rays, disease, pollution, and destructive pests. When we consume whole foods, the phytonutrient protection is passed on to us. Some of the recognizable characteristics of phytonutrients are their sensory attributes of scent, color, and flavor that provide culinary enjoyment and protection against disease.

Sometimes it's a "tug of war" between parents and kids over breakfast food choices—a sugary cereal or a nutritious food. To avoid starting the day in turmoil, the parent often lets the child win. But why is that cereal in the pantry? According to a study released in October 2009 by the Rudd Center for Food Policy and Obesity, cereal manufactures spent a staggering $156 million in 2008 in promoting children's cereals in the media. Six-hundred-and-forty-two of the ads bombarded pre-schoolers!

Of the 43 cereals investigated that were marketed to children, 85 percent had more sugar, 65 percent less fiber, and 60 percent more sodium than those marketed to adults. They failed every reasonable nutrition test. However, all qualified as "better-for-you" foods according to industry-derived standards brokered by the Council of Better Business Bureaus. They also received the industry-funded "Smart Choices" designation. Both statements are in total disregard for children's health; but with these bogus health decrees printed on the boxes, parents are fooled into buying the cereal, which makes you wonder how much control cereal marketers have in determining your family's diet.

As an alternative to boxed cereal, make your own and store it in the freezer. Or prepare cooked whole grains in minutes. It just takes a little ingenuity in thinking outside the box. There are a number of recipes in this chapter that you'll love, and then you can springboard from them to create your own signature cereal! ▶

*Buckwheat Banana Pancakes (recipe on page 54).*

## Buckwheat–Banana Pancakes (Bobby's Breakfast Tacos)

2 cups pitted dark sweet cherries, fresh or frozen (or use mixed berries)

1 cup chopped, peaches, fresh or frozen

1 teaspoon honey (cherries probably won't need sweetening)

1 teaspoon cornstarch

1/4–1 jalapeño, seeded, deveined, and minced

1 cup whole-grain spelt or wheat flour

1 cup buckwheat flour

2 teaspoons baking powder

3/4 teaspoon sea salt

2 teaspoons ground cinnamon

2 tablespoons evaporated cane juice

2 pastured eggs

2 cups unsweetened soy beverage or nonfat milk

1 tablespoon canola oil

1 tablespoon pure vanilla extract

1/2 cup toasted buckwheat groats

1/2 cup chopped pecans

2 tablespoons chia seed, optional

4 bananas, thinly sliced and chopped

1 cup nonfat Greek yogurt

---

**Makes about 10 six-inch pancakes or "tacos"**

Calories per serving: 299
Total fat: 8g
Saturated fat: 1g
Calories from fat: 72
Protein: 10g
Carbohydrates: 50g
Dietary fiber: 7g
Sugars: 19g

*These tacos started out as buckwheat pancakes and then Bobby, our son-in-law, got creative. Rather than putting the fruit sauce on top, he lined the pancake with fruit sauce, added a dollop of yogurt (instead of sour cream), folded it like a corn tortilla, and called it a breakfast taco! We enjoyed a relaxing breakfast full of laughter and good food with Bobby, his mom Patty, and our grandchildren, Ty and Aaron. Hope you, too, take the time to enjoy the tacos and the good times that friends and family bring to a relaxing dining table. This recipe uses a version of the fruit sauce from Meme's French Toast Fingers with Berry Dip, except this time we add jalapeño! The optional chia seeds in the pancakes will make the batter a little thicker and add a healthy punch.*

▼ ▼ ▼

Make the fruit sauce as follows: Slightly warm the cherries or berries over medium heat. (Heat frozen fruit until warm.) Mash half of the fruit, then mix in the minced jalapeño; if needed, add a little honey and blend with a spatula. To thicken, blend in the cornstarch and heat until it reaches the desired thickness. Not everyone is an aficionado of hot and spicy, so you might add jalapeño to only part of the sauce. Set aside.

Sift the next 6 ingredients (flour through evaporated cane juice). Beat the eggs on high speed until thick and pale. Add milk, oil, and vanilla to the eggs, beating on medium to blend. Pour the wet ingredients into the dry mixture and beat on low speed until integrated. A few lumps are okay. Stir in the buckwheat groats, pecans, and chia seeds. It will be a fairly thin batter, but the chia seeds will start gelling and it will thicken.

Preheat the oven to 200 degrees F. As the pancakes come off the griddle, place them in the oven until there is enough for everyone.

Pour about 1/4 cup of batter onto a non-stick griddle, sprinkle banana pieces over the cakes. When bubbles appear in the batter, flip the pancakes. Serve warm with fruit sauce and a dollop of yogurt.

**Variation: Buckwheat Apple–Cinnamon Pancakes** Follow the same directions as for the Buckwheat Banana Pancakes but substitute chopped apples for the banana.

## Whole-grain Pumpkin–Pecan Waffles

Apple-Pomegranate Strudel Topping (recipe follows)

¾ cup whole-grain spelt flour or whole-wheat flour

½ cup old-fashioned rolled oats

3 tablespoons cornstarch

1 ½ teaspoons baking powder

¾ teaspoon sea salt

2 teaspoons ground cinnamon

1 ½ teaspoons ground ginger

¼ teaspoon ground cloves

½ teaspoon ground nutmeg

¼ teaspoon ground cardamom

½ cup pecan pieces

2 pastured eggs, separated

1 cup canned solid-pack pumpkin, or cooked and puréed fresh pumpkin, drained

1 cup nonfat milk or unsweetened soy beverage

1 teaspoon pure vanilla extract

2 tablespoons canola oil

2 tablespoons evaporated cane juice

2 tablespoons chia seed

Canola oil spray

---

**Serves 5–6**

Calories per serving: 263
Total fat: 16g
Saturated fat: 0g
Calories from fat: 142
Protein: 12g
Carbohydrates: 46g
Dietary fiber: 9g
Sugars: 18g

*Comforting aromas of pumpkin spices ready the palate for this wonderfully flavorful autumn breakfast. Unlike most waffles, these offer fuel to take you through the morning. Spelt is similar to wheat, but has a nuttier and slightly sweeter flavor, has more protein, and is easier to digest. I used evaporated cane juice mainly for its molasses flavor, and it's easier on the environment than white sugar, but it is not less caloric than white sugar. Chia is added to increase protein and fiber. Cornstarch and canola oil tend to make the waffles crisp, and lightness is achieved by beating the egg whites with the evaporated cane juice and folding them into the batter. Be sure to use organic cornstarch, which is non-GMO.*

*Time-saver Tip: Make a double batch, freeze leftover waffles, and then later in the week, reheat in a toaster oven. The strudel topping can also be frozen and thawed in the microwave.*

▼ ▼ ▼

Make the Apple-Pomegranate Strudel Topping first (page 56). You can start the waffles while the strudel is simmering.

In a large mixing bowl, thoroughly stir together the next 11 ingredients (flour through pecan pieces).

In a small bowl, beat the egg yolks on high speed for about 1 minute or until the yolk is a couple shades lighter in color. Add pumpkin, milk, vanilla, and canola oil, and thoroughly blend on medium speed. Pour mixture over the dry ingredients and mix with a spatula just to combine.

Beat egg whites on high speed until they start getting frothy; continue beating while slowing adding the evaporated cane juice and until the egg whites hold soft peaks.

Preheat waffle iron.

Fold egg whites and chia seeds into the flour-egg mixture until combined.

Even though the iron may have a non-stick surface, spray the waffle iron with canola oil for the first waffle. Pour batter onto the iron plate and bake according to manufacturer's directions.

To serve crispy-warm waffles to everyone at the same time, keep waffles in a preheated 200-degrees-F oven.

## Apple-Pomegranate Strudel Topping

3 large unpeeled Granny Smith or pippen apples, cut in eighths and then into ½-inch pieces

2 cups fresh orange juice

1 teaspoon ground cinnamon

1 teaspoon cornstarch

Zest from 1 orange

2 teaspoons honey

5–6 tablespoons pomegranate seeds

**Serves 10**

Calories per serving (½ cup:) 63
Total fat: 0g
Saturated fat: 0g
Calories from fat: 2
Protein: 1g
Carbohydrates: 16g
Dietary fiber: 2g
Sugars: 12g

*If you think you need syrup—whether it is pure maple syrup or the fake stuff—hold the syrup and go for the healthy whole-food strudel topping. Since the red pomegranates glisten against the green-skinned apples, my husband refers to the pumpkin waffles with strudel as Christmas waffles.*

*Note: Be sure to use organic cornstarch, which is non-GMO.*

▼ ▼ ▼

Mix the apples, orange juice, and cinnamon together in a saucepan; set over high heat. Bring to a boil, reduce heat to low, and simmer until the apples are soft. In a cup, mix a tiny bit of the sauce with the cornstarch to form a smooth, thin paste; then mix into the sauce to thicken. Thoroughly mix in the orange zest and honey. Pour strudel over waffles and top with pomegranate seeds.

## Nut-Butter Covered Apple Slices with Grains

1 unpeeled apple, cut in quarters

2 tablespoons raw almond butter or lightly roasted peanut butter

¼ cup or more raw wheat germ

1 tablespoon ground chia seed, optional

**Serves 4–5**

Calories per serving: 123
Total fat: 7g
Saturated fat: 1g
Calories from fat: 55
Protein: 4g
Carbohydrates: 15g
Dietary fiber: 4g
Sugars: 6g

*Many people enjoy a nut-butter sandwich with a coarse piece of organic whole-grain bread. This recipe is an alternative to a sandwich; dip apples in nut butter and then dip in wheat germ. Our grandchildren enjoy this not only for breakfast but also for a snack. Pumpkin Spice Granola (page 57) is also great for dipping.*

▼ ▼ ▼

Serve the nut butter in a small bowl and the wheat germ or mix of wheat germ and chia seed in another bowl, and serve the apple slices on a plate. Then dip an apple slice in nut butter and then into the wheat germ to coat the butter. Enjoy!

## Pumpkin Spice Granola

1 cup orange juice, pulp removed

3 tablespoons evaporated cane juice

2 tablespoons macadamia oil

1 tablespoon pure vanilla extract

3 cups old-fashioned rolled oats

½ cup oat bran

1 cup buckwheat groats

1 cup raw wheat germ

1 teaspoon sea salt

2 tablespoons chia seed, whole or ground

1 cup chopped raw walnuts, almonds, or macadamia nuts

2 teaspoons ground cinnamon

½ teaspoon ground cloves

1 teaspoon ground ginger

¼ teaspoon ground nutmeg

¼ teaspoon ground cardamom

¾ cup raisins

### Serves 14

Calories per serving (½ cup): 337
Total fat: 12g
Saturated fat: 2g
Calories from fat: 99
Protein: 11g
Carbohydrates: 51g
Dietary fiber: 8g
Sugars: 10g

*Not too sweet, just a little oil, a mix of healthy grains, nuts, and fruit, warm pumpkin spices, and lots of love make this granola a wholesome, deliciously healthy breakfast or snack food. Sprinkle on yogurt, or serve with nonfat organic milk or unsweetened soy beverage. Preparing food in large batches saves time—double or triple the recipe and freeze part of it, making it more available with less effort.*

▼ ▼ ▼

Line 2 jelly-roll pans or 3 baking sheets with parchment paper; set aside. Preheat oven to 275 degrees F. Heat orange juice in the microwave for 1 minute on high; then stir in evaporated cane juice, oil, and vanilla; set aside. In an appropriate size bowl, mix the remaining ingredients; then pour in the orange juice mixture. Grease your hands with oil and mix the granola thoroughly with your hands, then spread it on the parchment-covered baking pans. Bake the mixture for about 45 minutes, turning every 15 minutes, or until lightly browned and dry. It will be made up of small clusters. Allow to completely cool, then store in a jar with a tightly fitted lid, or freeze.

## Organic vs. Conventionally Grown Grains

The United States is the number-one producer of corn and one of the top producers of wheat, oats, and rice in the world. The majority of soy and corn in the United States are now genetically modified, often requiring more herbicides and pesticides to control invasive predators. GMO corn shows up in the form of a grain, corn syrup, high-fructose corn syrup, dextrose, fructose, malt, malt syrup, malt extract, starch, food starch, and modified food starch. Aside from chemical consumption, GMO foods may carry as-yet unforeseen hazardous side effects.

According to the USDA, total grain cropland acreage was 141,573,000 in 2008. The bounty reaped from all is reflected in a pesticide footprint in millions of pounds. According to the USDA Economic Research Service, organic grain acreage in 2008 was 907,916, which is less than approximately 0.5 percent of total grain-cropland acreage. The report also stated that between 2002 and 2008, there was a 15 percent average annual increase in total organic cropland acreage. Even though it has been slow coming, consumer demand for organic has caused this increase in organic plant production, which shows that the consumer can force change in agriculture.

By choosing nutrient-dense chemical-free non-GMO grains, we are ensuring the health of our planet, which goes full circle back to promoting our health! Support farmers who concentrate on promoting plant health to ward off disease rather than relying on GMO seeds and chemicals to feed and protect the plants.

Buying organic cereals still requires vigilance. Making sure it is organic is the first hurdle in selecting an organic cereal. Statements such as "natural ingredients" or "made with all natural ingredients" are empty words. The USDA Organic symbol is printed on the package, certifying that its contents are either 100 percent or 95 percent organic. Not all organic cereals are equally healthy. Read the label!

▶ The first ingredient in a nutrient dense cereal should be whole grain, not wheat flour, rice, or corn meal. If the grain is not preceded by "whole," it is not whole grain. Multiple whole grains such as spelt, buckwheat, oats, barley, rye, amaranth, and quinoa mixed with omega-3 and protein-rich seeds such as chia, flax, and hemp, and nuts are even better. The mix provides different amino acids and nutrients and works together to provide more antioxidant punch.

▶ Cereal should be void of sugar or with just a little sugar. Sugar comes under various names, such as concentrated fruit juice, molasses, maple syrup, agave nectar, honey, raw sugar, evaporated cane juice, high-fructose corn syrup, corn syrup, dextrose, glucose, maltose, sucrose, xylitol, or mannitol. Raisins or other dried fruits also add sugar, which is not differentiated from added sugar on the label.

▶ Look for cereal that is low in salt. The American Institute of Cancer Research recommends that our daily intake of salt be less than 2,400 mg per day.

▶ Cereals should be low or void of total fat and saturated fats and should contain no hydrogenated fats. Nuts and seeds contain good fat, which will be listed in the amount of fat but not distinguished from added fat. Commercial granolas are usually high in sugar and fat, most of which are unhealthy fats.

▶ According to the 2005 Dietary Guidelines for Americans, 14 grams of dietary fiber per 1,000 calories each day is recommend by The Institute of Medicine. Thus, if 2,000 calories are consumed during a day, the foods should have a total of at least 28 grams of fiber. The average American consumes only 14 grams of dietary fiber a day. Shoot for 5 or more grams of fiber for breakfast. To boost fiber consumption, add oat bran, wheat bran, or chia seeds to your cereal and a side of fruit.

▶ Packaged cereal serving sizes, which are frequently only ½ cup, are often not enough to satiate your appetite, and you wind up eating 1 cup or more and doubling the calories, sugar, etc.

## Good Old-fashioned Oatmeal Made Quick

½ cup old-fashioned rolled oats

1 cup water

Tiny pinch of sea salt

Nonfat milk or unsweetened soy beverage

1 chopped pitted dates or a little honey
or evaporated cane juice (optional for sweetening)

### Serves 1

Calories per serving: 315
Total fat: 5g
Saturated fat: 1g
Calories from fat: 46
Protein: 14g
Carbohydrates: 53g
Dietary fiber: 8g
Sugars: 2g

1 cup old-fashioned rolled oats or ½ cup steel-cut oats

2 cups water

Pinch of sea salt

Nonfat milk or unsweetened soy beverage

1 teaspoon evaporated cane juice
or 2 pitted dates, chopped (optional for sweetening)

### Serves 2

Calories per serving: 315
Total fat: 5g
Saturated fat: 1g
Calories from fat: 46
Protein: 14g
Carbohydrates: 53g
Dietary fiber: 8g
Sugars: 2g

*When in a rush, don't sacrifice good nutrition by eating inferior instant oats, which usually contain added sugar and salt, have less dietary fiber, and lack the delicious full flavor and texture of oats. Instead, turn old-fashioned rolled or steel-cut oats (Irish or Scottish) into a healthy instant porridge by soaking either type overnight and cooking instantly in the morning.*

*A study published in the June 2004* Journal of Nutrition *suggests that when oats are consumed with a food high in vitamin C, the two synergistically interact, providing the body with almost double protection against free radicals compared to eating each alone. Whole foods such as strawberries, currants, oranges, and grapefruit are excellent sources of vitamin C. A well-ripened fresh local fruit will have the highest levels of vitamin C and the best taste. Freshly picked fruits that are frozen in a timely manner also retain a good amount of vitamin C.*

*To complete your meal, add milk or unsweetened soy beverage, and serve warm with a side of fruit high in vitamin C.*

*Note: Stovetop is the only method recommended for quick steel-cut oats.*

*Note: Replace sugar with fiber-filled nutrient-rich dates.*

▼ ▼ ▼

### Microwave Method

The night before, mix oats, water, and salt in a microwave-safe glass or ceramic cereal bowl and cover it with a small plate. In the morning, stir, place in the microwave, and cook on high for 2 minutes. For a creamier texture, add a little unsweetened soy beverage or nonfat milk, stir, and cook for another 30 seconds to 1 minute. If it starts to boil over, turn off microwave. Sweeten by adding dates or a little honey or evaporated cane juice.

### Stovetop Method

The night before, in a small saucepan, swirl oats and salt in the water, and cover with a lid. The next morning, place the uncovered saucepan over high heat and bring to a boil; then cover, turn off heat and let it sit for a couple minutes or turn to low and simmer for a minute or two or until oats have reached the desired consistency. Sweeten by adding evaporated cane juice or dates.

**Variation: Quick Mixed Grains**  Variety is a key to healthy eating. Mixing a number of different grains in cooked cereal provides a greater variety of fiber, protein, nutrients, and phytonutrients than if only one grain was consumed. What is lacking in one grain, you may pick up from another. Choose 2 or more grains from any number of organic grains— spelt, wheat, kamut, barley, rice, millet, amaranth, rye, oats, quinoa, buckwheat, etc.—and mix them together. Figure out which grains you like the best, and then mix together 5 or 6 and freeze for later use. Use the stovetop method, because they are whole grains.

## Oats 'n Apples with Warm Mulling Spices

1 cup old-fashioned rolled oats or ½ cup steel-cut oats

2 cups water

Pinch of sea salt

½ teaspoon ground cinnamon

Hefty pinch of ground nutmeg

Hefty pinch of ground cloves

¼ teaspoon ground ginger,
or ½ teaspoon freshly grated ginger

½ teaspoon evaporated cane juice

1 apple, chopped (or use chopped fresh
or frozen peach or sweet pitted cherries)

½ teaspoon pure vanilla extract

1 tablespoon chopped walnuts

1 tablespoon chia seed, optional

Nonfat milk or unsweetened soy beverage

**Serves 2**

Calories per serving: 437
Total fat: 10g
Saturated fat: 1g
Calories from fat: 85
Protein: 17g
Carbohydrates: 72g
Dietary fiber: 13g
Sugars: 14g

*Chopped apples, walnuts, and a sprinkling of cinnamon, nutmeg, cloves, and ginger will add warm, comforting flavors reminiscent of apple pie. Walnuts also provide healthy alpha-linolenic acid (omega-3), which according to a Spanish study published in the* Journal of the American College of Cardiology, *October 2006, helps to maintain the elasticity of the arteries and reduces the risk of hardening of the arteries.*

*Chia is another excellent source of omega-3 that has a good balance of omega-3 to omega-6, is protein- and fiber-rich, and is high in calcium, potassium, and iron.*

▼ ▼ ▼

The night before, in a small saucepan, combine and swirl together the oats, water, salt, cinnamon, nutmeg, cloves, ginger, and evaporated cane juice, and cover with a lid. The next morning, add the chopped apple, place the uncovered saucepan over high heat and bring to a boil; then cover, turn off heat and let it sit for a couple minutes or turn to low and simmer for a minute or two or until until apple pieces are soft but a little crunchy; then stir in vanilla and top with walnuts and chia. Add milk or soy beverage and serve warm.

### Nutty Breakfast

Take a lesson from America's Blue Zone—a group of Seventh-day Adventists in Loma Linda, California—one of five pockets in the world where people live into their hundreds with able bodies and lucid minds. They, as a group, currently lead the nation in longest life expectancy. Dan Buettner, author of *The Blue Zones* points out that some Seventh-day Adventists believe that a large breakfast consisting of whole grains, nut butter, fruits, and milk fuels their bodies for most of the day with less cravings for sugary or fatty foods. Most are vegetarians and consume nuts at least five times per week.

## Meme's French Toast Fingers with Berry Dip

### French Toast

4–5 pieces slightly dry or toasted
Ezekiel Cinnamon Raisin or coarse whole-grain
or whole-grain sourdough bread,
cut into 1½-inch "fingers"

¼ cup whole-grain spelt or wheat flour

2 tablespoons chia seeds

½ teaspoon baking powder

2 teaspoons ground cinnamon

¼ teaspoon ground nutmeg

½ teaspoon sea salt

1 egg yolk

1 cup nonfat milk or unsweetened soy beverage

1 teaspoon pure vanilla extract

1 tablespoon orange zest

3 egg whites

¼ cup old-fashioned rolled oats

¼ cup toasted buckwheat groats

⅓ cup chopped almonds or walnuts

### Berry Dip (Fruit Sauce)

2 cups mixed berries or pitted dark sweet cherries,
fresh or frozen

1 cup chopped, peaches, fresh or frozen

1 teaspoon honey
(cherries probably won't need sweetening)

1 teaspoon cornstarch

---

### Serves 4

Calories per serving: 337
Total fat: 11g
Saturated fat: 1g
Calories from fat: 96
Protein: 18g
Carbohydrates: 44g
Dietary fiber: 12g
Sugars: 2g

*French toast covered with syrup or powdered sugar is an age-old favorite breakfast treat—usually made with white bread and fried in butter—that causes a spike in blood sugar, provides little protein, and is pretty much void of fiber and wholesome nutrients. It's not a healthy choice for starting the day. As an alternative, I (Meme) created healthy French toast fingers from Ezekiel sprouted whole-grain cinnamon raisin bread bathed in fluffy egg whites and chia seeds, sprinkled with oats, buckwheat groats, and nuts, and cooked in a tiny bit of oil, then served with fruit sauce. My granchildren, Ty and Aaron, love the dipping ritual and don't miss the syrup! They consider unsweetened fruit as an acceptable option. Chia seeds are the most important ingredient. Not only do they hold the batter together, but they add protein and omega-3, and are loaded with fiber.*

*Note: Cardiologist Dr. Dean Ornish, who has successfully reversed cardiovascular disease through lifestyle, recommends using a non-stick skillet or griddle to limit or eliminate oil. This French toast recipe is best suited for a non-toxic, non-stick skillet or griddle.*

▼ ▼ ▼

If you don't have day-old dry bread, toast the bread slightly. Cut bread into 1½-inch pieces.

Thoroughly mix together the first 6 dry ingredients (flour through salt). To avoid powdery clumps, beat the egg yolk with a fork and mix with a little milk, vanilla, and zest, and then mix with the dry mixture. Continue adding milk until a smooth batter is achieved. Beat the egg whites until light and fluffy; fold them into the batter.

Place the bread fingers in a 12 x 8 x 2-inch or larger casserole dish. Pour the batter over the bread and soak for about 5 minutes.

While the bread is soaking, place the oats, buckwheat, and almonds or walnuts in a mini food processor and finely chop the mix. There may be a few large pieces of nuts. Either pick them out or leave them in for an added crunch.

Heat a large non-stick skillet or griddle over medium-low heat. If necessary, spray with canola oil. Remove a bread finger from the glass dish, turning it over a couple times in the batter while scooping up a generous amount of batter. While holding the bread over the casserole dish, sprinkle with the grain-nut mixture; then place the bread finger in the skillet or on the griddle with the grain-nut mixture side down, and sprinkle the other side with more of the mixture. Repeat until the skillet/griddle is full, allowing enough room to turn the bread fingers; brown lightly on each side.

Slightly warm the cherries or berries over medium heat. (Heat frozen fruit until warm.) Mash half of the fruit; if needed, add a little honey and blend with a spatula. To thicken, blend in the cornstarch and heat until desired thickness. Pour into small individual cups. Serve the bread fingers with a side of this fruit sauce.

Freeze leftover French toast to serve on a busy morning and enjoy a hassle-free breakfast.

# Eggs

An egg carton labeled "cage-free," "free-range," or "natural," illustrated with a picturesque red barn amid a green pasture, is tricky and deceptive, causing us to envision hens soaking up rays of sunshine in the fresh outdoors. We pick up the egg carton and think, "happy naturally raised hens produce healthy wholesome eggs." Unfortunately, this is not always the case. Agribusiness factory eggs—organic or conventional—are labeled free-range even though thousands of hens subsist crammed in warehouses and never step out into the fresh air, while hens confined to wire cages are still labeled "natural."

Ninety-five percent of the eggs sold in the US are from hens confined in massive warehouses. Within each are thousands of tiny wire cages, tiered high and each holding four to five hens. Existing in a floor space the size of a folded newspaper, they are unable to spread their wings.

They rub against wires, causing severe feather loss, bruising, and sores, and are often splattered with dung from other chickens. Their beaks are painfully clipped off to prevent them from pecking each other. And to increase their egg production, they are forced to molt (lose feathers) by being starved for up to two weeks, which manipulates the hormones responsible for egg production. Their egg production decreases after one to two years, at which time they are slaughtered and used to make chicken broth, pot pies, or other foods for human or animal consumption. A pastured chicken's life span is about ten years. On egg cartons this cruelty is labeled as "natural."

The Humane Society of the United States lists caged laying hens as one of the worst animal practices in agribusiness and calls the hens biological "machines." They ask that we eat with a conscience by reducing the amount of egg consumption, which can be done by replacing eggs with plant-based foods, and switching to cage-free eggs.

Living conditions of organic, free-range egg-laying hens that are confined to corporate agrifactories don't differ much from those of conventional laying hens. Both are raised in densely populated warehouses totaling thousands of hens trudging around in chicken poop; but the organic hens do have a bit more room. To be labeled free-range eggs, the USDA requires a door in the warehouse for the hens to access outdoors; however, they almost never make their way out the door. These hens are still painfully de-beaked and are forced to molt. The organic hens are fed an organic diet void of prophylactic antibiotics and pesticides in accordance with the USDA. (In contrast, conventionally raised hens eat food laden with antibiotics, pesticides, growth stimulants, by-products from other animals, manure, and arsenic, among other ingredients.)

Truly free-range eggs come from small flocks of pastured hens, such as on Josh Koehn's Willcox, Arizona, ranch, where hens roam over green pastures and really do soak up sunshine in the fresh outdoors. They forage for food from a smorgasbord of grasses, weeds, grubs, bugs, and worms, and if needed, are provided with supplemental feed free of pesticides and antibiotics. They roost and lay eggs in small, usually portable, hen houses. I have noticed that pastured eggs differ from organic free-range factory-farm eggs in that the shells are stronger and have plump, bright orange yolks rather than runny whites and pale flat yolks.

Pastured eggs are available as both organic and non-organic. Many small farmers, such as Josh, raise chickens in organic pastures and supplement with organic food or pesticide-free food; but due to the hefty costs of certification, they may never officially become "certified organic" farmers. Most pastured eggs are available at farmers' markets, some health food stores, and through Community Supported Agriculture (CSA) cooperatives.

In 2007 the *Mother Earth News* Egg Testing Project compared official USDA data on factory-raised hens' eggs to data for pastured eggs and found that pastured eggs may provide a third less cholesterol, one-fourth less saturated fat, twice the omega-3 fatty acids, two-thirds more vitamin A, three times more vitamin E, and seven times more beta carotene. In addition, Mother Earth's latest tests show that pastured eggs have anywhere between four and six times as much vitamin D as typical supermarket eggs. Other studies in the twentieth century and into the twenty-first century from reputable research scientists have also shown that pastured eggs are more nutrient-dense than factory eggs.

## Huevos Rancheros con Nopalitos

4 nopalitos (4–5 inches tall)

2 Key limes, cut in half

Dash of sea salt

1 medium sweet yellow onion, sliced

1–2 garlic cloves, run through garlic press

1 medium red bell pepper, chopped

1–2 cups coarsely chopped tomato

1 small zucchini or crookneck squash, thinly sliced

1 tablespoon finely chopped serrano chile

1 cup finely chopped basil

8 pastured eggs, or 4 eggs plus 6 egg whites, or 12 egg whites

¼ cup nonfat yogurt, optional

½ Haas avocado

6 corn tortillas

---

**Serves 6**

Calories per serving: 201
Total fat: 9g
Saturated fat: 3g
Calories from fat: 81
Protein: 12g
Carbohydrates: 20g
Dietary fiber: 5g
Sugars: 7g

*Traditionally, huevos rancheros (fried eggs, smothered with salsa and served on fried corn tortillas) were served to ranch hands in Mexico, thus the name, ranch-style eggs. A side of beans and a mix of potatoes with onions and chiles also usually accompanied the dish. Nopalitos (young cactus paddles), a traditional food in Mexico, were often included in the salsa. Since we have an abundance of prickly pear cactus in our backyard and due to their awesome health-worthiness, nopalitos have been tossed into this dish. To make a healthier breakfast, we cut the fat by not frying the tortillas and by scrambling the eggs with fiber-rich, nutrient-dense vegetables. Having vegetables for breakfast also makes it easier to meet our goal of consuming nine servings of vegetables and fruit within the day. Even though salsa ingredients are mixed into the dish, additional salsa is always welcome.*

*We buy eggs laid by happy, healthy chickens from sustainable farmers at the farmers' market, whose free-range foraging chickens naturally provide omega-3 fatty acids. If you are concerned about the amount of cholesterol in eggs, use only the egg whites, which provide a good dose of protein, riboflavin, and selenium.*

*Serve with Seasoned Black Beans (page 156) and fresh fruit.*

▼ ▼ ▼

Remove cactus stickers (see Cleaning the Nopalitos, page 164), cut the pads into ¼-inch strips, then cut the strips in half or chop them, then squeeze lime juice and sprinkle with a pinch of salt; set aside. (If this can be done the night before, flavors develop, and some of the mucilage or slime from the cactus pad will ooze and can be drained. We don't mind the mucilage; besides, it's good for you!) In a dry skillet, sauté the onion, garlic, bell pepper, and nopalitos over medium-high heat for about 2 minutes. Add tomatoes and squash; sauté for about a minute while thoroughly mixing all the vegetables. Beat the eggs with a whisk or fork until somewhat fluffy. Add the yogurt and beat, and then combine with the vegetables in the skillet. (The eggs are cooked in the liquid from the vegetables, which prevents them from sticking to the bottom of the pan.) To firm up the mix, allow the eggs to set for a bit then mix again while scraping the bottom of the skillet. Repeat a couple times until the eggs are done; then add salt, pepper, serrano chile, and basil and mix thoroughly. Top off with avocado pieces. Heat corn tortillas over a gas flame or in a toaster oven until pliable and there is a scent of roasted corn.

### Variations

▸ Replace nopalitos, peppers, tomatoes, and squash with vegetables that are in season; but always include onions and garlic. If you use greens like spinach, chard, or arugula, they should be mixed in when the eggs are just about done, to prevent overcooking.

▸ Eggs and Herbs: Cook the onion, tomato, and eggs as above. Just before serving, toss in fresh oregano, thyme, basil, or cilantro, or a combination, to add wonderful flavor and an abundance of beneficial antioxidants.

## Fragrant Herbed Salsa-poached Eggs

1 cup chopped fresh herbs (oregano, basil, thyme, Thai basil, rosemary, marjoram, etc.)

3 cups chopped fresh tomatoes

1 medium onion, chopped

4 garlic cloves, run through garlic press

¼ –1 jalapeño or serrano chile, finely chopped

1 small cactus pad, cleaned and chopped, optional

2 tablespoons Key lime juice

4 pastured eggs

1 medium Haas avocado, chopped

4 slices whole-grain bread or whole-grain tortillas

**Serves 4**

Calories per serving: 284
Total fat: 11g
Saturated fat: 2g
Calories from fat: 96
Protein: 13g
Carbohydrates: 37g
Dietary fiber: 8g
Sugars: 9g

*Poaching eggs in freshly made salsa from a bounty of ripe garden tomatoes imbued with freshly snipped herbs and chile peppers will deliver a lively, light tasting, lowfat breakfast. (Avocado adds some good monounsaturated fat and vitamin E.) I use one or two herbs or a mix of several, depending on what is available in the garden. Serve with organic whole-grain toast or an organic whole-grain flour or corn tortilla.*

*Note: Herbs contain anti-inflammatories, and according to the USDA Database of the Oxygen Radical Absorbance Capacity (ORAC), many herbs have more antioxidants than most other foods. Oregano, sage, thyme, and marjoram are some of the most potent. Fresh herbs are more potent in antioxidants than dried ones.*

▼ ▼ ▼

Reserve ¼ cup of the fresh herbs for garnish; then mix together the tomatoes, onion, garlic, jalapeño or serrano, cactus pad, and lime juice. Over medium-high heat, cook the salsa until it begins to bubble; then turn to low and crack 4 eggs over the salsa separating them from each other enough to scoop out 4 servings. If you want to be assured of unbroken yolks, crack each in a cup and gently pour each onto the salsa. Cover with a lid and steam a couple minutes or until the yolks are set. Scoop up a generous serving of salsa with an egg and place on a plate topped with more salsa, avocado, and a sprinkling of fresh herbs. A splash of lime juice over the avocado brings out incomparable flavors!

## Yogurt Breakfast Parfait

¾ cup nonfat Greek yogurt

¼ teaspoon pure vanilla extract

1 cup blackberries or a mix of berries

1 heaping tablespoon coarsely chopped raw pecans

1 heaping tablespoon ground chia seed (grind ½ cup whole seeds in blender or coffee grinder)

1 tablespoon raw oat bran or raw wheat germ

**Serves 1**

Calories per serving: 229
Total fat: 6g
Saturated fat: 1g
Calories from fat: 53
Protein: 14g
Carbohydrates: 34g
Dietary fiber: 9g
Sugars: 22g

*This yummy, crunchy-creamy parfait with a kiss of sweetness and bursts of refreshing berries is a wholesome breakfast that is void of bad fat and won't cause disastrous spikes in blood sugar. The secret ingredient is ground chia seeds, which provide protein, fiber, antioxidants, and omega-3. It will energize you through the morning without any hunger pangs or a drop in blood sugar. Berries are considered a superfood, too. Densely dark-colored blackberries are loaded with flavanols, high-powered antioxidants that research indicates may enhance daily mental performance and protect the brain from dementia. Mix them with other berries to work synergistically in increasing their antioxidant effects in fighting free radicals.*

▼ ▼ ▼

Thoroughly combine the yogurt and vanilla in a small bowl. Reserve 3 berries and a few nuts to top off the parfait. In a tall wine or parfait glass, layer with ⅓ cup berries, a few nuts, 2 tablespoons of yogurt, a sprinkling of chia and oat bran or wheat germ, and 2 more tablespoons of yogurt. Repeat 2 times. Top with the reserved berries and nuts.

## Strawberry Smoothie

1 tablespoon chia seed

1 cup unsweetened soy beverage, nonfat milk, or nonfat or lowfat kefir

1 cup (or more) strawberries, fresh or frozen

½ cup (or more) fresh or frozen red grapes

1 small banana (optional)

½ cup crushed ice (use more if using fresh strawberries)

### Serves 1

Calories per serving: 288
Total fat: 6g
Saturated fat: 1g
Calories from fat: 55
Protein: 12g
Carbohydrates: 30g
Dietary fiber: 7g
Sugars: 20g

*Since strawberries aren't always very sweet, grapes, a banana, or both are added to increase sweetness instead of adding sugar. These fruits are whole foods, having fiber and nutrients, which sugar lacks. One cup of strawberries provides more than the daily-recommended dosage of vitamin C. According to the American Institute of Cancer Research, berries are one of the highest-ranking fruits in antioxidant content.*

*Note: When grapes are in season, I buy a bunch and freeze them for snacks or for sweetening drinks. Thank you, my good friend, Patty Friedman, for giving me this idea!*

▼ ▼ ▼

Add chia and soy beverage or milk or kefir to the blender jar and pulse a few times. Let set for 5 minutes, and then pulse again. Add the remaining ingredients, except for the ice, and thoroughly blend. Taste and adjust for sweetness by adding more grapes. Pulse a couple times to blend; then add ice and blend until smooth. Serve immediately.

**Variation: Ginger Peach or Mango Smoothie** Mangos are much sweeter than peaches and usually do not require added sweetener. Banana pieces can be added as an optional sweetener, but do take away from the peach or mango/ginger flavors. More grapes will not affect the flavor. Substitute 1 cup (or more) chopped frozen or fresh peaches or frozen mangos and add 1-inch piece of fresh ginger, peeled and cut in half.

**Variation: Blueberry Smoothie** Blueberries deliver a deliciously healthy smoothie full of antioxidant goodness. Unless a banana flavor is desired, sweeten only with grapes. Substitute 1 cup (or more) blueberries, fresh or frozen, and add 1–2 tablespoons of lime juice.

## Chia

Chia provides an excellent balance of omega-3 to omega-6 essential fatty acids, a good dose of full protein, vitamins, minerals, phytonutrients, and protective antioxidants. Forget the powdered protein drinks and mix up a healthy chia smoothie bursting with satisfying fruit flavors. Whether you are competing in an iron-man triathlon or you need brainpower for a brain-a-thon, chia will provide energy and endurance throughout the morning by slowing the conversion of carbohydrates into sugar, thus stabilizing blood sugar and squelching hunger. It absorbs 8–12 times its weight in water, which enables prolonged hydration, encourages nutrient absorption, maintains the electrolyte balance, and keeps you feeling full. Blending it with fruit makes it a deliciously potent complete-nutrition mix, replenishing your brain with fuel it is craving. According to Wendy Hodgson, Head of Herbarium, Desert Botanical Garden, Phoenix, and author of *Food Plants of the Sonoran Desert,* chia was a traditional food of many Native Americans living in the Southwest. Tell kids who are into superheroes the following story, which goes something like this: Way back when, young Native American men would run from the Colorado River to the coast to trade their turquoise, while packing only a bag of chia seeds and some water—sounds like supermen to me, or maybe a superfood.

*It is my view that a vegetarian manner of living by its purely physical effect on the human temperament would most beneficially influence the lot of mankind.*

—ALBERT EINSTEIN

# VEGAN & VEGETARIAN

**Americans have an** insatiable appetite for meat and dairy—especially beef—made available relatively inexpensively due to government subsidies and industrialized, large-scale confinement animal feeding operations (CAFOs). These meat factories are dependent upon massive amounts of pesticide-, hormone-, and antibiotic-laced food for animals. To produce food for livestock, conventional agriculture uses enormous amounts of pesticides and chemical fertilizers and depletes natural resources of topsoil, water, and biodiversity in the process. Mass-produced meat also constitutes inhumane and often unethical treatment of animals. According to David Pimentel, PhD, professor of Ecology and Agricultural Science, Cornell University, grains fed to US livestock could feed about 840 million people who follow a plant-based diet.

Aside from saving the environment for future generations, limiting meat consumption is health promoting. Total abstinence from meat has proven to be heart healthy and cancer protective. Over 25 years of clinical research by cardiologist Dean Ornish (director, Preventive Medicine Research Institute) and cardiac surgeon Caldwell Esselstyn (Cleveland Clinic) have revealed that lowfat, vegan, and vegetarian whole-food diets not only can prevent cardiovascular disease, but progression of the disease can be halted and in some cases it can be reversed. Former president Bill Clinton consulted with Ornish after learning that a bypass stent put in during his quadruple by-pass surgery had begun to clog from cholesterol. He started following a strict vegan diet but occasionally eats fish. He told Sanjay Gupta (an MD on CNN), "All my blood tests are good, and my vital signs are good, and I feel good, and I also have, believe it or not, more energy." Dr. Esselstyn told Wolf Blitzer of CNN, "When you do what President Clinton has done, when you completely try to remove any foods that are going to injure your vessel, the body has this remarkable capacity to begin to heal itself."

Dr. Pimentel also commented that Americans are eating twice as much mixed (animal and plant) protein as the Recommended Daily Allowance of 56g. Simply put, Americans in general eat too much, which is causing an obesity epidemic, the basis for many life-threatening diseases.

So, kick the meat and dairy habit once a week, or join others around the world by participating in the grassroots movement, "Meatless Mondays" (meatlessmondays.com)—a nonprofit initiative of The Monday Campaigns, in association with the Johns Hopkins Bloomberg School of Public Health. Its goal is to assist individuals reduce meat consumption by 15 percent to improve individual health, reduce our carbon footprint, and lead the world in the race to reduce climate change.

Leaving out meat need not mean leaving out taste. I've compiled a collection of tasty meals to delight your taste buds with satisfying flavors. No salty, processed fake meats are used in place of meat. Instead, I rely on the combination of the flavors and textures of a variety of whole foods to satisfy, causing you to forget about the absent slab of meat or cheese. Whether you choose to become a full-fledged vegan or vegetarian or simply cut back on your ingestion of meat, you'll be doing yourself and our planet a favor. ▶

*Tempeh Tacos (recipe on page 68).*

## Tempeh Tacos

1 ½ cups vegetable or mushroom broth

1 ½ cups mushroom broth

1 teaspoon Worcestershire sauce (vegan is available)

1 teaspoon hickory liquid smoke

1 teaspoon tamari sauce or Bragg® Liquid Aminos

1 crushed garlic clove, peeled

¼ cup coarsely chopped onion

1 chipotle chile

1 package soy or mixed-grain tempeh (8 ounces)

1 medium eggplant,
sliced lengthwise into ¼-inch thick slices

1 crookneck squash (7-inch),
cut into ¼-inch vertical slices

1 red bell pepper

1 Anaheim chile

1 loosely packed cup of chiffonade-cut cilantro leaves
and stems, or basil leaves

½–1 serrano chile, deveined, seeded, and minced

½ cup dry vermouth or dry white wine

1 tablespoon or spray pump of canola oil
or extra-virgin olive oil

1 large sweet onion, thinly sliced

6 medium garlic cloves, run through garlic press

1 ½–2 cups chopped Roma tomatoes

1–2 Key limes, quartered

1 avocado, sliced and peeled

Fresh Salsa (page 44)

2 cups salad greens

8 corn tortillas or 4 Ezekiel 4.9 sprouted grain tortillas

---

### Serves 4

Calories per serving: 331
Total fat: 15g
Saturated fat: 2g
Calories from fat: 131g
Protein: 17g
Carbohydrates: 39g
Dietary fiber: 10g
Sugars: 17g

*A harmony of beautifully colored vegetables and herbs provide a healthy dose of multiple antioxidants that, when combined, boost their individual benefits and preventive properties. To boot, tempeh tacos provide full protein and a generous amount of fiber and micronutrients. During taste testing, Beth Kniffin commented that she preferred tempeh tacos over chicken and favored using the eggplant as a wrap rather than tortillas. Our friends Victor Beer, an internist who is including more vegetarian meals in his diet, and his wife, Meg, commented that they were totally satisfied with this delicious meatless meal!*

*Fire-roasting (grilling) peppers and vegetables are the most time-consuming part of this recipe; but the full, deep flavors developed by doing so are worth the time. Grill a large batch of peppers and vegetables at a time, then refrigerate to have on hand for the next few days for sandwiches, tacos, or other recipes.*

▼ ▼ ▼

To make the tempeh strips, mix the first 8 ingredients (broth through chipotle chile) in a 1-quart saucepan; bring to a boil. Add the tempeh and simmer while grilling the vegetables.

Grill the eggplant, squash, red bell pepper, and Anaheim chile (see Fire-roasting, page 15). Slice the grilled red pepper. Peel, devein, and seed the grilled or roasted Anaheim chile, then process it with the cilantro, serranos, and vermouth or wine in a blender; set aside.

Drain and reserve the broth the tempeh was simmering in.

Heat a large skillet over medium heat. When hot, coat bottom with 1 tablespoon of oil (or lightly spray oil to coat a non-stick skillet). Add the drained tempeh; brown both sides, adding broth mixture as needed to prevent tempeh from sticking. Toss in the onions and garlic and sauté over medium-high heat until onions are translucent, adding broth as necessary to prevent sticking. Stir in tomatoes and remaining broth; bring to a boil for a minute or so. Reduce heat to medium and cook until the broth is absorbed. Stir in the Anaheim/cilantro mixture and cook until liquid is almost gone.

Serve family-style by attractively arranging on a large platter the tempeh sauté, grilled vegetables, and lime quarters for squeezing over the taco filling. In separate bowls, serve the avocado, salsa, and salad greens. Warm the tortillas and place in a napkin or towel. Suggest using the slices of grilled eggplant as a wrap.

### Variations

▸ Substitute the garnish with a side of Southwest Kale Salad (page 131) to stuff in the tacos or eat as a side salad or maybe a little bit of both.

▸ Whatever the season, these tacos offer up numerous variations in stuffing—yams, butternut squash, figs, arugula, roasted or raw fennel, basil, spinach, etc.

## Southwest Curry Salad

14 ounces sprouted tofu, firm or extra-firm (non-sprouted is also okay)

1 tablespoon fresh lemon juice

1 medium–large garlic clove, run through garlic press

⅓ cup finely chopped sweet yellow onion

3 tablespoons Dijon mustard

1 teaspoon umeboshi plum paste

1–2 teaspoons yellow curry powder

1 teaspoon smoked paprika (optional)

1 tablespoon capers or 2 tablespoons chopped dill pickle

1 medium red bell pepper, finely chopped

1 fresh-roasted (see Fire-roasting, page 15) finely chopped green chile, or 1 fresh raw minced serrano or poblano chile (seeded and deveined)

1 tablespoon minced fresh dill weed

3 tablespoons chopped fresh cilantro or basil (optional but tasty)

Freshly ground pepper

4 pieces Ezekiel 4.9 Cinnamon Raisin bread

1 peeled and mashed medium avocado

½–1 teaspoon lime juice

Sea salt

4 thin tomato slices

Baby spinach

### Serves 4

Calories per serving: 227
Total fat: 8g
Saturated fat: 1g
Calories from fat: 71
Protein: 14g
Carbohydrates: 27g
Dietary fiber: 7g
Sugars: 5g

*You curry-loving foodies may want to add additional curry to this recipe. Curry contains turmeric, which reduces inflammation—thus making it a worthy addition to food, so add it whenever taste permits. In lieu of spreading mayo, we spread avocado, which is a whole food made up of monounsaturated fat, a wide spread of essential nutrients, and lots of fiber. The Ezekiel bread was a hit for my editor, Caroline, who added it to her Trader Joe's shopping list. She also commented that it was an easy weeknight dinner and a great summer dish.*

*Note: Umeboshi plum paste is recommended to add a satisfying salty tartness to blended tofu dishes; 1–2 teaspoons of cider or balsamic vinegar with a little salt may be substituted for the plum paste, but its flavor will not be duplicated. Ezekiel is flourless, low-glycemic sprouted whole-grain bread. Sprouted tofu is made from soy beans that have been sprouted. Sprouting is supposed to reduce phytic acid, and by doing so, increases mineral absorption and also aids in digestion.*

▼ ▼ ▼

Drain tofu by placing it between two small chopping boards or flat plates. Apply pressure to expel water, drain, apply pressure, and drain again. Pat the tofu with a dry, clean lint-free towel. In a medium-size bowl, mix together the lemon juice, garlic, onion, mustard, plum paste, curry powder, and paprika. Using your fingers, crumble the tofu into the mixture and blend until an egg-salad-like consistency is achieved. Add capers or pickles, bell pepper, green or serrano or poblano chile, dill, and cilantro or basil (if desired), and toss until thoroughly mixed. Add pepper to taste. As pickled plum paste and other ingredients contain salt, additional salt may not be needed. If time permits, allow the flavors to meld for about 30 minutes in the refrigerator. Slightly toast the bread, spread mashed avocado on it, splash with a tiny bit of lime juice, and sprinkle sparingly with salt. Add a tomato slice, blanket with baby spinach, and then pile on the salad for an open-face sandwich.

**Variation** Instead of cinnamon bread, use another sprouted whole-grain bread, and add ½ cup raisins or ½ cup finely chopped crystallized ginger or dates, 1 teaspoon ground cinnamon, and a pinch of nutmeg to the salad; mix thoroughly.

## Roasted Butternut Squash Salsa over Lentil Stew

4 servings of prepared brown rice or Forbidden Black Rice (page 158), or mixture of both

Roasted Butternut Squash Salsa (page 46)

**Stew**

1 teaspoon extra-virgin olive oil

1 cup finely chopped sweet yellow onion

6 medium garlic cloves, run through garlic press

2 cups orange lentils

4 cups vegetable broth

1 cup white wine or dry vermouth

2 inches ginger root, cut into ¼-inch rings and then quartered, lightly pressed to release juice

1 teaspoon chili powder

2 broken bay leaves

½ teaspoon ground nutmeg

1 teaspoon ground cumin

1 teaspoon ground cinnamon

1 tablespoon Mexican oregano leaves, crushed to release flavor

1 teaspoon turmeric

2 teaspoons stone-ground mustard

Water, as needed

4 cups Swiss chard or flat kale, tough veins removed, and sliced into narrow ribbons

**Serves 8**

Calories per serving: 508
Total fat: 6g
Saturated fat: 1g
Calories from fat: 58
Protein: 15g
Carbohydrates: 92g
Dietary fiber: 21g
Sugars: 14g

*This quick, protein-rich, deliciously hearty fall stew will warm your soul and nurture your body with a healthy dose of wonderfully flavorful wholesome vegetables for a totally satisfying meal. Yum! Yum!*

*Timing note: You should start the rice first, and prepare the salsa while the lentils are cooking. The ingredients for Forbidden Black Rice and Roasted Butternut Squash Salsa are listed on their respective recipe pages, not with this recipe.*

▼ ▼ ▼

After the rice has been started, preheat oven to 400 degrees F.

Heat a 4-quart stew pot over medium heat; when hot, add 1 teaspoon of oil. Sauté onion and garlic until the onion is translucent. Add lentils, vegetable broth, wine or vermouth, ginger root, chili powder, bay leaves, nutmeg, cumin, cinnamon, oregano, and turmeric; bring to a boil over high heat and boil for 2–3 minutes. Reduce heat and simmer, uncovered, until the lentils are done, about 20 minutes, adding water as necessary to achieve a stew-like consistency.

While the lentils are cooking, prepare the salsa.

After the lentils are cooked, whisk in the mustard and stir to combine. If desired, remove the pieces of ginger.

In a blender, purée 1 cup of the lentils and then mix back into the rest of the stew. (To avoid being burned, start on low speed and blend with the lid cap ajar, to allow steam to escape and keep the lid from shooting off.) Stir chard into the stew; cook over low heat until bright green and wilted, adding water as needed. Serve stew over rice and top with squash salsa.

# Sleeping Frog Farms

As a social worker, Debbie Weingarten witnessed diet-related health issues that were rooted in a broken food system. Wanting more than a band-aid fix, she left social work to work on a local organic farm in Amado, Arizona. She quickly became friends with two organic farmers, C.J. Marks and Adam Valdivia, who shared a strong desire to change how food makes its way to our plates. The trio left Amado to form a partnership in 2008—the beginning of Sleeping Frog Farms.

Inside of a year, they transformed fallow horse property into a nutrient dense, verdantly thick edible landscape, and were coaxing enough organic vegetables from the soil to fill 50 CSA shares, stock their farmers' market stand, and provide produce to the Food Conspiracy Co-op and a few restaurants in Tucson. These holistic farmers were rapidly becoming an icon for local sustainable, incredibly fresh organic produce. Within two years, they bought a 75-acre farm in Cascabel, Arizona. The expansion made room for another partner: Adam's long-time friend Clay Smith who added business expertise.

They have opted against organic certification but follow the tenets of sustainable organic agriculture with a paradigm exceeding USDA organic certification guidelines. Sleeping Frog embraces the very ideals of organic by practicing permaculture design and biodynamic growing principles that build and maintain healthy, vibrant soil necessary to grow healthy food, for today's generations as well as for all future generations.

Always trying to choose the best methods for improving soil and the environment, they recycle the farm's organic waste by using bokashi for high-speed composting. Based on fermentation, it eliminates odor and pathogenic bacteria and produces nutrients and antioxidants; and unlike normal composting, doesn't emit greenhouse gases.

When we visited Sleeping Frog, we saw a diverse farm of a thousand laying hens, a few goats, a field of grasses to feed the chickens, a newly planted orchard, and 12 acres of vibrantly colored vegetables, herbs, and flowers, most of which were heirloom. C.J. noted, "Heirlooms have great flavor, but they also assure the same type of crop year after year, or pretty close." Also, by practicing biodiversity, Sleeping Frog has increased soil fertility and plant productivity and created a parasite- and disease-resistant environment.

Instead of fossil-fuel-driven machinery, Sleeping Frog uses sweat and muscle and able fingers to round up pesky weeds and to gently pick the crops, which are then washed with purpose, knowing that someone will be feeding a family with these healthy jewels.

CSA members are invited to quarterly potlucks, to volunteer, and to participate in planting parties on the farm. At a garlic planting party, over 50 people turned out to help shuck garlic heads and plant 1,500 pounds of garlic. After just a few hours, we left with sore calf muscles, skinned knuckles, rough fingertips, and stubs of fingernails dyed brown, which gave us pause to appreciate what is being done for us by our farmers on a daily basis.

Sleeping Frog's truly free-range hens eat organic grains, forage in green pastures of alfalfa and buckwheat, roost in family-size moveable mobile homes, and are protected from predators by a pair of Great Pyrenees, Lily and Gus, and a solar-powered electric fence.

Civano Community School (named "America's Greenest School" in 2008) partnered with Sleeping Frog Farms to provide fresh, seasonal produce each week for their school lunch program. Debbie noted that it is one of the first successful "Farm-to-School" programs in southern Arizona.

Educating local communities in the importance of building and supporting local food systems is the strongest tool in revolutionizing the fabric of our landscape. In addition to the Civano program, Sleeping Frog stands out in their community as supporters of community wellness and food literacy by sharing their knowledge and talents through farm-based education opportunities (on and off the farm), speaking engagements, writing articles, sitting on community boards, and participating in community-driven organizations.

They are part of a small, but growing culture of young farmers—risk takers—who are chipping away at reclaiming and establishing healthy local food systems, which have been lost to industrial agriculture and food conglomerates. But they can't do it alone! Supportive voices, actions, and investing in sustainable local farmers with our food dollars are essential in building a healthy affordable-for-all food system, which will serve everyone equally.

## Vegetable Lasagna with Vegan "Ricotta"

**Vegan Ricotta**

³/₄ cup cashew pieces or whole cashews

5 tablespoons lemon juice

6 medium garlic cloves, cut in thirds

1 pound sprouted-bean tofu, medium or firm (or use any medium or firm tofu)

1 teaspoon sea salt

1 teaspoon chopped fresh rosemary leaves

1 teaspoon oregano, crushed to release flavor

1 teaspoon extra-virgin olive oil, optional

¼ cup vegetable broth or unsweetened soy beverage

1 cup torn and loosely packed fresh basil

**Lasagna**

1 teaspoon extra-virgin olive oil

1 large onion, finely chopped

¼ cup vermouth

1 large red bell pepper, coarsely chopped (roasted is recommend, see Fire-roasting, page 15)

2 cups chopped eggplant (½-inch dice)

2 teaspoons minced fresh rosemary

1 teaspoon oregano, crushed to release flavor

2 cups chopped zucchini (½-inch pieces)

4 handfuls baby spinach leaves or 1 cup fresh oregano leaves and 1 cup chiffonade-cut fresh basil leaves (whatever is in season)

⅓ cup vegetable broth

½ cup finely chopped flat-leaf parsley

24 ounces pasta sauce

1 large salad tomato, thinly sliced

Sea salt and freshly ground pepper

10 ounces (9 sheets) brown rice (non-gluten) or whole-grain lasagna sheets

---

**Serves 6–8**

Calories per serving: 413
Total fat: 14g
Saturated fat: 2g
Calories from fat: 118
Protein: 14g
Carbohydrates: 61g
Dietary fiber: 6g
Sugars: 15g

*Instead of buying processed vegan cheese, make homemade vegan "ricotta"—but plan ahead, because cashews have to soak for eight hours. The creaminess and flavor of the cashew-based sauce complements the fresh vegetables. Cashew nuts also have a fatty acid profile that contributes to good health through phytosterols, tocopherols, and squalene, all of which lower the risk of heart disease. This vegetable lasagna contains a high amount of dietary fiber due to the cashews, whole-grain pasta, and vegetables. Eating a small salad and a reasonable serving of lasagna will control hunger and help in weight management.*

*Cashews can be soaked and stored in the refrigerator for up to five days, but must be rinsed a couple of times each day to prevent spoilage. Whole cashews will probably sprout, which is even more nutritious. Cashew pieces are generally less expensive. Select a pasta sauce with no cheese and little or no oil (oil should be canola or olive).*

▼ ▼ ▼

To make the vegan ricotta, soak the cashews for 8 hours, which will yield approximately 1 cup of soaked cashews; then rinse thoroughly.

Place 1 cup of the soaked cashews and all other ricotta ingredients in a food processor, with the exception of the basil, and blend until it resembles ricotta cheese. Add the basil and pulse until the basil is chopped and mixed into the "ricotta."

Before preparing other ingredients for assembling the lasagna, preheat the oven to 350 degrees F. If you are going to roast the red bell pepper, do so prior to preparing the other vegetables.

Heat a large skillet over medium-high heat, add the oil, and sauté onions until browned and sticking to the pan, or use a nonstick skillet without oil, over medium heat. Deglaze the pan with vermouth, releasing the flavorful bits of caramelized onion stuck to the bottom of the pan (onions in a nonstick skillet will brown but not stick or only stick slightly). Stir in the red bell pepper, eggplant, rosemary, and dry oregano, and simmer over medium to medium-low heat, frequently tossing, until eggplant is tender. Stir in the zucchini and cook for no more than 2 minutes. If you are using spinach, fold in a couple handfuls of spinach now, then pour broth over spinach, and continue folding while allowing it to wilt a bit; then fold in more spinach, continuing this process until all the spinach fits in the pan. When spinach is still bright green and wilted but not overcooked, remove the skillet from the burner. Add salt and pepper to taste, and stir in the parsley. If fresh oregano and basil are used instead of spinach, add them now, with the parsley.

Prepare pasta according to package directions.

Pour one-third of the pasta sauce into the bottom of an ungreased 12 x 8 x 2-inch glass baking dish. Place 3 strips of pasta over the sauce. Spread half of the vegan ricotta over the noodles and then spread half of the vegetable mixture over the ricotta. Repeat with another layer of 3 pasta sheets half of the remaining pasta sauce, followed by the remaining ricotta and then the remaining vegetables. Add the final 3 pasta sheets and then pour the last remaining sauce over the pasta. Cover the dish with thin slices of tomato. Cover the lasagna and place on the middle rack of the oven and bake for 30–40 minutes or until bubbly and hot.

## Spinach and Squash Pasta

1 tablespoon extra-virgin olive oil, divided

1–2 butternut squash (6–7 inches long), peeled and cut into ¼-inch cubes to yield 4 cups

4 garlic cloves, run through garlic press

½ cup diced onion

1 can (14.5 ounces) diced fire roasted tomatoes, drained (reserve juice)

½ teaspoon dry-leaf thyme, crushed to release flavor

½ teaspoon dry leaf sage, crushed to release flavor

1 teaspoon oregano, crushed to release flavor

1 teaspoon smoked bittersweet paprika

½ cup finely chopped parsley

7.5 ounces dry whole-grain penne pasta, yields about 4 cups cooked

Splash of olive oil for pasta

¼ cup ricotta cheese

1 ½ cups vegetable broth

1 tablespoon finely chopped fresh rosemary leaves, or 1 teaspoon dry rosemary, crushed between fingertips

6 large handfuls baby spinach

2 tablespoons Parmesan cheese

½ teaspoon sea salt

Freshly ground pepper

**Serves 4**

Calories per serving: 400
Total fat: 8g
Saturated fat: 2g
Calories from fat: 58
Protein: 13g
Carbohydrates: 72g
Dietary fiber: 7g
Sugars: 9g

*Grandchildren Ty and Aaron go through stages of banning certain foods from their diet. When winter squash was on their taboo list, they still enjoyed ravioli stuffed with squash or spinach. So, inspired by stuffed ravioli, I bathed pasta in squash sauce. Both boys happily gobbled down almost every morsel. Just a few chunks of squash were left behind. This makes a great meal, served with a tossed salad.*

*Note: The wheat in the pasta does not contain all of the essential amino acids to form a complete protein. By adding a little bit of cheese, the protein in the wheat becomes a complete, high-quality protein with a good balance of the essential amino acids. Look for smaller butternut squashes if you can find them; slender short squashes are easy to peel, and larger squash often can't be peeled.*

▼ ▼ ▼

Preheat oven to 400 degrees F. In a large roasting pan, toss the squash cubes in 2 teaspoons of the oil and roast uncovered in the oven until a knife can penetrate through the middle of a cube, about 20 minutes. Stir in the garlic and onion, roast for another 3 minutes; then thoroughly mix in the tomato, half of the reserved tomato juice, and the thyme, sage, oregano, paprika, and parsley. Roast for another 4 minutes.

Start cooking the pasta according to package directions. When done, drain and splash with a little extra-virgin olive oil; toss.

Reserve about 1 cup of the squash mixture. Place in your blender jar the remaining squash mixture, ricotta, and broth; then blend until smooth, venting the blender cap allowing heat to escape. (This may need to be done in two batches.) Transfer this sauce into an 8-quart saucepan and set over medium to low heat; stir in the fresh rosemary. Gradually toss handfuls of spinach into the pan while folding it into the sauce. Cook and stir until the spinach is wilted and limp. Remove from the burner and mix in the Parmesan cheese. Fold in the cooked pasta, or serve the sauce over the pasta. Taste, adding salt and pepper as needed. For a thinner sauce, add a little more broth. Serve immediately.

## Summer Southwest Pizza

1 Vicolo® Spelt & Corn Meal pizza crust

1 teaspoon Mexican oregano, rubbed between fingertips (toasted is preferred, see page 17)

1 teaspoon extra-virgin olive oil

1 garlic clove, run through garlic press

1 ½ cups black beans, rinsed and drained

½ teaspoon ground cumin

1 crookneck or zucchini squash (5 inches), finely chopped

1 roasted green chile, finely chopped (see Fire-roasting, page 15)

½ red bell pepper, coarsely chopped (preferably roasted, see page 15)

Freshly ground pepper, optional

Fresh squash blossoms, optional

1 large tomato, sliced

¼ cup goat feta cheese

2–4 tablespoons sliced black olives

¼ cup thinly sliced onions

Extra-virgin olive oil spray, or about 1 teaspoon

¼ medium avocado, sliced, then chopped

1 Key limes, cut in half

Pinch of sea salt

---

### Serves 4

Calories per serving: 482
Total fat: 17g
Saturated fat: 4g
Calories from fat: 148g
Protein: 18g
Carbohydrates: 69g
Dietary fiber: 15g
Sugars: 4g

*My British son-in-law, Ben, said, "This is bloody good. Your food is always so vibrantly colorful and is truly a reflection of you." Now is that buttering up your mother-in-law or what? It's not an ordinary pizza with oodles of cheese and "cardiac" fat. Instead, it's a delightful crust overloaded with lightly cooked vegetables and seasoned beans, imparting spicy fresh flavors with a pinch of cheese in each bite. Olé!*

▼ ▼ ▼

Preheat oven to 400 degrees F.

It only takes a few minutes to toast the oregano; do it, and you will be pleasantly surprised.

Rub each pizza crust with 1 teaspoon of olive oil and 1 minced clove of garlic.

In a small bowl, mix together beans, oregano, cumin, squash, green chile, and red bell pepper; spread evenly over crust. Top with a few squash blossoms; then completely cover with sliced tomatoes, scatter feta cheese and olives over tomatoes, and finish with sliced onions. Bake on the top-middle oven rack for about 10 minutes or until the crust is golden and the filling is hot. Remove from the oven, lightly spray with olive oil, and allow the pizza to rest for a couple minutes. Cut into serving pieces, top with avocados, splash with lime, and if necessary, sparingly salt the tops of the pizzas.

## Chipotle–Orange Tempeh

**Marinade**

2 teaspoons whole coriander seeds

¼ teaspoon whole cumin seeds

½ cup brown rice vinegar

2 tablespoons fresh Key lime juice

1 tablespoon orange zest, finely grated with microplane

1 cup fresh orange juice (about 3 oranges)

¼ cup honey or evaporated cane juice

¼ cup tamari

2 tablespoons fresh ginger, grated with microplane

2–4 medium garlic cloves, run through garlic press

½–1 whole chipotle chile in adobo sauce, minced (canned, or see recipe, page 50)

1 teaspoon adobo sauce

¼ cup organic canola or extra-virgin olive oil

1 tablespoon toasted sesame seed oil

2 packages (8 ounces each) tempeh

---

**Serves 4**

Calories per serving: 414
Total fat: 25g
Saturated fat: 4g
Calories from fat: 216
Protein: 22g
Carbohydrates: 30g
Dietary fiber: 0g
Sugars: 15g

*Captivated by the beautiful colors and freshness of Sleeping Frog Farms' produce at the Tucson Farmers' Market, I started preparing dinner in my mind—"oranges from Jessie, sweet-bitter greens, perfect with chipotle-orange tempeh, great combo of sweet, sour, bitter, salty, and pungent flavors." With the menu set, I was impelled to pick a bouquet of vibrantly colored dewy-fresh greens and bunches of pinkish-orange carrots.*

*Healthy Note: To reduce the amount of oil, eliminate the canola oil from the marinade. About 20 minutes into baking, liberally spray the tempeh with canola oil. After 30 minutes of total baking time, turn the tempeh and liberally spray again with canola oil. During broiling, spray each side of the tempeh with canola oil once more. For less heat, remove the chipotle seeds before mincing.*

*Serve with Mexican Red Rice (page 158) and Sweet Bitter Greens (page 134) surrounded by Chipotle-Orange Tempeh pieces.*

▼ ▼ ▼

Timing: To ensure that everything is warm and ready at the same time, while tempeh is baking, start the Vegetable Brown Rice; then prep the onions, garlic, and greens for sautéing (see Sweet Bitter Greens recipe, page 134) and set aside until the tempeh is finished baking.

Preheat the oven to 250 degrees F.

To release the perfume in the coriander and cumin seeds, toast them together in a small dry skillet over medium-low heat, while shaking the pan to prevent them from burning, until fragrant. Transfer to grinder or mortar, allow to cool, and then grind; mix with other marinade ingredients in a 14 x 9 x 2-inch non-reactive baking pan.

Horizontally cut across each tempeh rectangle to make eight 1-inch slices; then cut the depth of each in half, making 32 slices, each one 1 x ¼-inch in size. Place the tempeh slices into the marinade in a single layer, turning to coat. Pieces should not be stacked. Bake for one hour in the oven.

When tempeh is done, remove from the oven, and transfer the pieces to a baking sheet, placing pieces in a single layer. Spray each side with olive oil. Set tempeh slices 8–9 inches under the broiler and broil for 3–4 minutes on each side or until crispy and browned. To avoid burning, check periodically. They may also be sprayed with olive oil and browned in a skillet, also lightly sprayed with olive oil.

**Variation** Add 1 tablespoon of chopped rosemary leaves to the marinade.

## Chile Lovers' Spicy Vegan Chili

2 teaspoons whole cumin seed

1 teaspoon coriander seed

2 teaspoons Mexican oregano

3 ½ cups mushroom broth, divided

3 tablespoons tamari sauce, divided

2 teaspoons hickory liquid smoke, divided

2 teaspoons Worcestershire sauce, divided

1 package (8 ounces) tempeh,
grated with large holes of grater

2 teaspoons olive oil

1 large sweet yellow onion, finely chopped

1 poblano chile, finely chopped

8 garlic cloves, run through garlic press

1 cup dark beer (Negra Modelo or Bass Ale)

2 teaspoons chili powder

2 teaspoons smoked bittersweet or sweet paprika

1 can (15 ounces) black beans, don't drain

1 can (15 ounces) pinto or kidney beans, don't drain

1 can (14 ounces) diced fire-roasted tomatoes with juice

1 piece of kombu, optional (helps digestion, reduces gas,
adds nutrients)

1 chipotle chile in adobo sauce, seeded and minced
(canned, or see recipe on page 50)

1–2 teaspoons adobo sauce

½ cup chopped cilantro

1 teaspoon honey or evaporated cane juice

2 teaspoons Key lime juice

¼ cup nutritional yeast, optional,
but what a great flavor

---

**Serves 6**

Calories per serving: 325
Total fat: 7g
Saturated fat: 1g
Calories from fat: 59g
Protein: 21g
Carbohydrates: 46g
Dietary fiber: 12g
Sugars: 5g

*This recipe is not for meek chili eaters! Our daughter, Amanda, loves hot, hot, hot foods, while her husband, Ben, enjoys the heat toned down a bit. Even so, Ben—while on his third serving—commented, "This chili is in a different class, and I don't miss the meat." Worcestershire sauce normally contains anchovies, but vegan Worcestershire is available at health food stores.*

▼ ▼ ▼

To release the perfume in the cumin and coriander, toast them together in a small skillet over medium-low heat until fragrant, while shaking the pan to prevent them from burning. Remove from skillet and set aside. In the same skillet, add the oregano and toast until the scent of oregano fills the air. Transfer toasted seeds and herbs to grinder or mortar; grind and set aside.

In a large skillet mix 2 cups of mushroom broth, 1 tablespoon of the tamari sauce, 1 teaspoon of the liquid smoke, 1 teaspoon of the Worcestershire sauce, and the grated tempeh. Bring to a boil, reduce heat to medium, and simmer until the tempeh has absorbed all the broth. Move the tempeh to one side of the skillet, and add 2 teaspoons of oil. Allow the oil to heat; then toss the tempeh in the oil and sauté until it starts sticking to the skillet. Deglaze the skillet with the remaining mushroom broth. Scrape the pieces of tempeh from the skillet. Remove from burner and set aside.

While the tempeh is cooking, cook the onion and poblano chile in a dry 5-quart saucepan over medium heat until the onion is crispy tender. Add the garlic and sauté until the mixture starts sticking to the pan. Stir in the beer to deglaze the pot; then add the chili powder, the ground seeds and herbs mix, the paprika, the black and pinto or kidney beans, tomatoes, kombu, chipotle chile, adobo sauce, and the remaining tamari sauce, liquid smoke, and Worcestershire sauce. When tempeh is done, transfer it to the chili mixture. Cover and simmer over medium-low for 30 minutes, stirring occasionally. Uncover, simmer for about 30 minutes more or until the desired thickness, stirring frequently.

Remove from heat, stir in cilantro, honey or evaporated cane juice, and lime juice; then stir in the nutritional yeast if you are using it. It will add a rich flavor and thicken the chili somewhat. Pass extra nutritional yeast for diners to add.

## Farmers' Market Quesadillas

1/3 cup finely chopped fresh red onion

1 handful of pea sprouts, finely chopped

1 handful of purslane, finely chopped

1 tomato, chopped

1 cup shredded zucchini

1 handful of fresh oregano or basil leaves from the garden (optional—but tasty and full of antioxidants)

1/2–1 whole serrano chile, seeded and minced

1/2 cup crumbled feta cheese

4 Tortilleria Arevalo's mesquite tortillas, or your favorite healthy whole-grain tortilla

**Serves 4**

Calories per serving: 179
Total fat: 5g
Saturated fat: 3g
Calories from fat: 41
Protein: 8g
Carbohydrates: 29g
Dietary fiber: 4g
Sugars: 3g

*Quesadillas—dewy fresh vegetables encased in freshly made tortillas—were the headliner on our Sunday brunch menu. At 7:40 a.m. my grandson Aaron and I headed for St. Philip's Tucson Farmers' Market. Knowing that Arevolo's homemade warm organic whole-grain flour and mesquite tortillas (made with olive oil) would be in short supply and fly out of the market, we bought those first. Next stop, Sleeping Frog Farms for organic veggies, purslane, and pea sprouts; and then we stopped at Leo's (who's 80-something) Leo Big D Farms for pesticide-free squash; last stop was for organic feta goat cheese from Fiore de Capra. When we returned home, Aaron helped pick oregano, basil, thyme, and arugula from our garden. The herbs added wonderful flavor and a load of antioxidants. The wild arugula gave it a bite, which was deliciously balanced by the feta. Also, combining all these greens synergistically increased their individual powers to fight disease.*

*Serve with Fresh Salsa (page 44) and avocado slices.*

▼ ▼ ▼

Toss all the ingredients together except for the feta cheese and the tortillas. On a griddle or in a large dry iron skillet, heat 1 side of a tortilla just until warm and pliable—not hard. Turn it over and spread 1 heaping tablespoon of crumbled feta cheese over one-half of the tortilla, while leaving 1 inch of edge free. Then scatter 1/4 of the vegetable/herb mix over the cheese, and top off with a tiny bit more cheese. Fold the empty half over the vegetables and press down with a spatula. Let it warm a bit. Then, flip it over and press down again. When the cheese is completely melted, remove from heat and enjoy.

## Winter Spinach–Sweet Potato Vegan Quiche

**Piecrust**

1½ cups whole-grain spelt flour

½ teaspoon sea salt

½ teaspoon baking power

1 heaping tablespoon fresh rosemary leaves

5 tablespoons extra-virgin olive oil

¼ cup ice water

*Quiche is not for those hoping to lose weight or following a heart-healthy diet. Try this healthy and very tasty vegan alternative. I set out to make a healthier crust by choosing olive oil, which the Greeks have used in pastries for centuries. Whole-grain spelt was used because compared to wheat, it's easier to digest, absorption of nutrients is better, it is higher in protein and fiber, and has a pleasant sweet-nutty taste. This crust is tender and crumbly, with exceptionally good flavor. The filling is packed with wholesome vegetables rich in fiber; saturated fat and cholesterol are reduced by using mushroom broth, nutritional yeast, and vegan cheese, and substituting chia seeds for the eggs, which also adds omega-3 and protein. It freezes nicely, making it a quick meal to pop in the microwave or oven for a later busy day.*

*Notes: The firmer the tofu, the higher the content of protein. The brand I used when I made this recipe (Soy Deli) is tightly sealed in plastic, with little water, and has 15 grams of protein per 3 ounces. It was not necessary to press water from this tofu. Firm tofu packaged in a tub usually has about 10 grams of protein and is floating in water. Thus, if using firm or extra-firm tofu from a tub, you need to drain off water. Place paper towels on the top and bottom of the block, put block between your hands, and press the block while holding over the sink.*

*Nutritional yeast is known for its "cheesy" taste and as a flavor enhancer. It's a good source of fiber and protein and is loaded with B vitamins, along with a good dose of other vitamins and minerals. Pickled plum paste or purée adds a salty, sour flavor that changes tofu from bland to zesty. Both are available in health-oriented grocery stores. I am not a fan of fake cheese, but Follow Your Heart® Vegan Gourmet Cheese and Daiya™ are okay on occasion, and they both use non-GMO oils.*

*Serve this quiche with a tossed salad.*

▼ ▼ ▼

To make the piecrust: In a food processor work bowl with the "S" blade in place, blend the flour, salt, and baking powder for about 30 seconds; then add rosemary leaves and press pulse a couple times. While slowly pouring the olive oil into the dry ingredients, pulse the mixture until it resembles a coarse meal. With the processor on, add ¼ cup of ice water, and blend until the dough forms a ball. (More or less water may be needed depending on flour and humidity.) Remove the ball and any loose dough from the work bowl and combine into one ball. Sprinkle the workspace with a little flour; then roll out the dough to fit a 10-inch pie plate. If the dough sticks to the rolling pin, sprinkle a little more flour on the dough. Transfer to a pie plate, flute the edges, then cover with plastic wrap and set aside. Another option is to form a ball, flatten it, and place it in the middle of the pie plate; then push it from the center out and up the sides. A 9-inch tart pan with a removable bottom can also be used.

**Filling**

12 ounces firm or extra-firm tofu, drained and pressed (not silken)

$^3/_4$ cup mushroom broth

2 tablespoons pickled plum paste

2 medium garlic cloves, cut in thirds

2 tablespoons chia seed

2 teaspoons olive oil, divided

2 cups chopped sweet yellow onions

4 medium garlic cloves, run through garlic press

$^1/_2$ cup rice wine

1$^1/_2$ cups cubed garnet yams, $^1/_4$-inch pieces

8 ounces baby or large portabella mushrooms, about 1$^1/_2$ cups sliced

8 handfuls fresh baby spinach, washed

3 tablespoons spelt flour

1 teaspoon baking powder

1 teaspoon freshly ground cumin

$^1/_2$ cup finely chopped sweet yellow onion

1 $^1/_2$ tablespoons fresh oregano

2.5 ounces Follow Your Heart® Vegan Gourmet Cheese or Daiya™ cheddar "cheese" alternative, about $^3/_4$ cup grated

$^1/_3$ cup nutritional yeast

Freshly ground pepper

Extra-virgin olive oil spray

Sprinkling of bittersweet smoked paprika

---

**Serves 10**

Calories per serving: 297
Total fat: 13g
Saturated fat: 1g
Calories from fat: 116
Protein: 12g
Carbohydrates: 33g
Dietary fiber: 7g
Sugars: 5g

For the filling: In the work bowl of a food processor, blend the tofu, mushroom broth, pickled plum paste, and the 2 garlic pieces cut into thirds for about 5 minutes or until mixture is very smooth. Add chia seeds and pulse a few times, allow to set for a couple minutes, then pulse again to keep the chia seeds from clumping together. Set aside while preparing the vegetables, to allow the chia seeds to gel.

In a 4 quart saucepan over medium heat, in 1 teaspoon of the olive oil, sauté the 2 cups of chopped onion until crispy tender. Add the pressed garlic and sauté until the onion is golden, aromatic, and starting to stick to the bottom of the pan. As the onion and garlic begin to stick, stir continuously. Deglaze the pan with $^1/_4$ cup of rice wine, add the yams, turn to low heat, cover, and cook until yam cubes are tender, about 10 minutes. Add more wine as needed.

While the yams are cooking, sauté the mushrooms in 1 teaspoon of olive oil over medium heat until tender, add wine as necessary, then remove from burner and set aside.

When yams are done, turn heat to medium, add the freshly washed spinach, frequently toss until spinach is wilted; then, remove from burner.

Preheat the oven to 375 degrees F.

Add the spelt flour, baking powder, and cumin to the tofu mixture in your food processor's work bowl, and pulse until blended. Transfer the tofu mixture and sautéed mushrooms to the vegetable sauté. Stir in ½ cup finely chopped onion, oregano, vegan cheese, and nutritional yeast, and thoroughly mix. Turn the mixture into the piecrust, smooth to level the filling, spray the top with olive oil, and sprinkle top with paprika. (I often wind up with excess filling. If this happens, simply oil a couple of ramekins and scrape the excess filling into them for crustless mini quiches.)

Place on the middle rack of the oven. Bake for 45–55 minutes or until the blade of a thin knife comes out almost clean, and the crust is golden. Remove from oven and cool for 10 minutes. Serve warm.

## Variations

▸ **Vegetarian alternative:** Substitute ⅓ cup goat feta cheese for fake cheese.

▸ **Broccolini-Sweet Potato Vegan Quiche:** Substitute 1½ cups raw chopped broccolini for the spinach. Fold into filling just prior to putting filling in crust.

## Shiitake Mushroom Enchiladas

½–⅔ cup Southwest Enchilada Sauce Concentrate (page 48)

2 cups mushroom broth

Zest from 1 lime

1 teaspoon cornstarch or flour, optional, for thickening

1–2 tablespoons extra-virgin olive oil

1 medium sweet yellow onion, finely chopped

6 garlic cloves, mashed, peeled, minced

4 cups sliced shiitake or grilled portabella mushrooms

¼ cup dry vermouth

1 cup finely chopped flat leaf parsley

½ cup chopped fresh purple sage

1 cup mushroom broth

2 tablespoons lemon thyme or plain thyme

3 handfuls of baby spinach or 2 cups coarsely chopped chard, tough stems removed

10 corn tortillas

Feta cheese, for garnish

Avocado, for garnish

Chopped onion, for garnish

Lime juice, for garnish

---

### Serves 4

Calories per serving: 270
Total fat: 8g
Saturated fat: 1g
Calories from fat: 69g
Protein: 10g
Carbohydrates: 40g
Dietary fiber: 7g
Sugars: 7g

*Add a touch of gourmet to enchiladas, along with a lot of health-promoting and immune-boosting properties, a meaty texture, and considerable protein, by stuffing tortillas with flavorful shitake mushrooms or portabella mushrooms. In addition to being such a wonderful complement to mushrooms, fresh sage is a powerhouse of antioxidants, having five times more per ounce than blueberries.*

*Serve this dish with tossed salad and beans.*

▼ ▼ ▼

Combine the enchilada sauce concentrate, the 2 cups of mushroom broth, and the lime zest, and simmer over low heat for at least 5 minutes to combine flavors. For thicker sauce, add a thin cornstarch paste (cornstarch mixed with a little water).

Over medium heat, sauté the onions, garlic, and mushrooms in the olive oil for about 5 minutes, adding vermouth to keep things from sticking. Add the parsley, sage, and the 1 cup of broth, and simmer over low heat until mushrooms are soft. If using grilled portabellas, don't sauté; fold in after spinach is cooked. Fold in the spinach and cook until limp; then remove pot from burner. Toss with thyme and set aside.

Spray an appropriate-size baking dish with olive oil. Preheat oven to 250 degrees F. Spray or rub oil over the tortillas and place them in the oven; heat until the tortillas are pliable, not crisp. Turn up the oven to 350 degrees F. Dredge a tortilla in the warm sauce, then lightly cover the tortilla with filling, and either roll it up and place it, seam down, in the pan, or fold the tortilla in half and lay it in pan. Repeat with rest of the tortillas. Any leftover filling, scatter on top of the enchiladas; then pour the remaining sauce over the enchiladas.

Place in the oven until enchiladas are hot, about 15 minutes. Remove from the oven and sprinkle with feta cheese, avocado, and chopped onion. Splash with lime juice.

# FISH & SEAFOOD

**Fish takes minutes** to cook, with effortless preparation while bringing to the table fabulous, deliciously healthy meals. I've crafted a menu of health-promoting meals full of color, shapes, and textures designed to lure family and friends to dig in and enjoy dishes that satisfy and intrigue their palates. Whether the fish or seafood complements roasted winter roots or a mélange of colorful tomatoes and peppers mixed with summer vegetables, whether it is used in a salad or chowder, the combinations are infinite for fashioning enticing meals. To keep it healthy and not smother the flavor of the fish, no rich sauces are used. As an added perk, life becomes a little simpler in the kitchen, allowing more time with family or friends at the dinner table.

In general, fish and seafood are low-calorie, high-protein foods and contain less total and saturated fat than most meats. Oily fish is one of the best sources for vitamin D, crucial for calcium absorption. Wild oily fish (salmon, sablefish, sardines, herring, anchovies, and mackerel) are top sources of omega-3, promoting a healthy omega-3 to omega-6 ratio, which is lacking in the American diet.

Due to the omega-3s (EPA and DHA) in oily fish, the American Heart Association recommends two 3.5-ounce servings of oily fish per week to reduce the risk of heart disease, particularly sudden cardiac death. In addition, evidence suggests that oily fish could decrease the risk of stroke and boost emotions by reducing depression. These same fats are also essential for sight and brain development in babies (especially DHA) from prenatal to postnatal, and may avert mental decline in old age and provide relief for achy inflamed joints. So, from the womb into old age, oily fish can help you live a life with fewer maladies.

Unfortunately, sometimes the good stuff has a downside. For almost a century, industry has dumped mercury waste into our waterways, causing all fish to have varying degrees of mercury, which may have negative effects on fetuses and children. Therefore, pregnant and nursing mothers and children under 16 must choose their fish wisely and may need to limit consumption. Studies have shown, in general, that most fish don't contain any more PCBs and dioxins than meat, dairy, and vegetables; fish from some lakes and rivers in the US, however, may be an exception. Your best bet is to check the Environmental Defense Fund and Natural Resources Defense Council websites for a list of fish containing mercury and other toxins. Also, the Environmental Protection Agency (EPA) website will link you to your local region for up-to-date toxin advisories.

We live on a small planet, where our food choices impact all aspects of our environment. Thus, our vote at the cash register is our most powerful weapon in promoting sustainable food sources and a healthy environment. Agriculture practices on land and aquaculture practices in the water both affect the sustainability and healthiness of our seas and waterways. If we buy plant foods grown in monoculture and doused with harmful chemicals, and if we consume ill-managed factory-farmed animals and fish, we are contributing to and condoning the pollution of our waterways and oceans. ▶

*Wild Alaskan Salmon Wrapped in Fig Leaves (recipe on page 84).*

## Wild Alaskan Salmon Wrapped in Fig Leaves

8 freshly picked fig leaves, or enough to wrap 4 pieces of salmon

Extra-virgin olive oil or olive oil spray

4 pieces (4 ounces each) wild Alaskan King, Sockeye, or Silver (coho) salmon, with skin

1–2 Key limes, cut in half for squeezing

Sea salt

Freshly ground pepper

Butcher string

4 fresh figs, thinly sliced (mission figs used in this recipe)

4 lime wedges

---

**Serves 4**

Calories per serving: 268
Total fat: 13g
Saturated fat: 2g
Calories from fat: 117g
Protein: 26g
Carbohydrates: 14g
Dietary fiber: 2g
Sugars: 11g

*Salmon wrapped in fig leaves will deliver a succulently moist piece of fish with an infusion of coconut flavor and a lovely coconut scent that will tantalize your senses. To keep it simple, I top the cooked fish with 1 thinly sliced fresh fig from our mission fig tree that bears fruit during the summer and early fall. If you want more color and have to be persuasive with picky fish eaters, dress it with Fig Salsa (page 45).*

*Serve with Simply Spinach (page 136) and Cilantro Lime Quinoa Pilaf (page 154).*

▼ ▼ ▼

Preheat oven to 375 degrees F.

Rinse fig leaves with water and pat dry; then spray or brush the top sides of the leaves with olive oil. Splash the salmon with a little lime juice, brush or spray the salmon with oil, and lightly sprinkle it with salt and pepper. Wrap the salmon with the top (oiled) sides of the leaves against the salmon, and tie with butcher string. If the leaves are small, use two or more leaves to wrap each piece. Some of the salmon may be exposed. Place in a shallow baking dish and bake 10–12 minutes. Remove from oven and allow to rest for a couple minutes; it will continue to cook outside the oven. Unwrap and test for doneness. If it is not done to your satisfaction, return it to the oven until it is cooked to your liking. Untie packets and serve salmon in opened packets with sliced figs atop. Pass lime wedges.

# Purchasing Fish and Seafood

To assure that we are eating an ethical catch, we need to choose fish wisely and with a conscience. Hopefully, the following guidelines will help. They are based on information from the Natural Resources Defense Council, Environmental Defense Fund, and Seafood Watch, among other sources advocating for clean sustainable seafood.

- Select seafood with the MSC (Marine Stewardship Council) label on it guaranteeing it is from a certified sustainable fishery. Fish markets and restaurants trading in sustainable seafood also post it. You can also search for a shop or restaurant on the MSC website.
- Before going to the market, check online with Monterey Bay Aquarium's Endangered Seafood Guide, Seafood Watch, for recommendations on which seafood to buy or avoid. It is updated twice a year. A Seafood Watch pocket guide can be printed, and an application for mobile devices can be downloaded from their website. They also offer Project Fish Map for the iPhone. The Environmental Defense Fund website offers web and pocket guides of eco-ratings that list good fish high in omega-3s with low environmental contaminants and less desirable fish high in mercury or PCBs. The Natural Resources Defense Council website has a mercury pocket guide and mercury calculator.
- Buy seafood from the US. With stricter fishing and farming standards in the US than other parts of the world, the variety of a particular type of fish is generally more sustainable and with a healthier profile than imported.
- Ask where fish is from. Then check one of the guides previously listed. Since the health and sustainability vary by region within the United States, check the Environmental Protection Agency website for regional updates. Alaskan seafood is generally good for you and the environment.
- Buy small fish and seafood such as herring, sardines, anchovies, clams, and mussels, which are lower on the food chain. They are more sustainable, more plentiful, and have considerably fewer toxins than the larger, longer-lived, and more predatory fish.
- Eat a variety of sustainable fish from different waters to reduce intake of toxins and to avoid depleting any one type of fish.
- Buy fish from reputable sources. Don't buy fresh or previously frozen fish that has been in the market for more than two days. Don't be shy; ask to take a sniff. It should have a sweet or mild smell, not a fishy or strong odor, and should never be slimy. Frozen or fresh, the health benefits are the same.
- When preparing fish, keep in mind that high heat used in deep-frying destroys omega-3. Therefore, bake fish at moderate (350–375 degrees F) to moderate hot (400 degrees F) temperatures for a short period of time and only until almost done. It will continue to cook out of the oven. Fish should be moist, not dry, and never overcooked. Steaming and quickly grilling and broiling are equally good methods. A "Grill-Per'fect" temperature sensor for fish is the perfect tool for determining if fish is ready. I remove the fish when it indicates that it is almost done.

## Chipotle Wild Alaskan Salmon Chowder

1 tablespoon plus 1 teaspoon extra-virgin olive oil

2 ½ cups finely chopped onions

4 medium garlic cloves, run through garlic press to yield 1 heaping tablespoon

1 ¼ cups finely chopped celery

1 teaspoon dried thyme leaves, crushed to release flavor

2 tablespoons unbleached wheat flour (or non-gluten thickener)

½ cup vermouth

2 ½ cups low-sodium vegetable stock

1 chipotle chile in adobo sauce, finely chopped (recipe on page 50, or canned)

1 tablespoon of adobo sauce

1 tablespoon finely chopped fresh rosemary leaves

½ teaspoon freshly grated nutmeg or ground nutmeg

1 medium-large unpeeled and scrubbed red potato, cut into bite-size pieces

1–2 medium unpeeled and scrubbed garnet yams, cut into bite-size pieces to yield about 2 ½ cups

2 ¾ cups nonfat milk

3–4 cups torn fresh beet or chard leaves, tough stems and veins removed

1 pound wild salmon, cut into 2-inch strips

1 cup fresh chiffonade-cut basil

Sea salt

Freshly ground pepper

Sweet smoked paprika, for garnish

2 tablespoons chopped fresh dill, for garnish

---

### Serves 5

Calories per serving: 424
Total fat: 10g
Saturated fat: 2g
Calories from fat: 90
Protein: 35g
Carbohydrates: 28g
Dietary fiber: 6g
Sugars: 14g

---

*This wholesome chowder isn't full of saturated fat but is pleasingly creamy and full of comforting, tasty flavors. Encourage your kids to eat it, since there is evidence that omega-3 may improve their learning ability. Try flaking the fish to make it not so obvious. The deep-orange yams not only add beautiful color but are packed with the antioxidant beta carotene, which might slow down aging and reduce the risk of some cancers. The purplish-green beet leaves add a lovely contrasting color and a hefty dose of vitamin A. All these vegetables are full of fiber, which slows down digestion, helping stabilize blood sugar. Fiber keeps you feeling fuller longer, curbing your appetite and helping you maintain a healthy weight.*

*Note: To reduce fat from olive oil and make the soup gluten-free, eliminate the oil and flour that thickens the chowder. Instead, blend more vegetables until the desired creaminess is achieved.*

*Serve with a tossed salad.*

▼ ▼ ▼

In a 6-quart soup pot, over medium-high heat, sauté the onion and garlic in 1 teaspoon of the oil for 2 minutes. Turn heat to medium, add celery and thyme and cook, stirring occasionally, until onions start to brown and are somewhat sticking to the pan. Add 1 more tablespoon of oil, stirring to coat the mixture with oil. Add flour, stirring continuously to thoroughly coat the mixture; then add a little bit of vermouth at a time, while stirring constantly to avoid clumps of flour. Add vegetable stock, chipotle chile, adobo sauce, rosemary, nutmeg, potato, and yams; turn heat to high and bring to a boil. Reduce heat to low, cover, and simmer for about 10 minutes, occasionally stirring, until potato and yams are done.

Remove pot from stove; then, using an immersion blender, blend a small amount of the vegetables for a thicker creamier consistency and appealing color. If you don't have an immersion blender, remove 1 cup of the vegetables and broth from the chowder and place in a blender jar. (To avoid burning yourself and to keep the lid from shooting off the blender container, make sure the lid is ajar to release the steam.) Pulse a few times and then blend on low until smooth; stir back into the chowder.

Stir in the milk, add the beet or chard leaves, and cook a couple minutes; then add the salmon, cover, and cook for about 3 or 4 minutes or until salmon is almost done and the leaves are limp. Remove from burner, stir in the basil leaves, cover, and allow it to rest for about five minutes. Taste, season with salt and pepper to taste, and serve with a sprinkling of smoky sweet paprika and scattered dill fronds.

**Variation** Replace the beet leaves or chard leaves with spinach. However, place the spinach in the individual bowls, pour hot chowder over the spinach, and allow the bowls to sit for a few minutes; then stir and add garnishes.

# Salmon

Due to the enforcement of environmentally sound fishing practices—no overfishing and use of catching methods that are least destructive to the habitat—Alaskan wild salmon is the healthiest and most sustainable option. Healthwise, wild-caught king salmon and sockeye are top sources of omega-3 and astaxanthin (a red-orange carotenoid with antioxidant power). According to the EDF, most Alaskan salmon are healthy and low in contaminants.

Conversely, Seafood Watch cautions that most farmed salmon, worldwide, should be avoided, including Atlantic farmed salmon. This is due to a host of negative environmental impacts and health issues. Farmed salmon contain higher levels of pollutants than wild and are treated with antibiotics. Waste is released into the ocean from salmon crowded in open ocean net pens in coastal waters, which allows parasites and diseases to spread to wild fish. If buying farmed salmon, Seafood Watch suggests those raised in confined inland recirculation tanks and currently recommends only US-labeled farmed freshwater coho salmon. Also, look for the blue MSC (Marine Stewardship Council) label verifying a certified sustainable fishery.

Whether it is land or sea, nutritional and environmental goals often conflict with each other. Such is the case with the resource-intensive farmed salmon. They are fed ground-up small fish and fish oil to provide necessary omega-3 in their diet, but this in turn shrinks the food supply available for wild carnivorous salmon. (It takes 3 pounds of small fish to produce one pound of farmed salmon—yikes!) As a solution, aquaculture has been replacing fish meal and fish oil with corn, other grains, and vegetable oils, resulting in higher amounts of omega-6, which means more omega-6 going into our already omega-6 tilted diet.

Salmon is on Dr. William Li's list of suggested anti-angiogenic foods to eat to prevent cancer. Due to an excellent source of omega-3 and its rich succulent taste, salmon has always been our family's fish of choice.

Unfortunately, there is not enough wild salmon to meet the demand. By mixing up the catch and including a variety of salmon species and other fish supplying omega-3, less pressure will be put on the Alaska wild salmon. In addition, only a 3.5 ounce serving of oily fish twice a week is recommend by the American Heart Association. So servings double that size, as is often the case, are not necessary to reap its health benefits.

# Scallops

Diver-caught (scallops manually collected by divers) causes the least habitat and wasteful "bycatch" (unwanted catch—fish, turtles, birds, etc., often dead or injured) damages, whereas trawling scoops up scallops, regardless of maturity, along with whatever else is in its path. The Interstate Shellfish Sanitation Conference suggests that scallops harvested in the US are a safe choice to eat because state and local jurisdictions monitor harvesting waters for excessive levels of contaminants. If harmful levels are found, commercial harvesting is halted.

Scallops are sold "wet pack" (treated with sodium tripolyphosphate solution (STP) and by law must be labeled as such) or untreated "dry pack." The STP solution prevents them from drying out, but is soaked up by the scallops, adding extra liquid weight, which you end up paying for by the pound. This added liquid also causes them to steam-cook in the pan, often resulting in overcooking, and they may shrink down to half their size. On the other hand, the dry pack scallops won't do this. Dry pack scallops retain their clean, sweet flavor and texture. They cost more per pound, but what you might have saved by buying soaked scallops just dwindled away in the pan.

## Chipotle–Almond-crusted Sea Scallops

3 zucchini squash (7 inches long)

1 crookneck squash (7 inches long)

Scant 1/2 teaspoon extra-virgin olive oil

1 1/2 pounds sea scallops, 1 1/2–2-inch diameter

2 tablespoons Key lime juice

1/2 cup almond meal

1–2 teaspoons chipotle chile powder, or New Mexico red chile powder

1 teaspoon Mexican oregano, crushed to release flavor

1 teaspoon ground smoked paprika

4 tablespoons minced lemon basil or sweet basil, divided

2 tablespoons minced cilantro or Italian parsley (flat leaf), divided

2 medium garlic cloves, run through garlic press

Sea salt

Freshly ground pepper

2 tablespoons grated Parmesan cheese (use microplane)

Extra-virgin olive oil spray

1/4 cup white wine or French vermouth

1 teaspoon cornstarch

1/3 cup chopped sweet yellow onion

2 finely chopped Roma tomatoes

1 medium–large garlic clove, run through garlic press

2 teaspoons lemon juice

2 tablespoons ultra-finely grated Parmesan cheese (use microplane)

1 teaspoon grated lime rind (use microplane)

4 lime or lemon wedges

---

### Serves 6

Calories per serving: 327
Total fat: 15g
Saturated fat: 2g
Calories from fat: 139
Protein: 33g
Carbohydrates: 12g
Dietary fiber: 4g
Sugars: 3g

*Frozen sea scallops are about all we can hope for in the Southwest. If on the East Coast during the scallop season, I would opt for the dry-packed diver scallops and prepare them the same day caught. Almonds are used for the crust in lieu of breadcrumbs. Although almonds are higher in fat than bread crumbs, a half stick of butter would probably be added to the breadcrumbs with a high amount of saturated fat. Almonds provide a healthier fat. Almonds are also packed full of heart-healthy nutrients and are gluten free. Served over colorful summer vegetables, this dish makes a beautiful easy dinner. Serve with a tossed salad.*

*Note: If scallops are frozen, allow them to thaw in the refrigerator overnight for best texture and taste.*

▼ ▼ ▼

Preheat oven to 375 degrees F.

Using a vegetable peeler, vertically slice thin, 1/2–1-inch wide strips of zucchini and crookneck squash, slicing first one side of the squash, and then turning and slicing the other side—slicing only to the seeds. Set aside.

Grease the bottom of a roasting pan with the olive oil. Quickly rinse the scallops in cold water to remove any shell particles, pat dry, and place in the pan so they barely touch each other; splash with lime juice. Thoroughly mix the almond meal, chile powder, oregano, paprika, 1 tablespoon of the minced basil, 1 tablespoon of the cilantro or parsley, and the garlic, 1/2 teaspoon of salt, and some pepper.

Cover the scallops with the almond meal mixture, sprinkle with Parmesan cheese, and spray liberally with olive oil. Bake for 10–15 minutes until almost done—they will be broiled later. Perfectly cooked scallops are opaque to somewhat white and have a firm feel. It is better to serve them slightly undercooked than chewing on rubbery, overcooked scallops. Remove scallops from the oven and transfer to the broiling grid of a broiler pan set, saving the broth to use in the pasta sauce.

In a small bowl, add enough wine or vermouth to the cornstarch to render a paste. Thoroughly mix the paste and remaining wine into the reserved scallop sauce. Stir in chopped onion, tomato, and pressed garlic; return this sauce mixture to the oven, until the sauce begins to bubble and slightly thickens. Remove from the oven, stir in the lemon juice, and toss 2 more tablespoons of the basil and the squash in the heated sauce; season with salt and pepper to your taste. Cover and set aside.

Broil the scallops for a few minutes until the topping is somewhat crispy and the scallops are done—don't overcook.

Plate the dish by placing the squash/sauce mixture on the plate, ladling any extra sauce over the squash, and sprinkle with Parmesan and top with scallops. Garnish the scallops with lime zest, and the remaining tablespoons of basil and cilantro or parsley. Serve with a lime or lemon wedge on the side.

## Chard-wrapped Chipotle Halibut

4–6 sweet oranges

1 teaspoon orange zest (use microplane or zester)

1/4–1 chipotle chile in adobo sauce, seeded and minced (canned or recipe on page 50)

1 teaspoon adobo sauce

1/3 cup chopped green onions, including some green

1–2 garlic cloves, run through garlic press or minced

1 tablespoon Key lime juice

1–2 tablespoons minced cilantro

1 teaspoon honey, optional

8–12 tender rainbow-colored Swiss chard, stems removed

1–2 tablespoons extra-virgin olive oil

Pinch of sea salt

Freshly ground pepper

4 pieces wild Alaskan halibut steaks or fillets (4 ounces each)

Butcher string

1/3 cup orange juice

Extra-virgin olive oil spray

1 teaspoon grated ginger (use microplane)

1/2 teaspoon sea salt

Freshly ground black pepper

3 tablespoons fresh herbs from garden (thyme, oregano, rosemary, etc.)

4 limes, quartered

### Serves 4

Calories per serving: 340
Total fat: 6g
Saturated fat: 3g
Calories from fat: 30g
Protein: 5g
Carbohydrates: 32g
Dietary fiber: 12g
Sugars: 3g

*Halibut is bundled up in colorful Swiss chard leaves and dressed with sweet, zesty chipotle–orange sauce, creating a tasty mix of flavors. It's loaded with colorful antioxidant power and delicious to boot.*

*Serve the fish packets over a bed of Heirloom Vegetable Brown Rice Pilaf (page 157), and top with chipotle sauce, allowing some sauce to run onto the rice. Serve with Spicy Roasted Winter Squash (page 144) and pass the quartered limes.*

*Note: Finely chop leftover kale and toss with the cooked rice.*

▼ ▼ ▼

Preheat oven to 350 degrees F. Prepare the chipotle–orange sauce as follows: cut off the ends of the oranges, and then cut off all of the rind including white pith. Using a bowl to catch the juices, cut the fruit into ½-inch slices, and then cut the slices in fourths and remove the seeds. Reserve the juice. Combine the orange zest, orange pieces, chipotle and adobo sauce, chopped green onions, garlic, lime juice, cilantro, and honey (if using); set aside while you prepare the fish bundles.

To make chard leaves more flexible for wrapping, run the back of a spoon down the tough center vein of each chard leaf to flatten. With the inside of the leaves facing up, lay 8 leaves on work space and brush or spray with olive oil. Lightly salt and pepper the halibut, and lay a piece of it on each of 4 leaves. Spread a little sauce over each halibut; then wrap the leaf around it, encasing as much as possible—more than 1 leaf may be needed for wrapping; then tie with butcher string. Coat the bottom of a baking dish with olive oil.

Place the wrapped halibut in the baking dish, pour the ⅓ cup orange juice over the bundles, spray or brush with olive oil, and place in the oven. Bake for about 6 minutes, then turn over and cook about 6 minutes more (approximately 12 total minutes per 1 inch of fish). Serve with quartered limes.

## Halibut with Grapefruit Sauce

Grapefruit Sauce (page 47)
2 tablespoons fresh Key lime juice
4 Alaskan halibut steaks (4 ounces each)
Extra-virgin olive oil spray
Sea salt
Freshly ground pepper

**Serves 4**

Calories per serving: 194
Total fat: 3g
Saturated fat: 1g
Calories from fat: 32g
Protein: 24g
Carbohydrates: 19g
Dietary fiber: 3g
Sugars: 14g

*A blanket of refreshingly piquant, tangy-sweet sauce adds beautiful color and pleasing flavors to the mild halibut and sautéed greens, delivering a delightfully satisfying meal. Serve with Cilantro-Lime Quinoa Pilaf (page 154) and Sweet Bitter Greens (page 134), starting the rice about 15 minutes before baking the halibut.*

▼ ▼ ▼

Preheat oven to 350 degrees F. Prepare the Grapefruit Sauce, and plan to prepare the greens while the halibut is baking.

Squeeze lime juice over each side of the halibut pieces, spray with olive oil, and sprinkle lightly with salt and pepper. Place in an appropriate-size baking pan and bake in the oven for about 13 minutes or until the halibut is almost done—don't overcook. (Prepare the greens while the halibut is baking.) Remove the halibut from the oven and allow it to rest for a couple minutes; it will continue to cook.

Serve the halibut over the Sweet Bitter Greens, topped with the Grapefruit Sauce.

## Halibut

MSC certifies Alaska, Washington, and Oregon halibut fisheries as sustainable. Halibut is a predatory fish, and the longer they live the more toxins they contain. Therefore, buy only young Alaska halibut (under 20 pounds) that is sustainably fished. Check the EDF website for consumption recommendations. Halibut has some omega-3, is rich in selenium, and is on Dr. William Li's list of suggested anti-angiogenic foods to eat to prevent cancer.

## Cornmeal-crusted Flounder, Chef Scott Uehlein

**Black Bean Salsa**

1 cup cooked black beans

2 tablespoons fresh corn kernels

1/2 avocado, diced

2 teaspoons fresh, chopped cilantro

3/4 teaspoon oregano

1/2 teaspoon olive oil

2 teaspoons fresh lime juice

Dash tabasco sauce

1/4 teaspoon minced garlic

1/2 roma tomato, diced

1 scallion, chopped

**Flounder**

4 corn tortillas, thinly sliced

1 yellow bell pepper, cut in half and seeded

1 red bell pepper, cut in half and seeded

1/4 cup cornmeal

1/4 teaspoon chipotle pepper powder

1/2 teaspoon cumin seed

1/2 teaspoon chili powder

1/4 teaspoon garlic granules

1/2 teaspoon salt

4 flounder fillets (4-ounces each)

4 teaspoons olive oil

### Serves 4

Calories per serving: 355
Total fat: 10g
Saturated fat: 1g
Calories from fat: 86
Protein: 29g
Carbohydrates: 39g
Dietary fiber: 5g
Sugars: 3g

*This delicious flounder, crusted with cornmeal and topped with black bean salsa, was generously shared by Corporate Chef Scott Uehlein of Canyon Ranch, Tucson, Arizona.*

▼ ▼ ▼

Combine all ingredients for salsa in a large bowl and mix well. Set aside.

Preheat oven to 350 degrees F. Lightly spray a sheet pan with canola oil. Place tortilla slices and peppers, skin side up, on sheet pan and roast in oven until tortillas are golden brown, about 5 minutes. Return peppers to oven and roast another 5 to 10 minutes or until the skin is golden brown. Slice peppers into strips.

Combine cornmeal, spices and salt in a medium bowl. Dredge fish in cornmeal mixture. Heat olive oil in a large sauté pan and add fish fillets. Cook until golden brown on each side and cooked through, about 3 to 5 minutes on each side.

Serve 1 flounder fillet with 1/2 cup black bean salsa and 2 ounces bell pepper strips.

# Southwest Shrimp Salad

**Shrimp and Marinade**

1/3 cup fresh Key lime or lemon juice

3 tablespoons extra-virgin olive oil

1 teaspoon Dijon mustard

1 tablespoon honey

2 teaspoons oregano, crushed to release flavor

4 medium garlic cloves, run through garlic press

1/2 teaspoon sea salt

1/3 cup minced cilantro

1 pound uncooked, deveined, and peeled shrimp (16–20 count)

**Dressing**

3 tablespoons fresh lime juice

2 tablespoons extra-virgin olive oil

1 teaspoon honey

1 garlic clove, run through garlic press

2 teaspoons Dijon mustard

1 teaspoon freshly grated ginger

**Salad**

1/2 cup quinoa, rinsed in ultra-fine strainer

3/4 cup water, mixed with leftover marinade

2 cups 1/2-inch diced peaches or Mexican papaya

1 serrano chile, deveined, seeded, and minced

1/4 cup minced red onion

1 tablespoon minced fresh mint

1/3 cup finely minced cilantro, include some stems

2 teaspoons lime zest

Sea salt and freshly ground pepper

**For Final Assembly**

1/2 medium avocado, sliced and cut into 1/2-inch pieces

Splash of fresh lime juice for avocado

4 cups arugula or baby spinach

**Serves 4**

Calories per serving: 467

Total fat: 23g

Saturated fat: 3g

Calories from fat: 205

Protein: 28g

Carbohydrates: 39g

Dietary fiber: 5g

Sugars: 18g

*Refreshing, zesty, and ever so delicious describes this colorful healthy salad.*

▼ ▼ ▼

Preheat grill to high.

Combine the marinade ingredients in a bowl that will accommodate the shrimp; then toss in shrimp and marinate for 30 minutes at room temperature. Reserve some of the marinade for the quinoa. Transfer the shrimp to the grill, and cook for about 2 minutes on each side or until shrimp turns orange—don't overcook! Remove from grill and refrigerate to chill.

Mix together the salad dressing ingredients and set aside. Prepare the quinoa by mixing 1 tablespoon of reserved marinade in a small saucepan with enough water to yield 3/4 cup. Stir in the rinsed quinoa and bring to a boil; reduce heat to low and simmer for 10–12 minutes or until quinoa has soaked up all the water. Fluff with a fork, transfer to large bowl, and allow to cool. Cut the cooled shrimp into bite-size pieces and toss with the quinoa, salad ingredients, and dressing. Serve on 4 individual plates over 1 cup of arugula each, top off with avocado, and splash with lime juice.

## Shrimp

According to the Monterey Bay Aquarium Seafood Watch, currently the most sustainable shrimp are British Columbia and Oregon wild-caught, farmed Pacific white shrimp and West Coast white shrimp grown in fully recirculation systems or inland ponds, and U. S. farmed freshwater giant shrimp grown in inland farm ponds. The Environmental Defense Fund (EDF) lists spot prawns (shrimp) from Canada and pink shrimp from Oregon as "Eco-Best" on their website. They also state, "Most shrimp sold in the US is imported from countries in Latin America and Southeast Asia, where environmental regulations are often lax or not enforced."

## Southwest Tuna–Kale Salad

½–1 cup seeds from 1 pomegranate

2–4 oranges or tangerines

1 medium avocado, mashed

1–2 garlic cloves, run through garlic press

1 bunch green onion, minced with some green or ¼ cup red onion

Zest from 1 Key lime

3 tablespoons fresh Key lime juice

1 bunch red or green curly kale, 8–10 leaves

2–4 teaspoons extra-virgin olive oil

1 teaspoon sea salt

2 water-packed cans (6 ounces each) wild pole-caught albacore tuna, drained

1 teaspoon orange or tangerine zest

2 teaspoons or more minced serrano or jalapeño chile

¼ cup pine nuts

Sea salt

Freshly ground multi-color pepper

**Serves 4–6**

Calories per serving: 277
Total fat: 12g
Saturated fat: 2g
Calories from fat: 100
Protein: 22g
Carbohydrates: 25g
Dietary fiber: 7g
Sugars: 4g

*This is a deliciously appealing fall or winter salad with colorful dots of bright red pomegranate seeds against hues of fresh tender greens. Fragrant limes and oranges from our yard inject incomparable notes of flavor and freshness while creating a tangy-sweet flavor that is in perfect harmony with tuna.*

*This recipe uses a variation on the Southwest Kale Salad on page 131, using pomegranate seeds and orange pieces in place of the other recipe's tomatoes.*

▼ ▼ ▼

Prepare the pomegranate seeds. Cut the ends off the oranges or tangerines, and then cut off all of the rind, including the white pith by cutting in strips from top to bottom; cut the oranges or tangerines into ½–inch slices, then cut each slice in fourths, and remove the seeds. Set aside.

Combine the mashed avocado, garlic, onion, zest, and lime juice; set aside.

Rinse the kale with cold water, shake off the water, and pat dry with a cotton towel. Remove the tough stem/spine from the leaves, cut the leaves into approximately 1-inch strips, and place in a large bowl. Pour olive oil over the kale and sprinkle with salt. Massage the oil and salt into the kale until the leaves glisten. It will weep its juices, reduce in volume, and lose some toughness and bitterness.

With a dinner fork, mix the avocado dressing into the kale, making sure that all the kale is covered. Gently toss the orange pieces, pomegranate seeds, tuna, and orange zest into the salad. Sprinkle pine nuts over the salad. Season with a little salt and pepper, toss, and serve immediately.

### Tuna

Buy troll or pole-and-line caught albacore tuna, which is more sustainable due to less bycatch of endangered species such as sea turtle, sea birds, and dolphins. Look for the (MSC) sustainable label and go to their website to source a sustainable brand of tuna. Since larger tuna have more mercury, buy from a source that cans smaller tuna. VitalChoice.com buys tuna that weighs 12 pounds or less. Tuna is a good source of omega-3, and if not cooked prior to canning, it retains more of its omega-3. It is also on Dr. William Li's list of suggested anti-angiogenic foods to eat to prevent cancer.

## Simply Sablefish

4 pieces (4 ounces each) wild Alaskan sablefish

2 tablespoons fresh lemon juice

4 teaspoons extra-virgin olive oil

Pinch of sea salt

Freshly ground pepper

2 teaspoons coarsely cut fresh dill weed

Pinch of calendula flower petals for each serving (optional)

4 lime or lemon wedges

—————————————

**Serves 4**

Calories per serving: 251
Total fat: 21g
Saturated fat: 4g
Calories from fat: 186
Protein: 15g
Carbohydrates: 2g
Dietary fiber: 0g
Sugars: 0g

*If you or family members have an aversion to fish, try sablefish. It has a pearly white meat with a sweet mild flavor and melt-in-your-mouth smoothness—you would think butter had been injected into it. Maybe that's why it is also known as butterfish. Forget heavy sauces or drenching with butter to cover up a fishy taste, because it doesn't have one. Since sablefish, with its rich succulent flavor, can stand on its own, I always fix it in a very simple fashion—lemon, a little olive oil, salt, pepper, and sometimes a slight sprinkling of dried or fresh calendula petals and an herb or two for color, all freshly snipped from my garden. As an added perk, you should be in and out of the kitchen in 45 minutes, including the side dishes.*

*Serve with Steamed Baby Bok Choy (page 151) and Forbidden Black Rice (page 158). Baby bok choy's mild flavor is a tasty accompaniment, and black rice will round it out for an extremely healthy meal.*

▼ ▼ ▼

If you are using the recommended sides: Start cooking the pilaf, then the fish, and then the bok choy about 5 minutes before the fish is done.

Preheat oven to 350 degrees F.

Place fish skin-side down in a baking dish. Dress it with lemon juice and olive oil and a light sprinkling of salt and pepper. Bake for about 10–13 minutes (about 12 minutes per 1 inch of fish) About a minute before the fish is done, sprinkle with dill weed and calendula petals. Be careful not to overcook! Since it will continue to cook after removed from oven, it should be slightly undercooked in the middle—you want it moist and buttery. Serve immediately over steamed bok coy with a lime wedge on the side.

## Sablefish (Black Cod or Butterfish)

According to Seafood Watch, Alaskan and British Columbian sablefish are the most sustainable, with California, Oregon, and Washington fisheries being less sustainable. It is considered a safe fish to eat. Sablefish can live to a ripe old age and become quite large, which means they could contain more mercury than the smaller and younger fish. Therefore, seek out a source such as VitalChoice.com, where smaller sablefish are sold. With a high fat content, it boasts more omega-3 per serving than salmon.

## Herbed Mahi-mahi

2 tablespoons lime or lemon juice

4 mahi-mahi steaks (4 ounces each)

1 tablespoon extra-virgin olive oil

Pinch of sea salt

Freshly ground pepper

2 garlic cloves, run through garlic press

2 tablespoons minced fresh parsley or cilantro

1 tablespoon minced fresh rosemary leaves

2 teaspoons chopped fresh English or French tarragon leaves

2 teaspoons chopped fresh spicy or regular oregano

1 tablespoon chopped lemon thyme

1 tablespoon finely chopped chives

Pinch of calendula petals from garden for each piece of fish (optional)

3 thin strips of red bell pepper for each piece of fish

1/4 cup vermouth

**Serves 4**

Calories per serving: 208
Total fat: 4g
Saturated fat: 0g
Calories from fat: 30
Protein: 40g
Carbohydrates: 2g
Dietary fiber: 0g
Sugars: 0g

*Deeply colored fresh herbs accented with a few calendula petals dress up the fish, and add vibrantly fresh flavors alive with a concentration of powerful antioxidants. Herbs grow like weeds, and fresh-from-your-garden are much less expensive than paying more than a buck an ounce in the store. Some might think that I went overboard with the number of herbs used, but it's hard to resist mixing up a bunch when they are so available in our garden. By combining their antioxidant powers, they collectively become more effective. Serve with Chipotle Sweet Potato Fries (page 141) and Southwest Coleslaw (page 148).*

▼ ▼ ▼

Preheat oven to 350 degrees F.

Pour lime juice over the fish, spray with olive oil, and sprinkle lightly with salt and pepper. Thoroughly combine the garlic, herbs (parsley or cilantro through chives), and calendula petals. Press this mixture onto the top and sides of the fish. Place in a baking pan, topping each piece of fish with 3 strips of red bell pepper. Pour vermouth in pan—not on fish. Bake for about 13 minutes (about 13 minutes per 1 inch of thickness) or until done.

### Mahi-mahi

Due to less bycatch, the EDF suggests buying pole- and troll-caught mahi-mahi from the US south Atlantic, the only region that proactively manages this species. It is largely unregulated in other parts of the world. It contains some omega-3. Check with EDF for how much can be safely consumed each month.

## Curried Sardine Salad

2 pastured eggs, boiled

12 ounces salt-free, water-packed sardines, drained

2 tablespoons coarse or Dijon mustard

2 tablespoons Vegenaise® (mayonnaise substitute)

1–3 teaspoons curry powder

$\frac{1}{4}$ cup minced sweet yellow onion

1 cup finely chopped red bell pepper

1 serrano or jalapeño chile, minced

1 celery stalk, finely chopped

1 cup finely chopped sweet, crisp apple

$\frac{1}{2}$ avocado, sliced and diced

Splash of lemon or Key lime juice

4–8 slices toasted Ezekiel 4:9® cinnamon raisin bread

---

**Serves 4**

Calories per serving: 328
Total fat: 15g
Saturated fat: 1g
Calories from fat: 130g
Protein: 22g
Carbohydrates: 29g
Dietary fiber: 5g
Sugars: 11g

*Having trouble getting family members to eat sardines? Shh! Don't tell them sardines are in this salad, and I bet they'll love it! Fragrant cinnamon, raisins, and apples add sweet-spicy-woody flavors to the salad that take away from the sometimes fishiness of sardines.*

*Note: If serving on plain whole-grain bread or in a wrap (instead of the cinnamon raisin bread), add 1 teaspoon of ground cinnamon and $\frac{1}{3}$ cup of raisins or dried cranberries to the sardine salad.*

▼ ▼ ▼

Mash the eggs and sardines with mustard, Vegenaise®, and curry powder; then add all other ingredients, except for avocado and lemon or lime juice, and mix with a fork. Taste, and then adjust seasonings if needed. Pile the mixture onto 4 slices of bread, topping each one off with avocado and a splash of lemon. Serve as an open-face sandwich or close with another piece of bread.

### Sardines

Sardines are in abundant supply and considered sustainable with little bycatch. They have very low contaminant levels, provide an excellent source of omega-3, and are on Dr. William Li's list of suggested anti-angiogenic foods to eat to prevent cancer.

## Baked Shrimp, Chef Ryan Clark

64 jumbo shrimp (U-12)
Extra virgin olive oil spray
1/2 cup all-purpose flour
1/4 cup mesquite flour
4 cups Sleeping Frog Farms braising greens
1 teaspoon aged Balsamic vinegar

**Corn Asparagus Salsa**

8 ears of corn, whole
24 asparagus spears, thin
2 tablespoons minced red onion
1 tablespoon minced Jalapeno
2 tablespoons diced roasted red pepper
4 limes, zested and juiced
1 teaspoon cumin
2 tablespoons cilantro

**Lime-Avocado**

4 avocados, diced
4 limes, juiced
Salt and pepper

**Red Pepper Puree**

4 Willcox tomatoes, rough chopped
8 garlic cloves, roasted
1 onion, small diced
4 red pepper, roasted
1/2 tablespoon smoked paprika
1 cup vegetable stock
1 tablespoon extra virgin olive oil

Salt and pepper

---

**Serves 4**

Calories per serving: 340
Total fat: 6g
Saturated fat: 3g
Calories from fat: 30g
Protein: 5g
Carbohydrates: 32g
Dietary fiber: 12g
Sugars: 3g

*This shrimp recipe was generously shared by Chef Ryan Clark of Lodge on the Desert, Tucson, Arizona.*

▼ ▼ ▼

For shrimp and greens: Remove stems from braising greens and slightly chop. In 1 teaspoon of oil, add greens to a hot pan and sauté. As they begin to wilt, add 1 tablespoon of aged balsamic vinegar and season. This should yield 1 cup after they are cooked. Squeeze out any extra water and set aside.

Mix the all-purpose flour with the mesquite flour. Spray the shrimp with the extra virgin olive oil and season. Coat lightly in the flour mixture. Bake at 350 degrees F until firm.

For salsa: Grill corn and asparagus. Cut corn off cob and slice asparagus into 1-inch pieces. Mix all ingredients.

For avocado: Mix avocado and lime. Season.

For puree: Sauté onions until translucent in 1 tablespoon olive oil. Add tomatoes, garlic, and peppers. Sauté another 10 minutes until tomatoes start to break down. Add remaining ingredients and bring to a boil. Puree until smooth and season.

# BEEF, PORK, LAMB & POULTRY

**Moving to a plant-based diet** doesn't mean eliminating meat from your plate. There will just be less of it—shoot for a 3- or 4-ounce serving. All the following health-promoting recipes combine meat with some type of plant food and suggest pairing additional vegetables, grain, and fruit recipes to complement the meat dish. By doing so, I believe, meat is less missed. And since plant foods, especially beans, provide fiber (meat is void of fiber), you will feel more satisfied and reach satiety faster. It also helps to eat slowly and savor every bite.

By cutting down on meat consumption, those dollars spent on larger quantities of commercially raised meats can be spent on clean, locally raised, pastured or open-range beef, lamb, goat, pork, and poultry. You will definitely enjoy their flavors and reap the benefits of leaner meats. Also, commercially raised animals, fed on a high grain diet—the typical feedlot diet—contain significantly more omega-6 over omega-3, compared to their pastured cousins, and this imbalance is passed on to the diner. Ideally, the ratio of omega-3 to -6 should be close to equal; this ratio in the typical American diet tips far to the omega-6 side and causes inflammation, which can lead to diseases such as heart disease, Alzheimer's, cancer, and diabetes.

So follow the wisdom of the centenarians and elders of Okinawa and other Blue Zones, who thrive on age-old traditional diets that serve up an abundance of plant foods and eat a little locally raised meat. I hope the following recipes will get you started on moving to a deliciously healthy plant-based way of eating.

As you get cooking, keep in in mind the following tips. Since there is less fat in grass-fed beef than in grain-finished beef, grill it over a low to moderate temperature for a longer period of time and serve medium-rare. High heat (above 350 degrees F) frying, grilling, and broiling change the natural sugars and amino acids in meat, poultry, and fish into cancer-causing chemicals known as heterocyclic amines (HCAs). According to the Physicians for Responsible Medicine Cancer Project, a study showed that grilled chicken produced more than 10 times the HCAs than grilled beef. The good news: a number of research studies have shown that marinating these foods prior to cooking with high heat cut the HCAs substantially—from 50 percent to over 90 percent.

The Food Safety Consortium project at Kansas State University suggest that spices such as oregano, rosemary, basil, and thyme, high in antioxidants, have an effect on reducing HCAs. In other studies olive oil, lemon juice, and garlic marinade; ginger teriyaki sauce; and wine- or beer-based marinades also reduced the HCAs. All of these contain antioxidants. Yes, beer—its antioxidants come from malted barley. Using dark beers and microbrew will provide even more antioxidants. Unfortunately, tomato-based barbecue sauce may increase the production of HCAs, which could be related to the sugar and its thickness, which cause charring. Frequently turning the meat, also, cuts down on HCAs. Vegetables can be grilled without HCAs forming, but don't expose them to flare-ups caused from meat, poultry, or fish. ▶

*Basil-stuffed Chipotle-crusted Flank Steak (recipe on page 102).*

# Basil-stuffed Chipotle-crusted Flank Steak

Approximately 1 pound flank steak

2 tablespoons Key lime juice

1 tablespoon extra-virgin olive oil, divided

2 garlic cloves, minced, divided

3–4 teaspoons Chipotle–Lime Rub (page 51), divided

### Filling

1 cup finely torn basil leaves

¼ cup finely chopped fresh parsley

1 medium red bell pepper, roasted, finely chopped (see Fire-roasting, page 15)

1–2 garlic cloves, minced

⅓ cup finely chopped yellow onion

1 small Roma tomato, chopped

½ teaspoon oregano, toasted (if time permits) and crushed to release flavor

¼ cup crumbled feta cheese

¼ cup pine nuts

Sea salt

Freshly ground pepper

Butcher string

### Serves 4

Calories per serving: 347
Total fat: 22g
Saturated fat: 7g
Calories from fat: 193g
Protein: 28g
Carbohydrates: 10g
Dietary fiber: 3g
Sugars: 4g

*To enjoy meat but consume less of it, liven up a strip of flank steak by deliciously transforming it into pinwheels of swirling colorful herbs and vegetables. Continue coloring your plate by adding Tepary Bean Desert Sauté, a vibrantly hued cornucopia of sautéed vegetables and tepary beans. By enjoying a full range of colorful vegetables, you'll soak up a profusion of unique health-promoting compounds from plants that work synergistically to provide the best all-around health benefits. The vegetable pigments represent protective phytonutrients (powerful antioxidants) in the plant that our bodies need to replenish daily. A good measure of fiber from beans and vegetables is also provided.*

*If you don't want to make the Chipotle–Lime Rub, you can substitute a mix of the following: 1 teaspoon lime zest; 2 teaspoons oregano, toasted (if time permits) and crushed; 1 teaspoon whole cumin seed, toasted (if time permits) then ground (or use ground cumin); 1–2 teaspoons toasted and ground chipotle chile (after toasting, remove seeds for less heat); sea salt and freshly ground pepper.*

*Serve this steak with Tepary Bean Desert Sauté (page 165).*

▼ ▼ ▼

Butterfly the steak. The objective is to have a thinner piece of meat, ideally about ¼-inch thick. Cut with the grain of the meat. Begin cutting at the thicker end, through the middle of the meat, leaving about 1 inch intact at the other end to yield 1 long strip of meat. Then, open the meat and lay it flat. To tenderize, beat the meat with the bumpy side of a butcher's mallet, but be careful not to masticate the meat! Then, to make the steak of uniform thickness, beat the thicker parts with the smooth side of the mallet. If you don't have a mallet, use an empty wine or coke bottle or a heavy wooden spoon.

Sprinkle both sides of the steak with lime juice. Lay meat flat with cut-side facing up, and rub with 1 teaspoon of the olive oil, half of the minced garlic, and 1½–2 teaspoons of the Chipotle-Lime Rub (or the substitute seasonings mentioned in the headnote). Place a layer of each filling ingredient (basil through ground pepper), one by one, over the steak; then tightly roll the filled steak into a log, stretching the meat as you roll. Tie it with butcher sting at about every inch. Rub the outside of the log with the remaining olive oil, garlic, and Chipotle-Lime Rub (or substitute seasonings). For extra flavorful and a little tenderer meat, marinate in the refrigerator for a couple hours or up to 24 hours. It may also be grilled or broiled immediately. Put a pot of water on the grill for moisture; then place the meat on a medium-hot grill. Sear and turn the log until it's browned on all sides (if necessary spray with olive to keep moist) for 10 or 15 minutes.

Transfer the log to indirect heat, cover the grill, and roast for another 30 to 45 minutes, turn occasionally, or until an instant-read thermometer reaches 125–130 degrees F for medium rare and 135–140 for medium. Remove from the grill and allow to rest for about 10 minutes. It will continue to cook off the grill. It may also be prepared in the oven by broiling all sides about 4 inches from broiler until browned; then baked in a 350 degree F oven for about 20 minutes or until above noted temperatures are reached. Slice against the grain into 1-inch pieces and serve with Tepary Bean Desert Sauté (page 165).

## Extraordinary Southwest Burger

4 Ezekiel sprouted whole-grain hamburger buns, whole or half

1 pound ground beef

2 red bell peppers

2 poblano or green chiles

1 large onion, sliced ½ inch thick

4 scant ½-inch slices of eggplant

½–1 avocado (mashed)

Key lime wedges

Fresh Salsa, (page 44), optional

———————————

**Serves 4**

Calories per serving: 306
Total fat: 17g
Saturated fat: 6g
Calories from fat: 153
Protein: 25g
Carbohydrates: 16g
Dietary fiber: 4g
Sugars: 6g

*As an alternative to the fast-food burger, prepare hamburgers and some vegetables at home, then sit down and enjoy a burger and a serving of Chipotle Sweet Potato Fries (page 141) and Southwest Coleslaw (page 148). Since all these vegetables are seasonally available in Southern Arizona during early fall, their combinations make for the perfect culinary grouping full of alluring color (and full of antioxidant power!) and incredible freshness. Have the coleslaw made, and pop the sweet potato fries in the oven just before grilling the vegetables.*

*Note: Since the meat is ground, tenderness is not of concern; but to keep it from becoming dry, try Greg Vinson's method for free-range burgers: place the patty on a grill over low heat, a griddle set at 200 degrees F, or in an iron skillet over low heat, and cook until done to your liking.*

▼ ▼ ▼

Form the ground beef into 4 patties, ½-inch thick; sparingly sprinkle with salt and some pepper, and set aside. Grill the bell peppers, poblanos or green chiles, onion, and eggplant (see Grilling, page 15). Remove the skins and seeds from the peppers and chiles, then cut them in half (do not run under water, as the oils will be lost); transfer to a platter and set aside. Preheat grill to medium temperature and cook the ground beef patties until medium or medium-rare; then transfer to the vegetable platter. Smear mashed avocado or guacamole on the buns, splash with lime; then stack the patties and grilled vegetables on top, or let the diners create their own. Pass the salsa!

**Variation: Vegan Burger** Substitute one portabella mushroom cap for the meat. Spray cap with olive oil and grill or broil until tender.

# Jojoba Beef Company: Tips on Cooking Brush-fed or Open-range Beef

At a few farmers' markets in Tucson you'll find Gregg Vinson cooking beef from his Jojoba Beef Company ranch and spinning yarns that amiably wrangle in passersby to have a taste. While he educates his audience on the art of cooking moist, tender, and incredibly flavorful free-range beef, you'll hear unsolicited testimonials from satisfied customers.

Once I asked if he tested the meat for doneness with a thermometer. Oh boy! His blue eyes peered from beneath the brim of his cowboy hat with an unspoken expression of "What?" and commented, "There is no science to it, cowboys don't use thermometers, you just know when it's done and tastes right for you." At the markets, he grills the meat in a smoker on low temperature and prepares juicy hamburger and brats on a griddle set at about 200 degrees F. If you are not using a smoker, he recommends setting the oven at 200 degrees F, place your steak in a dry cast-iron skillet, and put it in the oven. Also put a pan with an inch or so of water in the oven for moisture, and roast the steak for 20 minutes. If you want it more done, cook it longer; however, never overcook it, or some flavor will be lost. Also, based on another recommendation from Greg, we have grilled brush-fed beef over low heat on a gas grill. Free-range meat will appear rare due to its color and the composition of the meat. He stresses the importance of allowing cooked meat to rest for five or ten minutes, depending on its thickness. Consequently, juices are evenly distributed throughout the meat and don't gush out of the center onto your plate, rather than being savored in your mouth. He also recommends cutting his steaks into very thin slices. Greg's low heat style of cooking beef does not form the cancer-causing chemicals heterocyclic amines (HCAs; see page 101 for more on this).

Comparing his brush-fed cattle to grain-fed, he explained that grain-fed's flavor is more about the fat in the meat, stating, "The first couple bites are full of fat flavor; but the meat itself tastes like cardboard." He believes open-range or brush-fed beef has "a ton of flavor without excessive marbling and that each bite gives you full, juicy flavor." It has a fat and meat flavor profile, rather than a mostly fat flavor profile. So, as you continue to chew the meat, the flavor just keeps coming.

His cattle are born and graze on the range for a number of years before harvesting. Throughout their lives they forage on more than 60 different types of nutrient-dense native plants (he attributes the meat's juiciness to jojoba) from land free of chemical fertilizers and pesticides. They are not finished on grass nor given supplements or hormones, making their total diet from the "brush," as Gregg calls it. Being a conscientious steward of the land, Gregg received the Arizona Game and Fish Commission's Wildlife Habitat Steward Award.

## Beef Fajitas

1 pound open-range or grass-fed skirt, chuck, or round steak

### Fajita Marinade

1/4 cup lime juice

1 teaspoon lime zest

1 tablespoon soy sauce

1 small chipotle chile, toasted and crushed, stem and seeds removed

2 tablespoons extra-virgin olive oil

3 medium garlic cloves, cut in thirds

1/4 cup finely chopped sweet yellow onion

1 teaspoon cumin seeds, toasted and ground

2 teaspoons Mexican oregano, toasted and crushed

1 tablespoon evaporated cane juice

1 tablespoon unsweetened cocoa

1 teaspoon sea salt

3–4 grinds of peppercorns

3 whole cloves

### Vegetables

1 large red bell pepper

1 large green bell pepper or poblano chile

1 large or 2 medium sweet yellow onions, sliced 1/2-inch thick

1 zucchini squash, cut into strips

1 yellow crookneck squash, cut into strips

### For Serving

Corn tortillas

1/2 avocado, sliced and chopped

2 Key limes quartered

Fresh Salsa (page 44)

---

### Serves 5

Calories per serving: 414
Total fat: 20g
Saturated fat: 6g
Calories from fat: 175
Protein: 30g
Carbohydrates: 33g
Dietary fiber: 7g
Sugars: 14g

*Yesteryear, vaqueros (Mexican cowboys) drove cattle across the range and prepared arracheras (fajitas) from the tough skirt steak. They marinated the tough, flavorful skirt steak, cooked it in an iron skillet, cut it into strips, stuffed them in tortillas, and ate with a side of beans. This humble meal became popular in Texas and spread far and wide, increasing in demand and escalating in price. As Arizona rancher Dennis Moroney puts it, "You only get two skirt steaks per cow, which isn't enough to meet today's demand. So for great value, take the lowly round or chuck steak and make something great out of it."*

*Note: This recipe will make enough marinade for up to 2 pounds of skirt, round, or chuck steak. You might want to marinate the meat several hours or even a day ahead of starting the rest of this recipe.*

*Serve with warm corn tortillas, beans (see page 156), and lettuce topped with thin slices of radishes and onions.*

▼ ▼ ▼

Trim any fat and membrane from the steak while leaving any tiny ribbons of fat within it, which will melt away during cooking. To tenderize, evenly pound the meat to 1/4-inch thickness.

Place all the marinade ingredients, except the cloves, in a blender and process until fairly smooth. Pour into a non-reactive container and add the cloves. Place the skirt steak in the marinade making sure that both sides are coated with the sauce. Marinate 8–24 hours, then remove the meat from the marinade.

Grill the meat and the vegetables (page 15). Peel and slice the grilled red bell pepper and the green bell pepper or poblano chile. For tender and incredibly juicy fajitas, grill the meat over low heat for 3–5 minutes on each side or until medium-rare (free-range and grass-fed meats cook faster). Remove from the fire and allow the meat to rest for 5 minutes before cutting diagonally against the grain into thin pieces. Mix the fajitas with the vegetables and serve. Pass the tortillas, salsa, avocados, and lime wedges.

# Dennis and Deb Moroney's 47 Ranch

Spinning windmill blades and solar panels are reducing the carbon footprint of energy required to operate Dennis and Deb Moroney's 33,000-acre 47 Ranch, situated in the Mule Mountains and Sulphur Springs Valley in southeastern Arizona. It has been a cattle ranch for over 100 years, and like much rangeland in the Southwest, suffered from human mismanagement. When the Moroneys purchased the ranch in 2002, their passionate beliefs about preserving working landscapes of the West for food production, wildlife habitat, watershed, and open spaces led Dennis to put together a long-term sustainable plan for restoring healthy rangeland, which will elevate the ecosystem health.

Dennis and Deb don't depend solely on commodity cattle, but have diversified livestock that are holistically managed through planned rotational grazing using multiple paddocks. They have a mix of crossbreed cattle, heritage Criollo cattle, and Boer Goats that roam and forage on native rangeland. Some cattle and goats are finished on pesticide-free grass, and heritage Navajo-Churro sheep are raised on irrigated, pesticide-free pasture. All this wipes out the necessity for transported feeds, which increase costs and cause a larger carbon footprint. Their livestock are never fed grains or administered hormones or prophylactic antibiotics. Dennis proudly told me, "They are here from conception to consumption; everything we sell we have raised, every step of the way."

Dennis has not only verbalized his belief, saying that, "Genetics is our link to a more sustainable past." But he and Deb have put that belief into action by bringing "placed-based" Navajo-Churro lamb and Criollo meats back to the tables of the Southwest (he says the best way to save these animals is by eating them.) Consumers may initially try a heritage meat because of its novelty or to support sustainability, but if it doesn't taste good, they won't buy it again. Both of the Navajo-Churro lamb and Criollo meats that we bought from Dennis were full of flavor, lean, moist, and tender. The lamb had a distinctive sweet mild flavor. It's no doubt people can get hooked on these wonderful flavors that took centuries to develop, which will in turn fuel demand for other heritage meats and cause a culinary movement, bringing about even more demand for them.

Dennis also states that it is "better to consider cuts that are more common and affordable if sustainability is a goal.

Many people follow their consumerist training and assume that the rare and expensive cuts are also the best. Not true in my experience. There is a movement among producers of grassfed products and 'slow foods' chefs to promote gourmet consumption of the entire animal, 'from nose to tail.' I strongly support that concept."

When there is a demand for rare breeds and raising them is profitable, ranchers like the Moroneys will continue to produce them. This will ensure the survival of these ancient breeds that were brought to northern Mexico and what is now the American Southwest from Spain over four centuries ago. Unlike commercial breeds that couldn't survive in an open environment, these have the genetic ability to adapt to adverse climate changes, and they provide species variety and biodiversity to ranching and farming, all of which are crucial for the future of agriculture.

For almost 40 years, Dennis and Deb have been raising livestock and have often felt the pangs of small food providers. When uncontrollable forces came together in 1996—severe drought, a large number of hungry mountain lions, and no profit in the commercial meat market, Dennis said, "We were desperate to make ends meet." Being creative and resourceful, he took a bunch of his yearlings, ran them on irrigated pasture, processed them through a mom-and-pop butcher shop in Chino, and put an ad in the Dandy Dime. It was the beginning of the Moroneys selling grass-finished meat to a niche market of health-conscious consumers who did not want excess levels of hormones and antibiotic residues in their food. Today, Dennis pulls a solar-powered trailer holding a portable meat market twice a week to Bisbee and Sierra Vista farmers' markets to direct-market his Sky Island brand meats to local consumers. He also by-passes middlemen by selling to local food co-ops.

Dennis admits that from raising the livestock to getting the animals processed and trucking meat to local farmers' markets, it takes considerably more work than just loading a semi full of calves to be sent off to feedlots. However, Dennis looks at it as linking his and Deb's stewardship with the products they sell, and they see their relationship with their customers as a partnership involving food and care of the land.

## Navajo-Churro Lamb or Goat Kabobs

**Marinade**

6 garlic cloves, crushed and chopped

½ small onion, finely chopped

1 teaspoon sea salt

4–5 grinds of pepper

1 teaspoon cumin seed, toasted and ground

1 teaspoon each, oregano and marjoram leaves, toasted together and crushed

¼ cup lemon juice

1 chipotle, toasted, seeded, and crushed

1½ pound leg of Navajo–Churro lamb, cut into 1-inch cubes for kabobs

**Vegetables for Skewers**

2 fennel bulbs, vertically cut in half, core removed, and sliced in 1-inch-wide strips

1 medium red onion, peeled and cut in quarters

1 zucchini squash (6 inches long), cut in half lengthwise and then in 1-inch slices

1 yellow squash (6 inches long), cut in half lengthwise and then in 1-inch slices

1 red bell pepper, roughly cut in 1-inch pieces

24 cherry tomatoes

8–12 rosemary stems (10 inches long), or metal or bamboo (soaked in water) skewers

---

### Serves 4–6

Calories per serving: 386
Total fat: 24g
Saturated fat: 11g
Calories from fat: 213
Protein: 27g
Carbohydrates: 17g
Dietary fiber: 4g
Sugars: 9g

*The first time I tasted churro lamb was at Native Seeds/SEARCH's Harvest Dinner at Janos restaurant in Tucson. The meat was lean, but moist and tender, with a distinctive, sweet, and very satisfying flavor. With such great flavor, and since it is a heritage breed, with a history in the Southwest, it needed to be a part of this cookbook. So in the spring I made the trip to the Sierra Vista Farmers' Market to meet Dennis Moroney, one of a few local ranchers who raise Navajo–Churro lamb.*

*Note: if you cut the meat off the bone yourself, save the bones for soup or freeze to make broth at a later time.*

*Serve this dish over Heirloom Vegetable Brown Rice Pilaf (page 157) and add a tossed salad.*

▼ ▼ ▼

Combine the marinade ingredients and marinate the lamb in a non-reactive, covered container for 4–24 hours in the refrigerator. If you are using rosemary stems for the skewers, remove the needles except at the tip of each stem. Remove the lamb from the marinade, drain, and thread onto the skewers, alternating lamb with vegetables. Grill over high heat for about 10 minutes. Allow to rest for about 5 minutes before serving.

*Gordon, Deb, Dennis, and Allie Moroney, with their dog Lizard at 47 Ranch.*

## Grilled Lamb Rack, Chef Ryan Clark

**Lamb Rack**

8 chops lamb, frenched, fat cap removed

Salt and pepper

**Tzatziki Sauce**

⅔ cup nonfat yogurt

1 tablespoon mint, chopped

1 tablespoon Meyer lemon juice

Salt and pepper

**Quinoa**

1 cup quinoa

16 Campari or cherry tomatoes, halved

4 Meyer lemons, juice and zest

½ cup cucumber, sliced in half moons

½ cup parsley, chopped

2–3 drops lemon oil

2 ½ cups vegetable stock

½ teaspoon salt

¼ teaspoon pepper

**Glazed Carrots**

48 baby carrots and tops

2 tablespoons honey

Salt and pepper

**Serves 4**

Calories per serving: 430
Total fat: 6g
Saturated fat: 1g
Calories from fat: 48
Protein: 29g
Carbohydrates: 54g
Dietary fiber: 8g
Sugars: 17g

*This tasty lamb recipe was generously shared by Chef Ryan Clark of Lodge on the Desert, Tucson, Arizona.*

*Note: A rack of 8 chops from pastured lamb may weigh between 1.2 and 2 pounds, of which only 40–50 percent is meat, rendering a 3 or 4 ounce serving per person. Grain-fed lamb raised in confinement renders a much larger rack. Chef Ryan prepared lamb chops from the Moroney family's pastured Navajo–Churro Lamb. He trimmed the outer layer of fat from a rack of 8 chops and then frenched the chops. (Frenching is scraping the meat and fat from the ends of the rib bones to achieve naked bones.) New Zealand lamb is sought by many lamb aficionados and also, it travels thousands of miles to market in the US. However, many of these aficionados rave about the tender, succulent, sweet flavor of Dennis Moroney's lamb. They suggest that it is well worth your time to seek out pastured lamb in your area and forgo the New Zealand type.*

▼ ▼ ▼

For the lamb: Lightly spray with canola oil and season with salt and pepper. Place on a hot grill and mark on each side for 5 minutes. Finish in the oven about 5 minutes until cooked to medium. Use a probe to reach 135 degrees F internal temperature. Let rest.

For the sauce: Zest Meyer lemon and reserve 1 tablespoon juice. Mix yogurt with mint and lemon zest. Add lemon juice to desired tartness. Season with salt and pepper.

For the quinoa: Bring water to a boil. Add quinoa and simmer for about 12-15 minutes until all water is absorbed. Spread out on a baking sheet to cool. Add all ingredients to cooled quinoa. Warm slightly just before serving.

For the carrots: Blanch carrots until just cooked.

To serve: Heat in a small amount of water and strain. Toss with honey and season.

# Pork Stir-fry with Soba Noodles

8 ounces 100% buckwheat soba noodles

1–1½ cups mushroom or vegetable broth, divided

2 tablespoons cornstarch

1 tablespoon extra-virgin olive oil

⅓ pound pork, trimmed of fat and finely chopped

3 cups (5–7 ounces) sliced fresh shitake mushrooms (without stems)

2 tablespoons mirin (Japanese sweet rice cooking wine)

1 red bell pepper or 3 Jimmy Nardello peppers, seeded and sliced (if in season)

1 medium carrot, thinly sliced

1 sweet yellow onion, chopped

6 garlic cloves, minced or run through garlic press

1-inch piece of fresh ginger, finely minced

1 bunch bok choy, chopped (keep stalk separate from leaves)

2 tablespoons low-sodium tamari sauce (naturally brewed soy sauce)

---

**Serves 4**

Calories per serving: 367
Total fat: 7g
Saturated fat: 1g
Calories from fat: 60
Protein: 19g
Carbohydrates: 59g
Dietary fiber: 7g
Sugars: 9g

*Since ancient times, bok choy has been cultivated in China and is one of the cancer-preventing foods recommended by Dr. Li of the Angiogenesis Foundation. It holds up nicely in a stir-fry and has an enjoyable fresh flavor with a hint of sweetness.*

*Note: Most soba buckwheat noodles provided by US grocers are made with wheat and buckwheat flours. Health-oriented grocers and Asian markets carry soba noodles made with 100-percent buckwheat flour, which makes the noodles dense, hearty, and flavorful. It has almost twice as much protein as rice, is a good source of B vitamins, and is high in the antioxidant rutin, which is believed to be good for the cardiovascular system and may help prevent cancer. 100-percent buckwheat takes about 8 minutes to cook, whereas the more refined wheat/buckwheat noodles take about 4 minutes.*

▼ ▼ ▼

Start water to cook the noodles; don't salt. If using 100 percent buckwheat, add the noodles to the boiling water when the pork is browning. If using refined soba, start cooking when the bok choy is put into the stir-fry. When the water returns to a boil, set on low and simmer for the specified time. If water starts boiling again, add 1 cup of water. When the noodles are done—not mushy and not al dente, but in between—drain and thoroughly rinse until the water runs clear, to remove starch from the noodles.

Using a couple tablespoons each of broth and cornstarch, make a thin paste; then thoroughly mix in an additional ¼ cup of broth; set aside. Over medium-high heat, heat oil in a wok or large skillet and sauté pork and mushrooms until pork is somewhat browned, add mirin and additional broth as needed. Then, stir in peppers, carrots, onions, garlic, ginger, and chopped boy choy stalks. When onions are crispy-tender, toss in the bok choy leaves and cook until the leaves are limp. Mix the paste with the remaining broth and stir into the stir-fry to thicken the sauce. Add soy sauce, taste, and adjust seasonings and thickness. Toss the stir-fry mixture with the noodles, or serve it over the noodles.

## Traditional Rural Chinese Food

Researchers of the China Study concluded that the traditional diet of people in rural China is the main factor responsible for their significantly low rates of heart disease, diabetes, certain cancers, osteoporosis, and obesity. The diet consists mostly of plant-based foods (rice, vegetables, soy) with 9–10 percent of total calories coming from protein, of which only 9 percent is from animal sources.

My son's wife Kim is our family's link to traditional Chinese food. Her grandparents, Buck and Mabel Dong, and father Ben's roots are in rural China. Shortly after Communist rule, Buck snuck out and emigrated to the US, where he proudly wore an American GI uniform during the Korean War. Twelve years later, Mabel was smuggled to the British Colony of Hong Kong; Ben joined her legally a year later; and then they traveled to the US to reunite with Buck.

Desiring to hold on to their Chinese food culture but with little or no availability of fresh, locally grown Chinese vegetables, Buck and Mabel covered their Tucson backyard with verdant rows, patches, and trellises of a variety of organically grown Chinese vegetables. And to assure the same hearty, flavorful vegetables season after season, they carefully save seeds and trade seeds with like gardeners. Their cornucopia of healthy vegetables doesn't come without effort. Now in their mid-eighties, they still till the soil, dig, shovel, spread manure, and squat to pull weeds, all of which helps to keep them fit. As a warm-up to working in the garden, they take a four-mile walk each morning with a group of friends.

I have seen them unselfishly and with expressions of sheer delight share their plentiful harvest with family and friends. Our family has received Chinese broccoli, long beans, bok choy, colorful Chinese spinach, and other vegetables from their garden, with instructions on preparation and comments on their medicinal values. Also, they gave me bitter melon seeds and Chinese eggplant plants for my garden. Buck and Mable set the perfect example of how backyard gardening can provide a variety of health promoting organic fruits and vegetables that otherwise may not be affordable for many people.

Mabel turns the harvest into soups, steamed dishes, or stir fries with a little bit of oil and small bits of meat for flavor, similar to how she prepared foods in China 50-some years ago. In China, they also ate a lot of tofu (they still eat some) and soybean sprouts, which were used in egg foo yung. However, Ben said they ate very few eggs in China and still don't eat many here. They consume no dairy because they are lactose intolerant, as are so many Cantonese. Both Buck and Mabel like meat and do indulge in it on special occasions, but don't eat much on a daily basis. Lots of fresh, vibrantly colored vegetables, white rice, and noodles are the prominent foods on their table.

Ben recalls, "In China red meat was not plentiful. It was a treat to have beef at a meal. Cows were used to plow the field. So, you didn't eat the cow." He explained that once a week, if you were lucky, a small amount of pork, free-range geese, chicken, or duck, or fish from the ponds or rice paddies was eaten. Ben translated for his dad, who said, "We ate mostly vegetables and lots of them. We ate what was available. Rice and sweet potatoes were eaten often because they were plentiful and easy to grow."

## Julio's Blue Corn Pozole Pork Soup or Stew

2 rounded tablespoons oregano

1 tablespoon marjoram

1 tablespoon thyme

2 teaspoons whole cumin

2 teaspoons coriander seeds

Pig's snout, ears, tongue, feet, and tail (or 2 pound pork roast or 4 pounds meaty neck bones)

Stewing hen, cut in pieces

1 large sweet yellow onion, cut in quarters

1 head garlic, toes crushed with flat side of wide knife blade and peeled

3 bay leaves, broken

1 teaspoon sea salt

Freshly ground pepper

Water for broth

1 whole chipotle chile, toasted

3 ancho chiles, stems and seeds removed, then toasted

3 guajillo chiles, stems and seeds removed, then toasted

3 cups water

1 cup sweet vermouth

**Garnish**

2–3 tablespoons toasted and crushed Mexican oregano

½ cup finely chopped sweet yellow or green onions

3–4 cups finely chopped cabbage

1–2 cups thinly sliced radishes

1 cup finely chopped cilantro

3 limes, quartered

___

**Serves 12–16**

Calories per serving: 297
Total fat: 17g
Saturated fat: 6g
Calories from fat: 156
Protein: 24g
Carbohydrates: 6g
Dietary fiber: 1g
Sugars: 3g

*Traditional pozole is made from the pig's head or parts of its head and often included chicken. Since most people are more than likely not going to have a 20- or 30-gallon pot, which is needed to cook the entire head and a whole chicken, we have used Chef Julio Hidalgo's scaled-down version. He says it's the fat from the head that gives the broth an incredibly rich, deep flavor, and the taste of oregano is essential. In addition to the pork, he added a stewing hen (a tough, old retired laying hen). Old hens are tough but hold an immense amount of flavor—much more than the younger meat chickens—but need to stew longer to develop a bold flavor and become tender. Pozole is traditional for festive dinners where many are served. It's also great to eat a little and reserve the rest by freezing in dinner-size portions for busy days. The broth should be made the day before or early, early in the morning so the hard layer of fat can be lifted off the top of the broth before cooking the corn in it.*

*Note: An alternative to pig's head parts, feet, and tail is noted in parentheses.*

▼ ▼ ▼

Toast together the oregano, marjoram, and thyme (see page 17), then crush to release the flavors; set aside. Next, toast together the cumin and coriander seeds, then grind them; set aside. In a 12-quart stockpot, place the pork pieces and stewing hen pieces, along with the onion, garlic, the crushed and ground herbs and seeds, bay leaves, salt, and pepper. Fill the pot with water to within 6 inches of the rim, bring to a rolling boil, and then turn to low and bring to a simmer and cover. Immediately start boiling 3 cups of water in small pot, add the chipotle, ancho, and guajillo chiles, reduce heat to low, and simmer covered for 1 hour. Cool, pull out the chipotle and remove its stem and seeds. Place it, the other chiles, and the chile broth in a blender jar. Blend until completely pureed, adding additional water as needed. Then, add this mixture to the stockpot, cover, and continue cooking for 2–3 hours or until chicken and pork are falling off the bones. About 30 minutes before meat is ready, add the vermouth. Remove from heat and allow to cool; then remove the meat—bones and all. Strain the broth through a fine sieve into a large container and refrigerate for the fat to harden at the top. Pick the meat off the bones and discard bones and fat; but leave a little cartilage—and don't throw away the skin. Not all people like tongue, cartilage, or skin; but at least there will be some for those who do. Chop each and put them in separate containers. Chop the chicken and pork meat. Refrigerate everything.

The next day, remove the fat from the top of the broth. In a large pot, add the nixtamal corn to the broth, making sure that there is enough broth for a soup consistency. If not, add water. The broth is strong enough to sustain its rich flavor. Bring to a boil and then reduce heat, cover, and simmer for about 3 hours or until the corn pops open. Place each garnish in individual condiment bowls. Serve the pozole in bowls, alongside the garnish, meats, cartilage, and skin, allowing people to choose what they like to eat in their pozole.

**Variation: Pozole Stew**   After the pozole has popped open, add 2 cups chopped fresh or fire-roasted canned tomatoes, and continue cooking, uncovered, until the pozole is reduced to a stew, stirring occasionally.

**Variation: Three Sisters' Pozole**   Following the farming and nutritional wisdom of the Aztecs and Native Americans, add 1 cup dry tepary beans (picked over and washed) when you start the soup or stew and add bite-size pieces of winter squash about 30 minutes before soup is done. Additional water may be needed during cooking. During the summer, add sliced zucchini to bowls and cover with soup. Such indigenous cultures planted the trio together in clusters where each nurtured the other. The beans provided nitrogen and climbed the corn stalks while the squash curbed weeds and provided moisture retention in the soil. This food triad also created nutritionally complementary meals. Due to the full protein achieved by combining corn with beans, meat can be eliminated for a healthy delicious vegan pozole.

## Nixtamal Corn

Blue nixtamal corn (field corn treated with lime) from a small farm in New Mexico, available at Native Seeds/ SEARCH in Tucson (sold as "posole"), is used in the following pozole recipes. "Nixtamalizing" mature, dry, field corn in lime (calcium hydroxide aka pickling lime) water releases the nutritional powerhouse locked within the hard kernels—niacin, other B vitamins, and essential amino acids—into a form more easily absorbed by the human body. Calcium hydroxide also makes calcium available and balances phosphorus in the corn. Nixtamal corn is a staple, which has sustained the Aztecs, other people of Latin America, and Native Americans for centuries. It gives the masa in tamales and tortillas a wonderful flavor and high quality nutrition. Canned hominy, available in most grocery stores, can be substituted for the blue or golden dry pozole (dried hominy); but the flavor of the hominy will not be as robust.

## "Nose to Tail" Philosophy

Our friend, Chef Julio Hidalgo from Veracruz, Mexico, shared a traditional pozole recipe, which follows the "nose to tail" eating philosophy of whole-animal consumption, leaving little animal to waste. By doing so, it lowers the impact of animal production on the environment by feeding more people from each animal at a lower price per pound. It is a centuries-old sustainable way of eating that has been practiced throughout the world and is still practiced in some cultures. Until the early 1900s many people in the United States lived on farms, raised their own meat animals, and customarily ate almost the entire animal. In the 50s and 60s, I remember eating tongue, brains, pig feet, blood sausage, head cheese, and chicken feet. Cows' and hogs' intestines were used for sausage casings, and pig fat was rendered into lard for baking and cooking. Today, over 50 percent of the animal is wasted. So if you buy a butchered whole hog from a local farmer, make sure you get the head or at least the tongue, cheeks, ears, snout, tail, and feet to make Julio's pozole.

## Stuffed Bitter Melon

1/3 pound pork loin or other cuts, cut into small pieces

1–2 teaspoons chipotle chile in adobo sauce, canned or recipe on page 50 (mince chipotle and include some sauce)

8 large shitake mushrooms, roughly cut in thirds (remove stems)

3/4 cup minced cilantro

1/2 medium sweet yellow onion

2 garlic cloves

1 tablespoon freshly grated ginger

1 tablespoon San-J wheat-free tamari sauce or oyster sauce

1–2 tablespoons extra-virgin olive oil

3–4 bitter melons (7 inches long), sliced into 1-inch-thick circles, pulp and seeds removed

1–2 cups mushroom broth or chicken broth

2 tablespoons powdered arrowroot or cornstarch

1 teaspoon sesame oil

### Serves 4

Calories per serving:243
Total fat: 8g
Saturated fat: 1g
Calories from fat: 77
Protein: 16g
Carbohydrates: 26g
Dietary fiber: 6g
Sugars: 2g

*Herbaceous bitter melon, part of the Asian food culture, is high in phytochemicals, protectors against disease, and is believed to lower blood sugar, while providing a good source of calcium and potassium, among other vitamins and nutrients. As a word of caution, in all the literature I've read, pregnant women are advised not to eat bitter melon.*

*Since our son Alex enjoys bitter melon and because of its healthy billing, I had to try it—but I was forewarned that its intense bitterness is an acquired taste. I enlisted the experts, the Dong family. Buck and Mabel brought the melons and some vegetables from their garden, and Mary, Ben's wife, taught me how to prepare this dish. I snuck in a little chipotle for smoky heat. We served it with steamed fish, which Ben prepared, brown rice, and a salad. It was a wonderful family evening filled with laughter and great tasting food— not too bitter!*

▼ ▼ ▼

In a food processor work bowl, mince the pork with the chipotle; transfer to a medium bowl. Mince the mushrooms, cilantro, onion, and garlic in the food processor work bowl, and then transfer to these chopped foods to the bowl with the pork. Thoroughly mix in the ginger and soy or oyster sauce. Pack tightly and slightly overstuff the melon circles with this mixture.

In a large heavy skillet, heat the oil over medium-high heat; brown the stuffed melon slices on each side. Remove the skillet from heat, transfer the stuffed slices to a steamer, retaining the juices in the skillet. Additional juices will be released during steaming, which will be used for the sauce. Steam until the pork is done and the melon is soft and light in color, about 20 minutes. Remove steamer from wok or pot. Bring the water/broth mixture to a boil and reduce its volume to about 1/2 cup.

Mix arrowroot or cornstarch with a little water to make a thin paste and set aside. Set the skillet containing the browning juices over medium-high heat and deglaze the bottom of the skillet by adding 1 cup of mushroom broth and the broth from the steamer. Reduce heat; then add the paste to the broth in the skillet, and simmer; stirring until a thin gravy is achieved, adding broth and additional paste as needed. Remove from heat, add sesame oil, taste, and adjust seasonings. Transfer the stuffed bitter melon to a platter and drizzle with the sauce.

*Stuffed Bitter Melon shown with Pork Stir-fry with Soba Noodles (recipe on page 110).*

## Okinawa Centenarian Study

Some of you may remember the hilarious 1980s Wendy's commercials starring three silver-haired ladies asking, "Where's the beef?" It's still asked by many Americans, who as a nation eat almost four times more meat (not including seafood) than developing nations, according to Environmental Working Group. Maybe the question should be, "Where's the vegetables?"

Dr. Bradley Willcox, co-principal investigator of the ongoing Okinawa Centenarian Study, may have the answer. In interviews with Allan Greg on YouTube, he describes elderly people of Okinawa in their 90s and 100s living illness-free and disability-free lives up until the end. He suggests that part of their good health is related to their low calorie, plant-based traditional diet. It's made up of a variety of home-grown or local vegetables and fruits covering a wide spectrum of colors, whole grains such as brown rice, soy (usually in the form of tofu), and complemented with fish or pork raised in the villages, which translates into a diet rich in antioxidant power and healthy omega-3 fat, but low in total fat, salt, and sugar.

Elderly Okinawans eat 2–3 pounds of food a day, as do Americans, but with half the calories. However, a third of the average American diet is junk food, and it is light on fruits and vegetables but heavy on processed foods, meats, and dairy. When Americans eat more calories than needed, their free radical production is increased; but the diet lacks needed antioxidants to stamp out the free radicals produced. On the other hand, by restricting caloric intake, Okinawans limit how much food their bodies have to process and convert to energy. Consequently, fewer calories decreases the amount of free radicals in their bloodstream, which promotes healthy aging void of dementia and other debilitating diseases that often accompany advancing age.

Too many calories cause weight gain, which is evident in American society—where the average American gains one to two pounds a year throughout most of adulthood. Due to a low-calorie diet, the Okinawa centenarians didn't gain weight with age. Willcox explains that body fat is an endocrine organ that generates hormones and can cause inflammation, which increases cancer risk. He said the elderly Okinawans also have lifelong lower blood sugar levels, adding that high blood sugar tends to make cells age more quickly and become "stickier" and less functional. These things—free radicals, inflammation, and high blood sugar levels—seem to work in concert in damaging cells or DNA, and in turn cause disease.

Aside from the study, in his article "History and Characteristics of Okinawan Longevity Food," appearing in the *Asia Pacific Journal of Clinical Nutrition* (2001), Hiroko Sho describes the Okinawa food culture as being built around the concept of food as medicine. It is *nuchi gusui*, or "medicine for life." In his interviews with centenarians, he said, "They always prepare their favorite meals and without fail explain its healthy properties." Their longevity food is part of their everyday diet and is based on combinations of foods that are found close at hand.

## Indian Chicken Curry Sauté with Southwest Nopalitos

1 tablespoon extra-virgin olive oil

1 pound chicken meat, skinned and cut in bite-size pieces

1 sweet onion, medium chopped

5 garlic cloves, run through garlic press

1–2 nopalitos, stickers removed, cleaned, and sliced in strips the size of green beans (page 164)

10 fresh sage leaves cut in 1/4-inch chiffonade

1–2 cups vegetable or chicken broth

1 inch of ginger root, peeled and minced

2 tablespoons hot Madras curry powder

2 carrots, sliced into rings

1/2–1 chipotle chile in adobo sauce, minced (canned or recipe on page 50)

1–2 teaspoons adobo sauce or 1 teaspoon ground chipotle

1 tablespoon arrowroot powder or cornstarch

1 handful of herb leaves (basil, lemon basil, oregano, thyme, etc.) from garden, chopped if needed

1/2–1 teaspoon sea salt

3–4 grinds of peppercorns

### Serves 4

Calories per serving: 210
Total fat: 5g
Saturated fat: 1g
Calories from fat: 45
Protein: 28g
Carbohydrates: 13g
Dietary fiber: 3g
Sugars: 6g

*In early April, prickly pear pads (or nopalitos) were perfect for the picking, and we were craving curry—besides, sliced nopalitos look a lot like green beans, which are commonly used in Indian curry. We had an abundance of snow peas and baby carrots in the garden, perfect complements to the cactus. Since chiles weren't in season, I used dry ones for the heat and flavor. So that's how the desert curry came about—totally seasonal and unbelievably fresh. You also can freeze grilled or sauteed cactus strips so they can be added to curries made with summer vegetables. Since not everyone has cactus readily available, substitute whatever is in season.*

*Note: Turmeric is the earthy spice that gives curry that brilliant yellow color, which comes from the phytochemical curcumin. The incidence of Alzheimer's disease (AD) in India is 4.4 times less than what it is in the United States. Researchers from UCLA concluded that curcumin is a promising agent in the treatment and/or prevention of AD and continue to study the use of curcumin in patients with AD. Nopalitos may be beneficial in controlling type II diabetes and cholesterol.*

*Serve this dish over Forbidden Black Rice (page 158).*

▼ ▼ ▼

Over medium-high heat, in oil, sauté the chicken, onion, and garlic for a few minutes or until the garlic begins to stick. Stir in the nopalitos, sage, and a little broth if necessary; sauté for 3 minutes. Add more broth, the ginger, curry powder, carrots, and chipotle. Bring to a boil and then reduce to a simmer, cover, and cook for about 10 minutes or until carrots are done. Mix the arrowroot or cornstarch with a little broth or water to form a thin paste, and then stir it into the curry to thicken. Remove from heat, taste, add pepper and salt if needed. Toss in the fresh herbs.

# Herbed Chicken Pasta Salad

Chile–Lime Chicken Shish Kabobs (page 120, prepare without vegetables), chilled

1 cup chopped tender cactus pads (nopalitos), fresh or marinated (see page 164)

8 ounces organic whole-grain or durum-wheat semolina pasta with 2 teaspoons sea salt, cooked al dente

1 garlic clove, run through garlic press

1/4 cup finely chopped yellow onion

Zest from 1 lemon

1/4 cup lemon juice

1/2–2/3 cup chopped kalamata olives

1–2 tablespoons extra-virgin olive oil

Sea salt

4–5 grinds of multi-color peppercorns

1 cup minced mix of fresh rosemary, lemon verbena, spicy or plain oregano, and lemon thyme

1 cup chiffonade-cut fresh basil leaves

1/2 cup fresh edible pansy blossoms, or a sprinkling of calendula petals (petals only)

1 cup peeled mandarin or orange slices

### Salad Ingredients

4–6 cups mixed salad greens

1–2 handfuls pea shoots or micro greens

1/4 cup fresh chocolate mint leaves (any mint will do)

1 teaspoon extra-virgin olive oil

1 tablespoon fresh lemon juice

Scant pinch of sea salt

Couple grinds of multi-color peppercorns

1/4 cup goat feta, optional

### Serves 4

Calories per serving: 534
Total fat: 17g
Saturated fat: 2g
Calories from fat: 145g
Protein: 36g
Carbohydrates: 58g
Dietary fiber: 6g
Sugars: 10g

*Twists of whole-grain pasta tossed with inviting bites of juicy Chile–Lime Chicken (page 120) and colorful specks of fresh herbs, ribbons of basil, and deeply colored pansies dress up this salad and imbue it with amazing fresh flavors. If you are not a desert dweller or you don't want to pick the cactus paddles, forget the cactus and add more herbs or maybe asparagus.*

*Note: According to a study in the* Journal of Nutrition, *May 2003, herbs may be a better source of antioxidants than many other food groups such as fruits, berries, vegetables, and cereals. Oregano, sage, and peppermint are at the top of the list, with lemon balm and basil not too far behind. All of them grow like weeds and must be cut and eaten often to keep them from taking over the garden!*

*If you can, try to prepare the Chile–Lime Chicken ahead of time so it can chill. While the Chili–Lime Chicken is chilling, prepare the cactus pads. Some people dislike the mucilage from the cactus pad. To reduce it, marinate the pads, and either grill or drain them and use fresh (see page 164).*

▼ ▼ ▼

While the Chile–Lime Chicken is chilling, cook the pasta, then rinse in cold water. Mix together the garlic, onion, lemon juice and zest, olives, and oil; then combine this with the pasta. Taste and season with salt and pepper as needed. Add the mixed herbs, basil leaves, pansy or calendula, orange pieces, and chicken pieces; toss, cover, and chill in refrigerator. Toss together the salad greens, oil, lemon juice, salt, and pepper. Plate salad greens topped with pasta salad and feta cheese.

*Free-range chickens at Chiricahua Pasture Raised Meats.*

# Joshua Koehn's Chiricahua Pasture Raised Meats

Joshua Koehn grew up on his family's row crop farm near Willcox, Arizona, where he and his siblings helped take care of a few cattle. His interest in animals and livestock fostered a desire to raise livestock and poultry in a spacious outdoors environment. He found mentors from other parts of the country and followed the pastured poultry model from Joel Salatin's book, *Pastured Poultry Profits*, but commented, "They helped a lot, but this is still a different climate and environment—I felt like I was a pioneer in the area." Today at 24 years old, he owns Chiricahua Pasture Raised Meats and mentors other farmers raising pastured livestock and poultry.

As I stood next to him amid the lush green pasture of his 70-acre farm, it was obvious that he holds respect for the land and raises animals with a conscience. We were entertained by spring lamb triplets following and nudging their mother for milk, while a couple hundred sheep grazed freely in two of the nutrient-dense green paddocks. In another paddock, a small herd of cattle were lazily enjoying their fresh chow, and flocks of chickens were busy in the distance. It was a perfect picture of natural agriculture, and it was the real thing!

After walking through an empty paddock of green grass, we crossed over the fence into a lush green pasture where six-week-old Red Rangers strutted around in a roomy, roofed open-floor shelter with airy netted sides, built for protection from predators, the sun, and inclement weather. Since they were old enough now to be safe from predatory birds, Josh opened the sides of the shelter that afternoon, allowing them to roam and forage freely in the large fenced (against coyotes) paddock of dense green pasture.

Josh explained that he initially raised Cornish Cross chickens—the most commonly raised hybrid pastured poultry, also grown in the factory-farmed broiler industry—but soon converted to Red Rangers. Cornish Cross was bred to be big breasted, but their legs aren't strong enough to support them. Josh commented, "They don't move as much as the Red Rangers, so they burn fewer calories and don't need as much food, which defies the purpose of pasture production. I want them to run around and eat as much as they will." The Red Rangers also take five more weeks to grow than the Cornish Cross before harvesting, which means they cost more to produce.

We stepped over another fence into an adjacent paddock of happily clucking laying hens. Like the Red Rangers, they were foraging in a smorgasbord of living grasses, weeds, bugs, worms, and Josh's wholesome grain mix. Then we made our way into the nesting area and gathered freshly laid eggs still warm from the hens' bodies. Unlike the factory-raised laying hens, there were a mixed stock of heritage chickens in different sizes and colors, and their eggs were as different as the hens. Josh made sure I got some turquoise, blue, and pinkish-colored shells for Easter.

His heritage hens are hardier than the hybrids used in factory egg production. Josh explained that they don't lay as frequently as the hybrids, but they lay for a longer time. When their laying days are over, he butchers and sells them as stewing hens—whereas, Josh remarks, "By the time the hybrids are done laying, they have laid so many eggs, they are reduced to a scrawny carcass."

When asked how his chickens compared to certified organic free-range chickens available in grocery stores, Josh chuckled and retorted, "You have this big chicken house with bare dirt yards outside, with maybe 50,000 chickens inside. Some go outside. But why would they go out there? There is not a lot of draw. They have a hard time keeping disease away. With my chickens, it's a non-issue for a variety of reasons. They have greater nutrients, access to green pasture, and there are less birds in one area. They live in a large paddock for a week to 10 days. Then they are moved to another paddock. The sun sterilizes the empty paddock, the pasture regrows, and bacteria is not an issue."

Josh explained that the chickens get about 25 percent of their nutrition from the pasture. He said the caloric content is not that great, but the vitamins, minerals, antioxidants, and chlorophyll from the live grasses make a huge difference in the quality of the meat and eggs. He also prepares a custom food mix for them, void of any animal by-products or drugs. It consists of a purchased organic mineral/vitamin pre-mix, local non-GMO corn, and organic soybeans. To get non-GMO soybeans, he has to buy organic from Kansas. His mix is not totally organic. He said, "If I did a total organic food, the cost would be astronomical. If I shipped in organic corn, it would be ridiculous. The grain doesn't cost that much, but the freight would be double the cost of the corn. I am also supporting local farmers who are growing non-GMO corn."

## Chile–Lime Chicken Shish Kabobs

**Marinade**

⅓ cup Key lime or lemon juice

1 teaspoon Key lime or lemon zest

1 tablespoon Dijon mustard

3 tablespoons extra-virgin olive oil

½–1 serrano chile, seeded and minced

4 garlic cloves, run through garlic press

2 tablespoons fresh lemon thyme leaves, bruised, or 1 teaspoon dried thyme, crushed

2 tablespoons fresh Mexican or spicy hot oregano, bruised, or 1 teaspoon Mexican oregano, crushed

½ teaspoon ground cumin

1 teaspoon sea salt

4–5 grinds of peppercorns

½ cup minced fresh cilantro (include some stems)

8–12 rosemary stems, 8–12-inches long, or bamboo (soak in water for 20 minutes) skewers

**Chicken and Vegetables**

1 pound chicken breasts, cut in rough 1-inch cubes

12 cherry tomatoes

1 medium zucchini squash

1 medium crookneck squash

1–2 small fennel bulbs

1 red onion

1 red bell pepper

---

**Serves 4–6**

Calories per serving: 170
Total fat: 2g
Saturated fat: 0g
Calories from fat: 15
Protein: 23g
Carbohydrates: 16g
Dietary fiber: 4g
Sugars: 6g

*Juicy pieces of chicken infused with pleasing notes of fresh aromatic herbs and lime make this a family favorite. The flavor changes with the choice of herbs (such as rosemary, dill, or cilantro) and vegetables, making it a perfect in-season meal almost year-round. The aroma is amazing! To make life easier, double the chicken recipe and refrigerate half; and then for the next day's lunch or dinner, toss pieces in a cold grain, quinoa, or pasta salad that's loaded with fresh or steamed seasonal vegetables.*

*Serve these just-cooked over warm Basil-Lime Quinoa with Squash Blossoms and Black Beans (page 153).*

▼ ▼ ▼

Mix the marinade ingredients in a non-reactive bowl; add the chicken and thoroughly coat. If time permits, marinate in the refrigerator for 1–4 hours. Otherwise, marinate while prepping the vegetables: Cut the zucchini and crookneck squashes in ½-inch slices; cut the fennel bulbs in quarters, remove the cores, and separate the layers (reserve the fronds); peel and quarter the onion, then separate the layers; and cut the red bell pepper in 1-inch rough squares.

Strip the leaves from the rosemary stem, top down, leaving a 1-inch spray of leaves at the top of the stem. Attractively thread the chicken pieces, separated by vegetables, onto the skewers.

Grill over high heat for about 5 minutes, turning to cook evenly. Cut into a piece of chicken to make sure it is done. Chicken should be juicy, not dry. Don't overcook.

*Chile–Lime Chicken Shish Kabobs shown over Basil–Lime Quinoa with Squash Blossoms and Black Beans (recipe on page 153).*

# Walking J Farm

Growing up in the ranch culture of hard work, having experience in organic gardening, and possessing a deep respect and a nurturing connection to the land, Jim McManus's dream of owning and operating a holistic, sustainable farm came to fruition in the spring of 2009. He, his wife Tina Bartsch, and their two children Maggie and Colm are living a new chapter in their lives by putting down roots on a 72-acre farm in Amado, Arizona, that they named Walking J Farm. The farm is centered around two adobe homes dating back to 1897 that are shaded by 100-year-old trees. It seems fitting that during World War II a victory garden was planted at the Sopori School, which was on this land. And now, some sixty years later, Jim and Tina—partners in life and on the farm—are working on realizing their goal of a homestead based on holistic farming that feeds itself with few outside inputs, while also feeding their family and people from nearby communities through Community Supported Agriculture (CSA) and farmers' markets.

They cultivate 1.5 acres of organic herbs and vegetables—more than 100 varieties—with plans for growing beans and grains as supplemental food for the livestock. On land void of chemical fertilizers and pesticides, they finish a small herd of beef cattle on grass, and in pastures they raise a few pigs, meat chickens, laying hens, heritage turkeys (for Thanksgiving and Christmas), and a couple of goats for milking. The livestock is also free of hormones and antibiotics.

In April 2011, they took raising hogs a step farther by making a home for a small breeding stock of Large Black Hogs, a rare heritage breed whose lineage goes back more than a century. The piglets will not travel miles to a new home, but will stay with their moms and grow up on the farm. By raising heritage animals, Walking J is committing to increasing agricultural biodiversity by preserving genetic diversity, which assures food security for present and future generations. As a tasty plus, Jim explained that the pork rendered is superior culinary pork of extra tender, micro-marbled cuts of meat that are moist with an exquisite flavor.

The McManus family is building their farm on the premise that rich, healthy soil is the foundation necessary for healthy animals and plants, which in turn puts safe, health-promoting foods on the dining table. Jim explained, "We have been slowly rebuilding soils with compost, effective microorganisms, and manure from the animals." He further stated, "A variety of crops and animals, rotational grazing, rotational cropping in paddocks, and rotational vegetable cropping are developing healthy soil that has both nutritional elements and the right probiotics in terms of beneficial bacteria." They aspire for their farm to be a self-contained entity that will mimic the symbiotic relationship of plants and animals as seen in a natural ecosystem.

For them, there are no days off, and work is endless—from before dawn to beyond dusk. We visited them on an unmercifully windy Sunday morning and caught a glimpse of their lives. Tina, in her knee-high rubber boots and knitted stocking hat positioned over her ears, loaded the small trailer (attached to a four-wheeler) with chicken feed, shot us a smile, and headed out to the pasture where chickens were in "chicken tractors," waiting for their supplemental food.

As we walked toward the pasture, Jim explained that the chickens live in bottomless pens, which are moved daily to fresh grass, saying, "They are actually fertilizing and preparing the land for us by harvesting the forage, depositing nitrogen-rich manure, and scratching (tilling) the ground. But moving these things and butchering 150 chickens every two weeks is killing our backs." Oh yeah, Jim and Tina work their tushes off doing a myriad of chores and working three farmers' markets fifty miles away each week. And there is no shortage of disruptions that must be dealt with, such as coyotes preying on their turkeys in the middle of the night or watching a gust of wind hurl a piglet structure forty feet in the air, resulting in a stunned little piglet and a damaged pen.

Since most people don't raise their own food, many children are clueless as to how or where it is raised or grown, thus, lacking connection to their food. With children being future consumers, Jim and Tina believe it's important that they understand the impact of their food choices on their health and on our planet, and that they understand somewhat the foundations of agriculture. With that in mind and being conscientious stewards of the land, Jim, Tina, other farmers, and educators started FERN (The Farm Education Resource Network), which serves to support the advancement of sustainable farming, local food systems, and healthy food choices through education.

## Crusted Baked Chicken Nuggets

**Marinade**

½ teaspoon sea salt

Freshly ground pepper

¼ cup lemon juice

¼ cup nonfat yogurt

2 teaspoons local honey

1 teaspoon Dijon mustard

1–1½ pounds chicken breast, cut in chunks

**Crust**

½ cup rolled oats

1 piece of dry or toasted whole-grain bread

⅓ cup whole-grain spelt or wheat flour

1 tablespoon oregano, crushed

3 tablespoons Parmesan cheese, finely grated (use microplane)

½ teaspoon sea salt

Freshly ground pepper

1 teaspoon garlic powder

2 teaspoons evaporated cane juice

Extra-virgin olive oil spray

**Dipping Sauce**

⅓ cup lemon juice

2 cups lowfat yogurt

½ teaspoon ground cumin

1 cup grated cucumber

1 clove garlic, minced

1 tablespoon finely chopped dill weed

½ teaspoon sea salt

**Serves 4–6**

Calories per serving: 358
Total fat: 5g
Saturated fat: 2g
Calories from fat: 48
Protein: 43g
Carbohydrates: 34g
Dietary fiber: 3g
Sugars: 13g

*While Elizabeth Mikesell was chairwoman of the American Culinary Federation's Chef & Child Foundation, she compiled health-promoting menus, and asked chefs and me for recipes. The menus were sent to family restaurants throughout the US, suggesting that they replace those that are so bad for kids. I submitted this recipe as an alternative to the ever-so-popular chicken nuggets served with French fries, catsup, and ranch dressing at not only McDonald's, but also at many non-fast-food restaurants. Elicia, my daughter, served them to her boys and their friends, ages 4–8. They all really liked them! I served them to a mixed group of adults and children. The adults gobbled them up, hardly leaving any for the kids. The dipping sauce is tasty and fun, but these nuggets can be equally enjoyed without sauce.*

*Suggested sides include Chipotle Sweet Potato Fries (page 141); a mix of carrot sticks, apples, and raisins; or salad greens with apple slices and raisins, tossed with lemon juice and a little extra-virgin olive oil.*

▼ ▼ ▼

Preheat oven to 350 degrees F. Line a baking sheet with parchment paper and set aside.

Combine the marinade ingredients (salt through Dijon mustard) and toss the chicken pieces in the marinade, making sure each piece is coated. If time permits, marinate for 1–2 hours.

When you are ready to finish preparing this dish, preheat the oven to 350 degrees F. Break the bread into small pieces and toss them into a mini food processor bowl; process into fine breadcrumbs, then turn into a small bowl. Process the oats until a coarse meal forms, then thoroughly mix this with the breadcrumbs and all other dry ingredients (flour through evaporated cane juice). Drain the marinade from the chicken, shake off any excess, and then roll the chicken pieces in the dry mix. Place them on the baking sheet, leaving space between pieces on the sheet. Generously spray the pieces with olive oil and bake in the oven for 5 minutes or until lightly browned.

While the chicken bakes, make the dipping sauce by combining all the ingredients (lemon juice through salt).

Turn the chicken pieces, spray again with oil, and bake for another 3–5 minutes or until lightly browned and the chicken is done. Serve plain or with the dipping sauce dished out into 4-ounce ramekins or other small bowls.

**Variation: Southwest Chicken Nuggets** Follow the instructions for Crusted Baked Chicken Nuggets while making the following changes: To the marinade add ¼ cup minced cilantro. Eliminate the salt and add 1–2 teaspoons Chipotle Rub (page 51) to the crust mixture, or leave the salt in and add ½–1 teaspoon chipotle chile powder (if unavailable grate toasted chipotle on fine microplane).

## Brown Rice Southwest Paella

1 large sweet yellow onion

4–6 garlic cloves, crushed and skins removed

3 medium tomatoes or 1 cup diced fire-roasted canned tomatoes

1 poblano chile or green bell pepper, roasted and then cut in quarters and seeded

1 cup coarsely cut, loosely packed cilantro, including some finely chopped stems

2 chicken thighs

2 chicken drumsticks

Sea salt

Freshly ground pepper

2 tablespoons extra-virgin olive oil, divided

1 teaspoon Mexican oregano

1/2 teaspoon thyme leaves

1 teaspoon dried sage leaves or 10 fresh sage leaves, cut in 1/4-inch chiffonade

1 teaspoon cumin seeds

Pinch of saffron threads

2 whole chipotle chiles

1 teaspoon smoked bittersweet paprika

1 1/2 cups short-grain brown rice

3–4 cups low-sodium chicken broth

1 can (15 ounces) or 1 1/2 cups cooked cannellini, butter, lima, or tepary beans, optional

2 cups fresh peas, snow peas, green beans, or whatever vegetable is in season

**Garnish**

1 sprig of fresh rosemary, plus 1 tablespoon finely chopped leaves

1 each California or New Mexico green chile and red bell pepper, roasted and then cut into strips (see Fire-roasting, page 15)

Avocado slices

1/2 cup finely chopped cilantro leaves

### Serves 4–6

Calories per serving: 340
Total fat: 6g
Saturated fat: 3g
Calories from fat: 30g
Protein: 5g
Carbohydrates: 32g
Dietary fiber: 12g
Sugars: 3g

*In my spin on paella, the chicken or seafood is played down and the vegetables are elevated to star in the dish. It's a little spicy, full of Southwest flavors, and made with fiber-rich whole-grain rice that delivers chewy, plump grains that don't stick together. Sometimes for get-togethers, we set a 20-inch (about 16 servings) paella over an open fire on our patio, where our friends or family gather while the paella cooks. One Christmas Eve, we sang Christmas carols and filled the air with song, laughter, and enticing aromatic paella flavors. Our friends Victor and Meg, from next door, followed their noses and joined us for dinner!*

*Note: If you don't have a paella pan, use a 12-inch shallow stainless-steel or iron skillet (not non-stick) to develop a thin bed of rice with the ideal texture. If you plan on frequently making paella, you might consider buying a paella pan. For a 12-inch or larger paella pan, I would recommend a gas grill or open fire, and not cooking over an electric burner.*

*I fire-roast the peppers on a grill and toast the spices to bring out their flavors and perfumes (see pages 15–17). Roasted, toasted, or not, the paella will be delicious.*

▼ ▼ ▼

To save time, use a food processor to finely chop the onions and garlic (in one batch), followed by a separate batch with the tomatoes, roasted poblano chile or bell pepper, and cilantro; set aside the 2 batches of chopped vegetables. If not using a food processor, finely chop the 2 batches of vegetables with a knife, and set aside.

Dust the chicken pieces with salt and pepper. Over a preheated grill at medium-high heat, heat 2 teaspoons of olive oil in a 12-inch or larger paella pan or set a shallow skillet (not nonstick skillet) over a burner and lightly brown the chicken pieces; don't cook them all the way. Remove the pieces and set aside. (When cooled, remove skin from the chicken.) Drain and wipe the grease from the skillet or pan.

While the chicken is browning, in a dry skillet toast the oregano, thyme, and sage (if using dried) together; remove from the skillet. Toast the cumin seeds and then crush or grind them. Toast the saffron threads, remove them from the skillet and set aside, keeping them separate from the other spices. Toast the chipotles and set aside (toasting releases flavors—see Toasting, page 17).

To prepare the tomato sauce: Add 2 teaspoons of olive oil to the pan, sauté the chopped onion, garlic, and fresh sage (if using fresh) over medium-high heat until onion is translucent. Stir in the tomato, poblano or bell pepper, and cilantro. Rub the roasted oregano, thyme, and sage (if using dried) between your palms while releasing into the sauce, then add the cumin and paprika then stir into sauce. Sauté the sauce, frequently stirring until liquid has almost evaporated and the sauce is thick.

Clear the center of the skillet by moving the sauce around to the edges of the skillet. Pour 2 teaspoons of olive oil in the center of the skillet, then add the rice and mix with the oil. Stir the rice and oil for 4–5 minutes or until it is golden and there is a slight aroma of toasted rice; then stir with the sauce to thoroughly coat the rice with sauce, spreading this rice-tomato mixture evenly over the bottom of the skillet. Sauté, while turning it a few times, allowing the rice to settle on the heat a few minutes at a time. Continue sautéing until the rice becomes translucent—a very important technique in order for the rice to soak up the broth and hold a sachet of flavors. Add 3 cups of the chicken broth, the beans, and the browned chicken pieces; mix thoroughly. Crush the saffron threads, sprinkle them over the broth, and stir to mix.

Push the whole chipotle chiles into the broth. Turn the heat to high and bring the paella to a rolling boil for about 5 minutes, or until the liquid is just above the rice mixture. Taste and adjust the seasonings. Reduce heat, scrape the bottom of the skillet with a spatula, mix, and then make sure that the rice is distributed evenly. Important note: this is the last time you will stir the paella.

Gently simmer the rice, uncovered, until the liquid is almost absorbed. Test rice for doneness. It should be a little chewy and moist but not hard. If it isn't done and is not soaking in broth, add a tiny bit more broth to just cover the rice. When the rice is almost done, add the peas or other vegetables, pushing them into the rice, but don't stir. Remove from the burner, cover, and allow it to rest for 5 minutes. Remove the chipotles. Garnish with a sprinkling of chopped rosemary, green chile strips, avocado strips, cilantro, and rosemary sprig.

**Variation: Winter and Spring Paella**  In place of fresh tomatoes, substitute 1 can (14.5 ounce) fire-roasted diced tomatoes with green chiles. Instead of fresh poblano chile, substitute ½–1 diced chipotle in adobo sauce, plus 1 teaspoon of adobo sauce. For the green chiles, substitute canned green chiles. Use your choice of in-season vegetables.

# Paella

From the field hands' humble, aromatic rice dish of seasonally ripe vegetables and wild game simmering in a paella (pan) over an open fire in the countryside of mid-1800s Valencia, Spain, to today's dish-of-plenty in restaurants and on dining tables throughout the world—you'll find the communal paella. Back then, field hands gathered around the paella with wooden spoons, partaking directly from the pan. Today, it remains the perfect centerpiece for "slow food," where food is shared in a friendly no-rush atmosphere, and every morsel of food and friendship is truly savored.

Even before Valencia paella became famous, rice was brought to Mexico by the Spaniards through the port of Veracruz in the early 1500s. The Spaniards learned of tomatoes from the Aztecs and took these red fruits back to Spain, where they eventually made their way into Spanish paella. Rice flavored with tomato–chile sauce also caught on in Mexico, evolving into Mexican paella (similar to "Spanish rice"). It was a fusion of two culinary traditions that created two similar rice dishes on two continents. Aside from a few essential ingredients—olive oil, rice, saffron, paprika, tomatoes, onions, garlic, and a flavorful broth—whatever else you add is up to your imagination. Let your garden or a farmers' market be your inspiration. It's also the perfect dish for leftovers.

## Roasted Heritage Turkey

1 heritage turkey, 14–16 pounds

½ cup extra-virgin olive oil, plus more for coating the turkey

Freshly ground pepper

Sea salt

1 handful or more of freshly picked oregano, lemon thyme, or thyme leaves

¾ cup fresh purple or green sage leaves, roughly chopped

4–6 sprigs fresh rosemary

1 stalk celery, coarsely chopped

½ large onion, cut in half

1 carrot, coarsely chopped

1 lemon, cut in half

Butcher string

1½ cups white wine or sweet vermouth, divided

1 flour-sack towel

---

**Serves 14–16 plus leftovers**

Calories per serving: 340
Total fat: 6g
Saturated fat: 3g
Calories from fat: 30g
Protein: 5g
Carbohydrates: 32g
Dietary fiber: 12g
Sugars: 3g

*Since I had an abundance of oregano, English thyme, lemon thyme, rosemary, and purple sage, I used aromatic fresh herbs to add flavor. If you don't have fresh herbs, salt and pepper will do fine, or you may choose to add a few dry herbs. The heritage bird has a lot of flavor and can stand or rest on its own laurels.*

▼ ▼ ▼

If the turkey is frozen, place it in a pan in the refrigerator to thaw. Allow 24 hours per 5 pounds of turkey (15 pounds will take 3 full days). It must be completely thawed to ensure even cooking.

Preheat oven to 400 degrees F. Remove the giblets and neck from the cavity. Thoroughly rinse the turkey with cold water and pat dry. Gently separate the skin from the breast, thigh, and drumstick meat without tearing the skin. Rub a couple tablespoons of olive oil under the skin, over the breast and dark meat, sprinkle with pepper, and lightly salt, distributing both equally over the meat. Tuck the oregano, thyme, and sage leaves between the skin and the meat. Add three sprigs of bruised rosemary between breast meat and skin. Lightly salt and pepper the cavity, and place 2 sprigs of rosemary and the celery, onion, carrot, and lemon halves in the cavity. Lightly salt and pepper the skin of the turkey and rub with olive oil.

Tie the legs together with butcher string, and secure the wings under the turkey; set the bird aside. Mix 1 cup of wine or vermouth and the ½ cup of olive oil. Soak the towel in this mixture and use it to cover the entire turkey. Reserve oil/wine mixture for basting the turkey.

Place the turkey on a rack in a roasting pan. Pour 1 cup of wine or vermouth in the pan. Place rack at lowest level in oven and set the turkey on it. Roast at 400 degrees F for 30 minutes. Reduce to 325 degrees F, basting about every 20 minutes over the towel, roasting for about 3 hours (approximately 15 minutes per pound of turkey). Remove towel from turkey and roast uncovered, about 30 minutes to 1 hour (basting frequently), or until the internal temperature of the thickest part of thigh reaches 175 degrees F, taking care that the thermometer does not touch the bone. If you run out of basting liquid, spray or brush with olive oil.

Remove the turkey from the oven and allow it to rest for 15 minutes before carving. Remove vegetables from cavity and discard.

## Heritage Turkey

Next Thanksgiving, heritage turkey will grace our table as it did so many dining tables for centuries prior to the 1960s. However, due to a couple naysayers' warnings of its toughness and gaminess, I thought it wise to experiment before the big day. Since Jim McManus and Tina Bartsch's Walking J Farm is one of a few hundred farms throughout the country raising rare heritage breeds, I set out for the Santa Cruz Farmers' Market and was lucky to get the lone turkey in Tina's freezer for my test run. With a prominent breast bone, narrow breast, and long drumsticks, it was a far cry from its engineered descendant, the Broad-Breasted White that makes up 99 percent of turkeys eaten. Even though it was only April, Tina was taking orders for their two heritage breeds, White Holland and Chocolate Turkeys, for Thanksgiving and Christmas. A decision had to be made—I ordered two fourteen-pounders for Thanksgiving and felt good that our turkeys would be antibiotic- and hormone-free and would be foraging on a smorgasbord of food in the pasture while enjoying life outdoors.

On our way home from the market, Mom and I were reminiscing about our yearly trips during the 1950s to Boss Hanke's farm to pick out our Thanksgiving bird. She commented, "Boss's turkeys were not dry like the ones today." I did some research and discovered from heritage breeders and the Heritage Turkey Foundation that heritage birds are prized for their flavor and are much more succulent than the fast-growing industrial breed of turkey that take about 18 weeks to meet average market weight. Heritage turkeys, on the other hand, take from 24 to 30 weeks, allowing them to develop a layer of fat, which enhances flavor and keeps the meat from drying during roasting. Running and flying around, they get plenty of exercise, which gives the meat a firm texture.

Over the years of struggling to keep the breast juicy, I've often thought of just cutting up the bird and roasting the dark meat separate from the white; but the pomp and circumstance of the Thanksgiving bird nixed that from ever happening, and so each year brings on the turkey challenge: how to prevent moist breast/raw thighs or dry breast/cooked thighs? So, up for the heritage turkey challenge, I stuffed fresh herbs under the skin, seasoned it, and soaked a flour-sack towel in olive oil and sweet vermouth and placed it over the breast and did a lot of basting. The breast came out unbelievably moist, the thighs were meaty but not tough, and, yes, they were done. The flavors were amazing. The true test, however, was thawed leftover turkey breast from the freezer; it too was juicy and full of flavor.

With a layer of fat and a close ratio of dark to white meat, I believe the heritage bird cooks fairly evenly, making it moist and flavorful. Since the commercial birds don't have these attributes, they tend to be dry and somewhat tasteless, which is why Butterball injects their birds with water, salt, modified food starch, sodium phosphates, and natural flavorings to retain a salty moisture. Cooks have come up with other options for creating moist white meat: deep frying, brining in a flavored salt solution for 24 hours, or injecting juices into the breast. And if it's not moist, smother it in gravy.

*Heritage turkeys at Walking J Farm.*

*Over the long haul of life on this planet, it is the ecologists, and not the bookkeepers of business, who are the ultimate accountants.*

—STEWART UDALL, *Arizona's Native Son*

# VEGETABLES & SIDES

**Plant-based diets** bring to the table an array of festive colors and a bounty of health-promoting properties. However, this doesn't mean that you have to kick meat off your plate. It just means that plant foods should hold the prominent presence at a meal—and for good reason. Most are low in fat and calories, nutrient-dense, and are the foremost food sources for phytonutrients (plant compounds that have health-protecting properties that may act as antioxidants or immune boosters). According to a study in *Nutrition Journal* in 2010, plant-based foods have a mean antioxidant content from 5 to 33 times higher than the mean antioxidant content of meat products.

Plants are also the only source of fiber in the diet. Meat, poultry, and animal products have no fiber! Nutritionists suggest that our bodies need between 25 and 35 grams of fiber per day; some even suggest 45 grams per day to promote good health. However, the average American is consuming about half that amount. By adding a cup of cooked black or tepary beans, you will be adding about 18 grams of fiber!

To assist you in including more plants in your meals, I not only incorporate plants in the meat and fish dishes, I also suggest pairing them with additional plant-based dishes from this chapter. Vegetable dishes usually feature not just one, but a number of vegetables (often fruits are mixed in, too) from a broad range of colors to achieve a broader spectrum of phytonutrients. Colorful grain and quinoa pilafs and salads may bring together a combination of grains, nuts, seeds, beans, vegetables, or fruits. This should make it easy to consume 9–10 servings of a variety of vegetables each day. Scientists know that by combining two or more plants, the different compounds within each plant work synergistically, or as a team, and become more powerful in protecting against diseases than when eaten alone.

Cooking may destroy some phytonutrients; but it may also increase others or make them more readily absorbed. For example, eat cooked tomatoes with a little oil, and the antioxidant lycopene becomes more bio-available. Cooked carrots also release more beta-carotene than raw. This holds true for a myriad of other vegetables, too. Lightly steaming, grilling, broiling, or baking under moderate heat are your best cooking options to bring out and preserve most phytonutrients. Raw vegetables provide more vitamins C and B, polyphenols, and folic acid, which are damaged by heat. Thus, to make sure that you reap a full array of phytonutrients, eat vegetables raw as well as cooked.

You'll also notice that most vegetables are not peeled in the recipes. When you peel most fruits and vegetables, you are also peeling away many of their nutrients, antioxidants, and fiber. One more reason for buying local organic, there won't be any wax or toxins on the fruits or vegetables. Citrus zest holds a much higher dose of vitamin C and the powerful cancer preventing antioxidant d-limonene than citrus juice and the zest is also a rich source of vitamins A and B-complex. It's not only health promoting but also gives dishes a wonderful orange or lemon flavor. Also, the aesthetics added to recipes come from the beautifully colored skin of fruits and vegetables. ▶

*Kale Salad with Fresh Fig Dressing (recipe on page 130).*

# Kale Salad with Fresh Fig Dressing

**Dressing**

2 pieces of fresh peeled ginger, the diameter of a quarter by ¼-inch thick

½ cup quartered ripe figs

1 garlic clove, run through garlic press

2 tablespoons Key lime juice

2 teaspoons balsamic vinegar

1 tablespoon coarse-grain yellow mustard

1 teaspoon evaporated cane juice or maple syrup (optional, as fresh-from-the-tree figs may not need sweetening)

½ teaspoon sea salt

½ cup thinly sliced red onion (sliced in half rounds)

**Salad**

8–10 purple-red kale leaves

1–2 tablespoons extra-virgin olive oil

1½ cups quartered figs

Freshly ground black or multi-color pepper

**Serves 4–6**

Calories per serving: 114
Total fat: 6g
Saturated fat: 1g
Calories from fat: 52g
Protein: 2g
Carbohydrates: 15g
Dietary fiber: 2g
Sugars: 9g

*Curly purplish-red kale dancing with colorful slices of tree-fresh mission figs brings out various degrees of sweetness and a tad of bitterness that play against each other to deliver a delightful tasting salad. Unlike other salads, it does not become soggy and can also be enjoyed the next day. There is an indescribable difference in taste, texture, scent, and freshness between ripe figs picked fresh and those bought in the store. For this reason, I believe that my fig tree is the most prized tree in our yard. We are sometimes lucky to still have some kale in the garden and a few ripe figs at the same time.*

▾ ▾ ▾

To make the dressing: Release the juice from the ginger by muddling, pressing, and crushing the ginger pieces with ½ cup of the quartered figs and the garlic until the fruit is pretty much masticated; add the remaining dressing ingredients (lime juice through sliced red onion) and set aside. You may prefer removing the ginger before tossing together the dressing and salad. (Some people enjoy biting into fresh ginger and others don't.)

Thoroughly rinse the kale with cold water. Tear the leaves from the tough spines and into tiny bite-size pieces. Remove excess water by using a salad spinner, or dry the leaves with a cotton towel. With fingers, massage 1 tablespoon of olive oil into the kale leaves until all the leaves glisten, adding more oil as necessary. This will break down the leaves somewhat, causing some juice to release from the leaves, and it tames any bitter flavor. Add and thoroughly toss the figs, dressing, and pepper with the kale. Taste and adjust the seasonings as needed. Refrigerate and serve in a couple hours or the next day.

## Southwest Kale Salad

1 medium avocado, mashed

1–2 garlic cloves, run through garlic press

1 bunch of green onion, minced with some green, or ¼ cup red onion

Zest from 1 Key lime

3 tablespoons Key lime juice

1 bunch red or green curly kale (8–10 leaves)

2–4 teaspoons extra-virgin olive oil

1 teaspoon sea salt

2 cups coarsely chopped tomatoes

2 teaspoons or more minced serrano or jalapeño chile

¼ cup pine nuts

**Serves 4**

Calories per serving: 313
Total fat: 26g
Saturated fat: 4g
Calories from fat: 221
Protein: 7g
Carbohydrates: 20g
Dietary fiber: 8g
Sugars: 4g

*For a short period of time, kale and tomatoes are both in season, making it such a treat to prepare this delightful salad fresh from our garden or from Sleeping Frog Farms through our weekly CSA allotment. Some friends refer to it as a kale–guacamole salad and like to tuck it into tacos. Either way, it's very satisfying and carries a powerhouse of health-promoting ingredients.*

*Serve with tacos, burritos, over black bean soup, or with a small side of fish or meat.*

▼ ▼ ▼

Combine the mashed avocado, garlic, onion, zest, and lime juice; set aside while preparing the kale.

Rinse the kale with cold water, shake off the water, and pat dry with a cotton towel. Remove the tough stem/spine from the leaves, cut the leaves into approximately 1-inch strips, and place them in a large bowl. Pour olive oil over the kale and sprinkle it with salt. Massage the oil and salt into the kale until the leaves glisten. It will weep its juices, reduce in volume, and lose some toughness and bitterness.

With a dinner fork, mix the avocado dressing into the kale, making sure that all the kale is covered. Mix together the tomato and chile and gently toss them into the salad. Sprinkle pine nuts over the salad. Serve immediately.

## Cruciferous Vegetables

Eight or more daily servings of a variety of fruits and vegetables are important for staving off chronic disease such as heart disease, cancer, diabetes, and many others. Among vegetable families, the cruciferous family stands out as a strong protector against cancer. The American Institute of Cancer Research (AICR) states that studies have shown a lower risk of several types of cancer among people who have eaten four or five weekly servings of cruciferous vegetables over the years. It is believed that phytochemicals called isothiocyanates, inherent in these vegetables, kill off carcinogens (which come from pollution, grilled or processed meat, etc.) taken in by the body, preventing the formation of cancer cells and also increasing the self-destruction of cancer cells. With a wide variety and local availability throughout the cool seasons (and some during the summer), eat up and enjoy one of the tasty health-promoting recipes every day that include cabbage, broccoli, cauliflower, kale, collards, chard, mustard greens, Brussels sprouts, kohlrabi, rutabaga, or bok choy.

# Kale–Pomegranate Salad with Grapefruit Dressing

**Dressing**

¼ cup pomegranate seeds

2 pieces of fresh peeled ginger,
the diameter of a quarter by ¼-inch thick

¼ cup chopped sweet pink or red grapefruit sections
(membrane-free)

2 pitted dates, chopped and mashed

1 garlic clove, run through garlic press

2 teaspoons balsamic vinegar

1 tablespoon coarse-grain yellow mustard

1 teaspoon evaporated cane juice or maple syrup

½ teaspoon sea salt

½ cup thinly sliced red onion (sliced in half rounds)

**Salad**

8–10 purple-red kale leaves

1–2 tablespoons extra-virgin olive oil

1 cup sweet pink or ruby-red grapefruit sections
(membrane-free)

1 cup pomegranate seeds

Freshly ground black or multi-color pepper

**Serves 4–6**

Calories per serving: 149
Total fat: 4g
Saturated fat: 0g
Calories from fat: 33g
Protein: 4g
Carbohydrates: 28g
Dietary fiber: 5g
Sugars: 17g

*Our pink grapefruit tree provides an abundance of grapefruit for at least 9 months out of the year, which delivers a refreshingly sweet tang to many dishes throughout the seasons. During the holiday season, this salad will cheerfully accent a festive dinner table décor with its shiny green leaves punctuated with glistening red edible ornaments. It is at its best if it is allowed to marinate overnight, making it perfect for a no-hassle luncheon the next day. Add chicken for a stand-alone main-dish salad. Ruby Red and Texas Pink are really sweet and need no extra sweetening. We have a sweet pink grapefruit tree that works well, but I may add a few dates for a little more sweetness. Unlike most salads, it does not become soggy and can be enjoyed the next day.*

▼ ▼ ▼

To make the dressing: Release the juice from the ¼ cup of pomegranate seeds by pressing the seeds against a mesh strainer or muddling the seeds in a cup. Remove the seeds and set the juice aside. Release the juice from the ginger by muddling, pressing, and crushing the ginger pieces with the ¼ cup of grapefruit pieces, dates, and garlic until all is pretty much masticated; add the pomegranate juice and the remaining dressing ingredients (vinegar through sliced red onion) and set aside. You may prefer removing the ginger before tossing together the dressing and salad. (Some people enjoy biting into fresh ginger and others don't.)

Thoroughly rinse the kale with cold water. Tear the leaves from the tough spines and into tiny bite-size pieces. Remove excess water by using a salad spinner, or dry the leaves with a cotton towel. With fingers, massage 1 tablespoon of olive oil into the kale leaves until all the leaves glisten, adding more oil as necessary. This will break down the leaves somewhat, causing some juice to release from the leaves, and it tames any bitter flavor. Add and thoroughly toss the grapefruit, pomegranate seeds, dressing, and pepper with the kale. Taste and adjust the seasonings as needed. Allow the salad to marinate for at least 4 hours or overnight in the refrigerator.

**Variation** Substitute fresh oranges or tangerines for the grapefruit.

## Crispy Kale

1 bunch curly or flat green kale (8–10 leaves)

1–2 tablespoons extra-virgin olive oil

Sea salt

Splash of fresh lime or lemon juice or cider or balsamic vinegar, optional

**Serves 2–4**

Calories per serving: 73
Total fat: 4g
Saturated fat: 1g
Calories from fat: 35
Protein: 3g
Carbohydrates: 9g
Dietary fiber: 2g
Sugars: 0g

*While in Savannah for our daughter Amanda's college graduation in 2004, we ate at Paula Deen's The Lady and Sons restaurant, where pretty much everything was fried, including the bright green, crispy, tasty kale. Since everyone liked it so much, I made a similar version in a dehydrator and pretty much got the same crispness and flavor, but without the grease. I needed a quicker method—low temperature roasting was the answer. So, when six-year-old Calisa Perry joined me in the kitchen one morning, preparing and testing healthy food for kids, we fixed crispy kale in the oven. It was a hit with her and is repeatedly requested by our grandchildren and our son Alex. It's a healthy alternative to chips—kids will easily eat 4 or 5 leaves. To top it off, it is baked on a very low temperature, thus retaining most of its nutrients.*

▼ ▼ ▼

Preheat the oven to 275 degrees F. Line 2 baking sheets with parchment paper and set aside.

Rinse and thoroughly dry the kale (steam during the baking will prevent it from crisping up), then cut or tear the leaves into small pieces, discarding the tough veins and stems. Pour about 1 teaspoon of olive oil into the palm of your hand, then massage the oil into the kale leaves. Add salt and continue adding oil and massaging into the leaves until they glisten with oil. Transfer the oiled leaves, in a single layer, to the baking sheets. Place the kale in the oven and bake for 10–15 minutes, checking often to prevent burning. When they are crispy on the edges—some might have slightly brown edges—remove them from the oven. The leaves will continue to crisp up slightly. If they are not totally crispy, return them to the oven. If more than 1 pan of kale is baked concurrently, it may take a little longer; also, after 4 minutes, rotate the pans in the oven. Remove from the oven, allow to cool, and serve in a bowl for snacking or instead of French fries at a meal. As an option, splash the Crispy Kale with a minute amount of lime or lemon juice or vinegar.

**Variation: Chipotle–Lime Crispy Kale** Add a touch of heat and smoky chipotle flavor. Eliminate the salt and sprinkle with Chipotle-Lime Rub (see page 51), or sparingly with chipotle powder (or New Mexico red chile powder, which is not smoky in flavor) and a pinch of salt. Just before eating, splash with a tiny bit of lime juice.

**Variation: Cheezy Crispy Kale** Grind 1–2 tablespoons of nutritional yeast and a pinch of salt in a spice or coffee grinder with a low-fitting blade, then sprinkle this mixture on the baked kale. It's a vegan's delight!

**Variation: Cheesy Crispy Kale** For added flavor, use a microplane to grate a little Parmesan cheese and sprinkle it over the leaves prior to baking.

## Sweet Bitter Greens

5–6 handfuls of flat kale leaves

5–6 handfuls of Swiss chard leaves

1–2 oranges

1 teaspoon canola oil or extra-virgin olive oil

1 medium sweet yellow onion,
cut in half and thinly sliced

2 garlic cloves, run through garlic press or minced

1 teaspoon Key lime juice or a splash of balsamic vinegar

Sea salt

Freshly ground pepper

**Serves 4**

Calories per serving: 103
Total fat: 2g
Saturated fat: 0g
Calories from fat: 16
Protein: 4g
Carbohydrates: 21g
Dietary fiber: 4g
Sugars: 9g

*Upon receiving this recipe for testing, Linda Luft (my most avid recipe tester) and her husband Roberto, who is native Brazilian, invited us to a dinner featuring Roberto's traditional Brazilian food. They served a few bite-size stewed beef pieces over rice with beans, a dish of sautéed chard topped with orange slices, and powdered yucca root to be scooped up with each bite. (Yucca root is supposed to aid in digestion.) It was a perfect afternoon spent with good friends and tasty food. So soon after that, I made a pot roast and served tiny pieces over Mexican red rice, and I added sides of beans and these greens with orange slices. Of course, salsa, avocado slices, and lime wedges were offered, too. It was a beautifully colorful plate, full of plant foods with a little meat to satisfy those craving meat.*

▼ ▼ ▼

Cut the stems from the kale and chard leaves and thoroughly rinse them with cold water. Vertically fold the leaves in half and tear the leaves away from the tough center vein, and into bite-size pieces.

Cut threads of zest from 1 of the oranges, using a citrus zester. Using a bowl to catch the juice, slice both of the oranges into ⅛- to ¼-inch-thick wheels; remove the rind and pith, then cut each wheel in quarters.

Over medium-high heat, in the oil, sauté the onion and garlic until the onion slices are crispy–tender. Toss in the kale; cook and toss until it's about ⅓ its original volume; then add the chard and sauté until all the greens are wilted but still have a little life to them. Remove from heat; splash with the lime juice or vinegar, add a little of the orange juice produced from cutting the oranges, and season with salt and pepper to taste.

Serve topped off with the orange pieces and sprinklings of orange zest.

### Variations

▶ Any winter greens that are available make tasty alternatives—collards, mustard, dandelion, beet, arugula, and spinach. The choice is yours. If mixing different greens, always start cooking them in the order of thickness or toughness, because the thicker ones will take longer to cook. When they are somewhat soft, add the other greens. In addition to the orange pieces, a handful of pomegranate seeds add beauty and a wonderful sweet flavor.

▶ Substitute pink or red grapefruit pieces for the orange slices, and add ½ teaspoon maple syrup, or evaporated cane juice.

## Spinach Salad, Chef Scott Uehlein

1 cup sliced apples

½ cup Apple Cider Vinaigrette (see recipe below)

4 cups organic spinach leaves

4 teaspoons chopped toasted walnuts

4 tablespoons crumbled chèvre cheese

4 tablespoons dried cranberries

**Strawberry Champagne Vinaigrette**

½ cup strawberries

2 tablespoons champagne vinegar

1 tablespoon evaporated cane juice

Pinch sea salt

**Serves 4**

Calories per serving: 340
Total fat: 6g
Saturated fat: 3g
Calories from fat: 30g
Protein: 5g
Carbohydrates: 32g
Dietary fiber: 12g
Sugars: 3g

*This spinach salad topped with strawberry champagne vinaigrette was generously shared by Chef Scott Uehlein, Canyon Ranch, Tucson, Arizona.*

▼ ▼ ▼

Place apple slices in a glass baking pan and cover with Apple Cider Vinaigrette. Marinate in refrigerator for at least 2 hours.

In a blender container, combine all ingredients for strawberry champagne vinaigrette and puree.

In a medium bowl, combine spinach and strawberry vinaigrette and toss together.

Serve 1 cup of spinach with ¼ cup of marinated apples, 1 teaspoon walnuts, 1 tablespoon crumbed chèvre cheese, and 1 tablespoon dried cranberries.

## Apple Cider Vinaigrette, Chef Scott Uehlein

¼ cup cider vinegar

2 cups apple cider

¼ cup honey

1 cinnamon stick

1 teaspoon sea salt

**Makes 2 ½ cups or 20 servings
(2 tablespoons each)**

Calories per serving: 340
Total fat: 6g
Saturated fat: 3g
Calories from fat: 30g
Protein: 5g
Carbohydrates: 32g
Dietary fiber: 12g
Sugars: 3g

*This vinaigrette is a component of Chef Uehlein's spinach salad, and can also be used to dress other salads.*

▼ ▼ ▼

Combine all ingredients in a jar with a tight-fitting lid. Refrigerate overnight. Remove cinnamon stick.

## Simply Spinach

⅓ cup thinly sliced red onion

Splash of lemon juice

12 handfuls of fresh tender spinach, about 14 or 15 cups loosely packed

Sea salt

Freshly ground pepper

**Serves 4**

Calories per serving: 24
Total fat: 0g
Saturated fat: 0g
Calories from fat: 3g
Protein: 2g
Carbohydrates: 4g
Dietary fiber: 2g
Sugars: 1g

*Often, simply cooked vegetables with just a little bit of salt and pepper are the tastiest. You are not hiding the flavor of the vegetable, but bringing it out. Fresh, in-season local ingredients make the difference between tasty and just okay. If you're lucky to have tomatoes in season with spinach, chop a couple and throw them in with the greens for beautiful contrasting colors and a delightful taste. The vitamin C in the tomatoes will also aid your body in assimilating the iron in the spinach (however, the vitamin C is drastically diminished by heat). Therefore, toss the tomatoes into the sauté just before serving.*

▼ ▼ ▼

To reduce the strength of the sliced onion, splash it with lemon juice and set aside. Thoroughly wash fresh-from-the garden spinach to remove the rocks and mud often found clinging to the leaves and stems. The water from washing will be enough moisture to steam the spinach. Place the spinach in a large stockpot, 8 cup-size or so, and set over medium heat. As the spinach wilts, toss it, sprinkle it with a little salt, and continue steaming and occasionally tossing until it's wilted, bright green, and still holding a little life. Toss with the marinated onion and some pepper and serve immediately as a bed for fish or chicken.

## Beets

Don't throw away those vibrantly colored beet greens! Greens and the root both provide some soluble and insoluble fiber that respectively keep a smooth-running intestinal tract and keep blood sugar and cholesterol levels in check. Both offer a wide spectrum of nutrients, phytochemicals, and antioxidants. However, in general the greens contain higher amounts of vitamins and minerals than the root and make an excellent source of calcium, iron, magnesium, potassium, vitamins A and K, and beta carotene. The root is a good source of folate and has a high concentration of betalains (phytonutrients), which research suggests have antioxidant and free-radical-scavenging properties, for protection against oxidative stress-related diseases such as heart disease, cancer, and Alzheimer's. Use the raw greens in salads, or cook them as you would spinach or any other green. Raw or cooked, the root is a delicious alternative for tomatoes in a salad, especially when tomatoes are out of season.

To avoid fibrous and woody beets, buy them in season, choosing beets of no more than three inches in diameter with vibrant green leaves, thus assuring sweet and tender roots. Beet season runs from June to late October in many parts of the country. In southern Arizona, beets are a cool-season vegetable, harvested through the fall and winter months.

Immediately after harvesting or buying them, cut the leaves from the bulb, leaving a one-inch stem and retaining the taproot that extends from the bulb. The greens sap moisture from the root, causing the bulb to shrivel and loose flavor, along with nutrients. Bulbs and greens should be stored separately in the refrigerator and not cooked together. However, when combined after cooking, they make wonderful dishes. Use the greens right away; bulbs will keep for several weeks in the refrigerator in a perforated plastic bag. Don't peel the beets or snip off the tap root for cooking, or valuable health-promoting compounds will be lost.

## Garnet Fennel Salad

1 1/4 cups thinly sliced fennel bulb (remove core and slice paper-thin; reserve fronds)

1 1/2 cups peeled and grated beets (use large holes of grater)

2 cups thinly chopped Fuji apple

1/2 cup thinly sliced sweet yellow onion

3 tablespoons lemon juice

1-inch ginger roots, peeled and grated with microplane

1 tablespoon balsamic vinegar

1 teaspoon extra-virgin olive oil

1/2 teaspoon sea salt

Freshly ground pepper

2 teaspoons orange zest (avoid white pith)

2 tablespoons orange juice

1–2 tablespoons chopped fennel fronds

1/3 cup dried cranberries or raisins (raisins are sweeter with more calories)

1/3 cup or more coarsely chopped raw pecans

---

**Serves 4**

Calories per serving: 192
Total fat: 8g
Saturated fat: 1g
Calories from fat: 69
Protein: 3g
Carbohydrates: 31g
Dietary fiber: 6g
Sugars: 19g

*An October harvest includes fennel, beets, and apples, which are combined raw to deliver a trio of freshness in a vibrantly colored salad imbued with contrasting and complementary flavors that will definitely wake up your palate. However, raw beets are a different culinary experience compared to cooked—they hold a fresh, sweet, crunchy, earthy flavor and retain all of their nutrients and antioxidants. Good-tasting tender beets are essential for raw salads. Therefore, pick firm small to medium-size beets with vibrant green tops.*

*Caution! Prior to cutting raw beets, roll up your sleeves, don an apron, and either put a pair of clean disposable gloves on or sport a pair of red hands for the remainder of the day. No gloves? Soaking hands in Polident evidently will remove the red, but no one in our house wears dentures! So, stay natural and try rubbing your stained hands with lemon juice or white vinegar, then rinse and dry.*

*Note: Save leftover fennel fronds—chop and use them on fish as you would dill fronds, or toss them in salads.*

▼ ▼ ▼

It's important that all the ingredients are thinly sliced or grated to absorb flavors. Toss the first 12 ingredients together (fennel bulb through orange juice), reserving the fronds, cranberries, and pecans; marinate, covered, for 4–24 hours. The longer it marinates, the better it tastes. When you are ready to serve the salad, toss in the fronds, cranberries, and pecans, adjust seasonings to your taste, and serve.

## Quinoa–Beet Salad

1/3 cup finely chopped sweet yellow onion

1 1/2 cups finely chopped unpeeled and seeded cucumber

1/4 cup lemon juice, divided

4–6 small beets, unpeeled and taproot intact, scrubbed (save beet leaves)

1 3/4 cups water for cooking beets, also for cooking quinoa

1/2 teaspoon sea salt

1 cup whole-grain quinoa

1–2 tablespoons extra-virgin olive oil

1 teaspoon oregano, crushed to release flavor

1/4 cup finely cut fresh dill fronds

2 tablespoons mandarin orange zest (use citrus zester for pith-free fine strips)

1 cup mandarin sections, seeded and cut in half or whole skinless orange sections, chopped

1/3 cup minced mix of lemon thyme, chocolate mint, and/or plain mint

1 tablespoon finely grated fresh ginger, optional

Sea salt

Freshly ground pepper

**Tossed Beet Leaves**

Reserved tender beet leaves

Splash of balsamic vinegar

1 teaspoon extra-virgin olive oil

Sea salt

Freshly ground pepper

1 tablespoon of cider vinegar, optional

---

### Serves 4–6

Calories per serving: 233
Total fat: 6g
Saturated fat: 1g
Calories from fat: 57
Protein: 7g
Carbohydrates: 39g
Dietary fiber: 6g
Sugars: 12g

*Edible Christmas Wreath variation shown.*

*Cooking beets brings out their sweetness, gives them a soft, buttery texture, and readies them to absorb other flavors—perfect for this light and refreshing grain salad. However, when beets are cooked in water, nutrients and antioxidants bleed out. Therefore, I reserve the beet broth and cook the quinoa in it, capturing most of the nutrients in the quinoa. It can be served solo or over fresh, tender beet leaves with a little dressing.*

*Since it is a vibrant red salad with specks of green, my friend Linda Luft turned it into a beautiful edible wreath, a festive accent on her Christmas dinner table—see Linda's Christmas Wreath below.*

▼ ▼ ▼

In a small bowl, begin marinating the onion and cucumber in 3 tablespoons of the lemon juice to tame the onion and neutralize any bitterness of the cucumber.

Place the beets, water, and salt in a 2-quart saucepan over high heat and bring to a boil; reduce heat to simmer, cover, and cook for about 30 minutes or until the blade of a paring knife slides easily through a beet. Fit a colander over a bowl and drain beet broth into bowl. Measure 1½ cups of broth (adding water if necessary) and return to saucepan. Place beets in bowl and set aside to cool.

Using an ultra-fine double-mesh strainer, rinse the quinoa thoroughly with cold water, then transfer the quinoa to the beet broth. Bring to a boil, then reduce to low heat, cover, and cook for about 15 minutes or until the water is completely absorbed. If using an electric stove, boil for a couple minutes, then save some energy by turning off the burner and covering the pan; it will be done in about 30 minutes.

After the quinoa is done, remove the pan from the burner, add the beets, and fluff the quinoa and beets with a fork. Transfer to an appropriate size bowl, add olive oil, toss, and allow for cooling. Then, add the remaining ingredients, including the marinated onion and cucumber, and their marinade. Adjust seasonings if needed by adding more olive oil, lemon, salt, and pepper to taste. If you want a little more zip, add 1 tablespoon cider vinegar. Refrigerate for 2 or more hours to release and bring together the tasty complex flavors. Serve over a bed of fresh beet leaves tossed in a little balsamic vinegar, olive oil, salt, and pepper.

**Variation: Linda Luft's Edible Christmas Wreath** Eliminate cucumber (not in season), add 1 cup finely chopped fresh cilantro, seeds from ½–1 pomegranate for garnish, and olive oil spray. Reserve beet leaves for bow (if none, use other green leaves from kale, chard, etc.) Prepare salad according to Quinoa Beet Salad directions while eliminating the cucumbers and tossing in the cilantro. Spray 5-cup ring mold with olive oil. Tightly pack the salad into the mold, then set it in the refrigerator for 2 hours. (If you are in a rush, place in the freezer for 20 minutes.) Release the wreath from the mold onto an attractive platter. Arrange beet leaves on the wreath creating a bow-like accent. Place a cluster of pomegranate seeds in the middle of the bow to resemble a knot. Scatter the remaining pomegranate seeds over the wreath and onto the platter.

## Roasted Yams with Beets

4–5 medium-size beets with tap root and short stem intact (save leaves)

2 tablespoons extra-virgin olive oil

4 large unpeeled garnet yams, sliced into $1/4$-inch circles, then halved

$2/3$ cup finely chopped onion

$1/2$ garlic bulb, peeled and minced

3 Medjool dates, finely chopped

$1/4$–$1/3$ cup lime juice

2 teaspoons Dijon mustard

1 teaspoon minced chipotle chile in adobo sauce, canned or recipe on page 50 (optional)

2 teaspoons finely grated ginger (grate with microplane)

2 teaspoons fresh orange zest

Sea salt

Freshly ground pepper

$1/3$ cup finely chopped onion

1 tablespoon minced rosemary

$1/3$ cup minced fresh cilantro or flat leaf parsley

Reserved beet leaves mixed with spinach to make 4 handfuls

$1/4$ cup crumbled goat feta cheese

$1/2$ cup pomegranate seed or 1 cup seeded and quartered orange slices or both

### Serves 4–6

Calories per serving: 317
Total fat: 8g
Saturated fat: 2g
Calories from fat: 70
Protein: 6g
Carbohydrates: 58g
Dietary fiber: 10g
Sugars: 16g

*Often the best tasting and most interesting recipes come about by accident. Such was the case for this vibrantly colored fall harvest dish I took to Uncle Burr and Auntie Alice's home for Thanksgiving dinner. Since I had forgotten to buy the usual dozen sweet potatoes to bake, I started scrambling through the fridge, pantry, vegetable bins, and garden, tossing together a little of this and that to come up with a dish. It was a hit. The caramelized sweet potatoes and beets brought about complex flavors that complemented the tangy bite of the beet greens and creaminess of the feta.*

*Note: Beet greens and spinach are a good source of iron, but by itself it is not readily absorbed by the body. The vitamin C in pomegranate seeds or orange slices makes the iron available to the body.*

▼ ▼ ▼

Preheat the oven to 375 degrees F. Rub the beets with oil, place them in covered casserole dish, and roast in the oven 45–60 minutes or until a paring knife slides easily through a piece of beet. If the beets are uneven in size, remove smaller pieces as they are done, to avoid shriveling. While the beets are roasting, toss the yams in oil and arrange them in a single layer on a baking sheet or large roasting pan. Roast the yams in the oven with the beets for about 30 minutes or until lightly browned and easily penetrated with a paring knife. After 20 minutes of roasting, spread the $2/3$ cup of chopped onion and the garlic over the yams.

While the vegetables are roasting, prepare the dressing: mash the dates with a fork and blend them with the lime juice until you get a smooth consistency. Mix in the Dijon mustard, chipotle, ginger, zest, and salt and pepper to taste; then pour the date dressing mixture over the $1/3$ cup of chopped onion and toss, set aside.

Mix yams with rosemary, cilantro, and beet greens and spinach; toss. Allow the beets to cool enough to handle, then peel and coarsely chop them. Add the dressing and beets to the yam mixture and gently toss (greens will wilt somewhat). Sprinkle with feta and pomegranate seeds, and serve warm or at room temperature.

## Chipotle Sweet Potato Fries

3–4 unpeeled garnet yams, sliced ¼-inch thick, then cut ¼-inch wide

1–2 tablespoons extra-virgin olive oil

1 teaspoon Chipotle-Lime Rub (page 51)
or mix
1 teaspoon salt,
½ teaspoon garlic power,
¼ teaspoon chile powder,
¼ teaspoon smoky paprika

Extra-virgin olive oil

---

### Serves 4–5

Calories per serving: 189
Total fat: 6g
Saturated fat: 1g
Calories from fat: 49
Protein: 2g
Carbohydrates: 33g
Dietary fiber: 5g
Sugars: 1g

*The earthy, smoky chipotle is one of the more distinctive flavors of the southwest. For sure, it adds spark to these sweet potato fries. If spicy is not your forte, skip the chile. With these fries (maybe without chile), you will never have to coax kids to eat their sweet potatoes!*

▼ ▼ ▼

Preheat the oven to 475 degrees F.

The ends of the fries should be blunt, since pointy ends will burn. In a large bowl, toss the yam strips in olive oil to coat, sprinkle with the chipotle rub (or the salt, garlic powder, chile powder, and paprika), and toss again. Line 2 baking sheets with unbleached parchment paper or spray with oil. Without crowding, lay the yam strips on the sheets. Bake for 20–25 minutes. After 10–12 minutes, turn each yam strip and continue roasting until they are tender and toasty brown. Serve warm.

**Variation: Gringo Sweet Potato Fries** Eliminate seasonings except for salt; and after roasting, sprinkle with freshly ground pepper.

**Variation: Rosemary Sweet Potato Fries** Eliminate seasonings except for salt. Immediately upon removing from oven, sprinkle with freshly minced rosemary.

## Sweet Potatoes

Sweet potatoes are a crop of the Americas and were taken to China and Japan where they became a food of sustenance. After World War II, the purple sweet potato made up the majority of the Okinawan diet and is believed to be one of the longevity foods of the Okinawa centenarians. Deep orange flesh and purple flesh sweet potatoes are high in phytonutrient compounds, fiber, and vitamin C. Deep orange sweet potatoes (skin and flesh) are abundant in bioavailable beta-carotene (converts to vitamin A). The purple are high in anthocyanin, a flavonoid compound which produces the deep purple color, such as it does in blueberries. Both also promote healthy blood sugar levels, and may guard against cancer, heart disease, and the effects of aging. Unfortunately, in the US today, purple sweet potatoes are a pricy gourmet food. So, reach for the deep orange garnet yams (sweet potato) for a real super healthy food. Or plant the purple variety and enjoy when blueberries are out of season.

## Squash Stuffed with Fresh Cranberry Salsa

1 hybrid hubbard, acorn, or carnival squash, or 4 mini dumpling squash (3–4-inch diameter)

1 teaspoon oregano, crushed to release flavor (toast if time permits)

Saigon cinnamon

Sea salt

Freshly ground pepper

Extra-virgin olive oil spray

5–10 pitted dates

Zest and juice from 1 orange (about ¾ cup juice)

½–1 whole chipotle chile, seeded and coarsely chopped, or 1 jalapeño or serrano chile, seeded and minced

1 teaspoon grated ginger (use microplane)

12 ounces fresh cranberries

1 unpeeled Fuji or other crisp sweet apple, cored, cut in quarters or eights and then in thirds

1 garlic clove, cut in thirds

1 tablespoon chopped yellow onions

⅓ cup coarsely cut cilantro (include some stems)

Chopped fresh mint, for garnish

Chopped pecans, for garnish

---

**Serves 4**

Calories per serving: 192
Total fat: 4g
Saturated fat: 0g
Calories from fat: 35
Protein: 2g
Carbohydrates: 42g
Dietary fiber: 8g
Sugars: 19g

*Since garden-ripe tomatoes are unavailable for fresh salsa during the holidays, why not fresh cranberry salsa? Cranberries may not be local, but they are an American tradition for the holidays, and according to the Cranberry Growers' Association, they are one of the few fruits native to North America. All the ingredients, with the exception of chipotle, are raw. Why reduce the healthy elements of the cranberry by cooking them and adding lots of empty sugar calories? Go raw and sweeten with other fruit! Cranberries are high in antioxidant phenols, and research has indicted that they may prevent heart disease and some cancers. They also have properties that inhibit bacteria growth, which may prevent urinary tract infections and tooth decay. If you can find the organic, buy it. Little sweet dumpling squash are cute, colorful, tasty, and make the perfect container for individual servings of fresh cranberry salsa; and hybrid hubbard, carnival, or acorn squash makes an attractive serving bowl.*

*The number of dates you decide to use in this recipe will depend on how sweet you want it.*

▼ ▼ ▼

Preheat the oven to 350 degrees F. Cut out a lid or cap from the squash, just as you would for a jack-o-lantern. Remove the seeds and stringy pulp and discard (or seeds may be saved for roasting). Sprinkle the squash meat with oregano, generously dust it with cinnamon, salt sparingly, add a few grinds of pepper, and then generously spray with olive oil.

Place the squash in a baking pan: Place the cap on the squash (covering keeps the flesh moist and holds in the flavors) and bake in the oven for 35–60 minutes (depending on the size of the squash) or until the flesh can be easily scraped from the skin.

Meanwhile, make the cranberry salsa. With a fork, mash the dates with a little bit of orange juice until a thin purée forms. In a food processor, pulse a few times the orange zest, chipotle chile, ginger, cranberries, apple, garlic, onion, and date purée until the cranberries are coarsely chopped. Taste for sweetness. If needed, make more date-orange purée and add it; if not, add the remaining orange juice, toss in the cilantro, and pulse a couple times to mince the cilantro and combine it with the other ingredients.

Remove the squash from the oven. Use the squash or smaller squashes as the serving bowls, filling them with the cranberry salsa, and dress with the mint and pecans for garnish.

## Desert Treasures Citrus and Date Groves

During citrus season, Chris Duggan can be spotted on Sunday mornings at St. Philips Plaza farmers' market offering samples of different varieties of oranges, mandarins, grapefruit, and other citrus. One taste and you are hooked on the juicy sweet flavors of grove-fresh citrus. Since citrus doesn't ripen off the tree, each variety is picked at its peak of ripeness and it travels just six miles from Peter Larsen's (Chris' father-in-law) Desert Treasures Citrus and Date Groves. Chris also sets up at the Oro Valley Farmer's market from January through March and Pete sells to the Food Conspiracy and New Life Health Center stores in Tucson.

Realizing that the "thermal belt" in northwest Tucson was an ideal microclimate conducive to growing citrus in the Tucson desert, a number of citrus groves were planted during the late 1920s and 1930s by realtor Maurice Reid and Rev. George Ferguson, the rector at St. Philips in the Hills back then. Peter Larsen's grove, covering 8 acres, was part of Ferguson's 25-acre grove, which was subdivided in the 60s. It is also the only commercial grove still standing and continues to produce some of the best tasting citrus in the world. Desert Treasures citrus is also grown without chemical pesticides and fertilizers.

Chris makes more appearances at the St. Philips' market in September and October just after harvesting fresh pesticide-free black Hayani and golden-caramel Halawi dates. He uses a lift to reach and hand-pick these luscious dates from 25–35 foot trees and his customers thank him for his efforts in delivering these soft, fresh, melt-in-your-mouth dates. They are not only full of flavor but hold a good dose of vitamin C, which diminishes as dates are dried. He recommends storing fresh dates in a box or paper bag in the refrigerator to avoid spoilage and allow moisture to escape enabling slow drying. He commented, "Fresh dates are probably best within a few months, but can last longer, up to 6 months. They can blow their sugar if the temp varies (sugar melts out, and then crystallizes)." I often use them instead of sugar—especially

the extremely flavorful, ultra sweet Halawi—to add lovely flavor and sweetness to baked goods, oatmeal, and drinks. For a sweet treat or a hors d'oeuvre replace the seed with an almond or stuff with humus. Unlike table sugar, they provide health-promoting fiber, antioxidant flavonoids, vitamins and minerals.

Oh, I have also bought perfectly seasoned salt-brine-cured black olives and water-cured ripe Kalamatas that Chris' wife Tara prepared. All the wonderful local flavors Chris brings to market are indeed desert treasures!

## Spicy Roasted Winter Squash

1 large turban, kabocha, 7-inch hybrid hubbard, or carnival squash

1 teaspoon oregano, crushed to release flavor (toast if time permits)

Saigon cinnamon

Sea salt

Freshly ground pepper

Extra-virgin olive oil spray

¼ cup finely chopped sweet yellow onion

4 garlic cloves, minced or run through garlic press, divided

1 chipotle chile in adobo sauce, seeded and minced

Zest from 1–2 oranges

1 tablespoon freshly grated ginger root

1 tablespoon or more of fresh minced rosemary

2–4 tablespoons orange juice, blended with 1–3 fresh dates, chopped and mashed with fork (optional)

1 tablespoon fresh minced cilantro

Pomegranate seeds for garnish

---

**Serves 4–6**

Calories per serving: 74
Total fat: 1g
Saturated fat: 0g
Calories from fat: 11
Protein: 1g
Carbohydrates: 16g
Dietary fiber: 2g
Sugars: 5g

*Pretty much any type of winter squash can be used for this sweet and savory delight. Since squashes differ in size and the varieties come in differing sweetness, the ingredients are rough estimates. Tasting is your best determinant for ingredient amounts—and it's easy in this recipe since most ingredients are added after baking the squash. These raw ingredients also retain powerful healthy nutrients. This preparation is a favorite for Thanksgiving or Christmas, because it doubles as a dish and table decoration. The colorful collection of squash is presented on a large stainless steel platter and accented with a scattering of glistening pomegranate seeds. The colors and shapes are magnificent—especially the turban squash, with its colorful knotted crown, and the deeply pleated round carnival squash, speckled with festive fall colors. If you can find the large heirloom hubbard squash, it also makes a nice tabletop appointment and will serve a large number of people—it takes much longer to cook and you may need a meat cleaver to crack open its hard shell! Freeze any leftover squash for later use.*

*Note: The kabocha is sweeter than the other squash and may not need sweetening. This recipe is for one squash, so if you want to make a few different varieties, repeat the ingredients for each additional squash prepared. Since hybrid hubbard and carnival are smaller, taste carefully to determine the amount of ingredients you want to use.*

▼ ▼ ▼

Preheat the oven to 350 degrees F. Cut the hubbard squash vertically down the middle, or cut out a lid or cap if you are using turban, kabocha, or carnival squash, just as you would for a jack-o-lantern. Remove the seeds and stringy pulp and discard (or seeds may be saved for roasting). Sprinkle the squash meat with oregano, generously dust it with cinnamon, salt sparingly, add a few grinds of pepper, and then generously spray with olive oil. Place 1 tablespoon of onion, ⅓ of the chopped garlic, and the chipotle in the squash cavity.

Place the squash in a baking pan: Hubbard squash should be placed cut-side-up and covered with a sheet of parchment paper. Place the cap on the turban, kabocha, or carnival squash (covering keeps the flesh moist and holds in the flavors) and bake in the oven for 35–60 minutes (depending on the size of the squash) or until the flesh can be easily scraped from the skin.

Remove from the oven; add the reserved onions and garlic, and the zest, ginger, and rosemary to the squash cavity. Without damaging the skin, scrape the squash pulp from the sides and mix it with the other ingredients. Taste and adjust the seasonings if needed. If more sweetness is desired, add the blended orange juice and dates. Use the squash itself as the serving bowl. (The hubbard squash won't have as much pulp; so put all the pulp in one of the halves and use the other half as a container for either rice or beans.) Sprinkle the squash meat with cilantro and top off with a scattering of pomegranate seeds.

Variation: **Stuffed Winter Squash** Don't scrape the sides of the squash. Stuff hybrid hubbard or carnival squash with a rice or quinoa pilaf, a mix of Seasoned Black Beans (page 156) and Forbidden Rice (page 158), or Sweet Bitter Greens (page 134).

## Winter Squash

One of the welcoming signs of fall is the glorious colors of winter squash appearing in the farmers' markets; and by Halloween there is an interesting and gorgeous collection. Many are of heritage varieties sporting funky shapes that look like they came from fairytale land. I couldn't resist a magnificent 12-pound white heritage Cinderella squash from Sleeping Frog Farms, which soon transformed into a magical looking jack-o-lantern. After Halloween, it was roasted, and some of the sweet, deep-orange meat was used for soup. The rest was frozen and later turned into Thanksgiving pumpkin pies, tamales, pasta sauce, muffins, and other delights. A far tastier and cheaper option than commercially canned! Aside from being delicious, squashes are abundant in vitamin A, provide a good source of vitamin C, contain some B vitamins, and provide iron, calcium, and other minerals, along with a lot of fiber. Squash with deeply colored meat carries the most beta-carotene, a powerful antioxidant that may protect against heart disease and some cancers. With their tough rinds (after curing at room temperature for about 10 days) many winter squash can be stored for two or three months in a cool dark place with little humidity. The heritage hubbard squash will last for five or six months.

## Roasted Roots

2 carrots, sliced about 1-inch thick

2 parsnips, sliced about 1-inch thick

6 small sweet young turnips (1½-inch diameter), cut in half

1 rutabaga, sliced about 1-inch thick, cut in quarters

1 medium potato, sliced about 1-inch thick, cut into quarters

16 Brussels sprouts, trimmed

3–4 tablespoons extra-virgin olive oil

1 tablespoon oregano, crushed to release flavor

2 teaspoons dry basil, crushed to release flavor

1 teaspoon fine sea salt

Freshly ground pepper

1 medium onion, coarsely chopped

4 garlic cloves, minced or run through garlic press

2 tablespoons coarsely chopped fresh rosemary

½ cup coarsely chopped cilantro

2 tablespoons fresh thyme or lemon thyme

½–1 minced chipotle in adobo sauce (canned or recipe on page 50)

¼ cup Key lime juice

### Serves 4

Calories per serving: 355
Total fat: 15g
Saturated fat: 2g
Calories from fat: 128
Protein: 8g
Carbohydrates: 54g
Dietary fiber: 13g
Sugars: 20g

*As colder weather sets in, most vegetables are out of season in many parts of the country and are transported from afar, which makes root vegetables an excellent local option for winter. For a beautiful, tasty dish, place a fillet of deeply colored wild Alaskan baked salmon, accented with specks of dill, over this colorful confetti bed of blended roasted roots, Brussels sprouts, and fresh herbs. Another option is to not blend the roots, but to toss the cooked vegetables with all the other ingredients together and serve.*

*Note: the carrots, parsnips, rutabaga, turnips, and potatoes should be scrubbed, not peeled.*

▼ ▼ ▼

Preheat the oven to 375 degrees F.

Toss the carrots, parsnips, turnips, rutabaga, potato, and Brussels sprouts in the oil, oregano, basil, salt, and pepper until coated. Spread the vegetables over a large roasting pan or a couple of baking sheets. Bake about 45 minutes. Remove the vegetables as they are done, to avoid shriveling of those that take less time. Turn the vegetables a couple times during roasting. When all the vegetables are done, thoroughly mix in the onion and garlic and roast for another 5 minutes. Remove from the oven, toss with rosemary, cilantro, and thyme. Cool slightly. In 2 or 3 batches, transfer this mixture to a food processor work bowl. Add chipotle, a little adobo sauce, oil, and lime juice, dividing them between batches. Pulse each batch a few times to render a rough consistency. Mix batches together and serve as a bed for fish or meat.

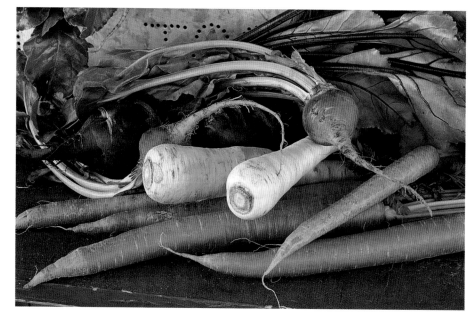

## Broccolini Quinoa Salad

**Dressing**

3 tablespoons lemon juice

1 tablespoon red wine vinegar

1 tablespoon coarsely ground mustard

½ teaspoon ground cumin

⅓ cup finely chopped red onion

1 garlic clove, run through garlic press

**Salad**

1 cup whole-grain quinoa, any color

1½ cups cold water

2 teaspoons Mexican oregano, crushed to release flavor

½ teaspoon sea salt

1 tablespoon extra-virgin olive oil

1 bunch broccolini or baby broccoli

2 Roma tomatoes, chopped
(for off season, see variation below)

¾ cup chopped fresh basil or lemon basil

1 tablespoon fresh lemon zest, (use citrus zester for pith-free fine strips or microplane for grated pieces)

1 teaspoon chipotle or New Mexico red chile powder, optional

1 chopped Haas avocado

Splash of lemon juice

¼ cup pine nuts

---

**Serves 4**

Calories per serving: 274
Total fat: 12g
Saturated fat: 2g
Calories from fat: 102
Protein: 8g
Carbohydrates: 36g
Dietary fiber: 6g
Sugars: 3g

*Rather than buying broccoli florets or whole broccoli and discarding the thick stems, try broccolini or baby broccoli. It has thin, tender stems and a sweet, delicate broccoli flavor, making it perfect for a salad. Little cooking is required and, to boot, it is high in vitamins and minerals, especially vitamin C and potassium. Even those who shy away from broccoli enjoy broccolini—give it a try with children.*

▼ ▼ ▼

Prepare the dressing by combining the lemon juice, vinegar, mustard, cumin, onion, and garlic; set aside.

In an ultra-fine double-mesh strainer, rinse the quinoa thoroughly with cold water; then transfer to a 1-quart pot and add the water, oregano, and salt; stir to mix. Bring to a boil, then reduce to low heat, cover, and cook for about 15 minutes or until the water is completely absorbed. If using an electric stove, save some energy by boiling for 3 minutes, then turning off the burner, covering the pot, and letting it sit for 30 minutes.

While the quinoa is cooking, steam the broccolini for about 3 minutes or until it is bright green and crunchy tender. Remove it from the pot and dunk it in ice water to stop the cooking.

Transfer the cooked quinoa to an appropriate size bowl, add the olive oil, and toss with fork to fluff. (Allow it to cool prior to adding the next ingredients.)

Cut the broccolini into bite-size pieces and toss them with the dressing; then if the quinoa has cooled sufficiently, add the dressed broccolini to the quinoa, along with the tomatoes, basil, zest, and chipotle or red chile powder, and toss to combine. When ready to serve, top the dish with the avocado pieces, splash the avocado with lemon juice, and sprinkle on the pine nuts. Serve cold or at room temperature.

**Variation**   If tomatoes are not in season, replace them with 1½ cups finely sliced steamed carrot slices. Or use 12 sun-dried tomatoes as follows: Rehydrate the tomatoes in hot water, drain, and finely chop them. To better absorb the flavors, add the rehydrated tomatoes to the dressing with 1 tablespoon of olive oil, and then set aside while preparing the quinoa and broccolini.

## Southwest Coleslaw

½ head of red cabbage, shredded

¾–1 cup thin matchstick slices of jicama

2 teaspoons lime zest

3 tablespoons Key lime juice

1 tablespoon cider vinegar (optional)

½ cup finely chopped cilantro (include some stems)

⅓ cup minced onion

1 garlic clove, run through garlic press

2 tablespoons chopped fresh oregano leaves

½–1 serrano chile, seeded and minced

Evaporated cane juice

Sea salt

½ avocado, finely chopped (optional)

Couple grinds of peppercorns

**Serves 4**

Calories per serving: 99
Total fat: 3g
Saturated fat: 0g
Calories from fat: 24
Protein: 3g
Carbohydrates: 18g
Dietary fiber: 6g
Sugars: 8g

*Cabbage offers a refreshing alternative to a tossed salad. During cabbage season, my mother used to fix coleslaw or braised cabbage practically every day, and we made sauerkraut for eating throughout the year. Cabbage is incredibly healthy; but red cabbage has more anti-oxidants than the green. The antioxidants are also increased considerably when the cabbage is cooked. However, vitamin C diminishes when cooked. Serve it cooked and raw, and all health-promoting aspects will be covered.*

▼ ▼ ▼

Toss all ingredients together and serve.

## Grilled Cauliflower Steaks

1 head cauliflower (white, purple, green, or orange)

2–3 tablespoons Key lime juice

1 tablespoon extra-virgin olive oil (oil pump suggested)

2 teaspoons oregano, crushed to release flavor

½–1 teaspoon garlic powder

Sea salt

Freshly ground black pepper

1 tablespoon of any chopped seasonal herbs, optional

---

**Serves 4**

Calories per serving: 68
Total fat: 4g
Saturated fat: 0g
Calories from fat: 31
Protein: 3g
Carbohydrates: 8g
Dietary fiber: 4g
Sugars: 4g

*Whether grilled or roasted, "quick, colorful, and deliciously healthy" describe painted scalloped-edged cauliflower steaks. They are perfect for a weeknight dinner or make a crowd-pleasing party tray by combining purple, orange, and green cauliflower and doubling or tripling the recipe. Blackening or browning a bit develops sweet, uniquely satisfying flavors and deepens the color, which is not achieved by steaming. Don't fear! Colored cauliflower is not a GMO crop. It couldn't be labeled organic if it were. The colored varieties are natural mutants of white cauliflower.*

*Flavonoids color the edges, which are beneficial compounds holding potent antioxidants that may prevent cellular damage by combating free radicals. As an added boost, combining different varieties of cauliflower increases their disease-fighting power!*

▼ ▼ ▼

If you plan to roast the cauliflower in the oven instead of grilling, preheat the oven to 425 degrees F. Slice the cauliflower from top to bottom through the core, yielding 2–3½-inch "steaks" held together by the core. Cut the remaining small-stemmed florets in half to make small steaks. Place the small leftover pieces in an appropriate size casserole dish for roasting or on a perforated grilling pan. On both sides of the cauliflower steaks and leftover pieces, splash the lime juice, spray or brush with olive oil, and sprinkle with oregano, garlic powder, salt, and pepper. Grill over a hot grill, or roast in the oven, for about 15 minutes or until crunchy-tender and browned in spots or branded with grill marks. Turn a couple times during cooking. Arrange attractively on a platter, sprinkle with the chopped herbs, and serve warm.

Variation: **Grilled Chipotle Cauliflower Steaks** Lightly sprinkle Chipotle-Lime Rub (page 51), chipotle powder, or red chile powder over the cauliflower "steaks" prior to grilling or roasting.

## Roasted Brussels Sprouts

24 Brussels sprouts

2–3 tablespoons Key lime juice

1–2 tablespoons extra-virgin olive oil

Sea salt

Freshly ground pepper

**Serves 4**

Calories per serving: 96
Total fat: 5g
Saturated fat: 1g
Calories from fat: 48
Protein: 4g
Carbohydrates: 11g
Dietary fiber: 4g
Sugars: 3g

*There's been many a nose turned up at Brussels sprouts. Not anymore. Roasting or grilling these miniature-looking cabbages to crispy-tender and golden brown in color will coax the Brussels sprouts haters to give them a try—and don't be surprised if they ask for seconds. Not only are these Brussels sprouts tasty, they are quick to fix and are loaded with extremely healthy phytonutrients that may provide protection against cancer and promote a healthy cardiovascular system.*

▼ ▼ ▼

If you will be oven-roasting, preheat the oven to 425 degrees F. Wash and thoroughly dry the sprouts. Make a fresh cut at the stem of each sprout and remove any discolored leaves; then cut the sprouts in half. Douse both sides of each sprout with lime juice, spray with olive oil, and sprinkle lightly with salt and liberally with pepper. Grill on medium-high or roast in the preheated oven until browned and crispy-tender, turning a couple times turning cooking. Serve warm.

**Variation: Parmesan Red Chile Brussels Sprouts** Prior to roasting, sprinkle the Brussels sprouts with 1–2 tablespoons of Parmesan cheese (to use less cheese, grate using a microplane for a fine, fluffy grate) and a little ground mild New Mexico red chile powder. Hard cheeses such as Parmesan, Asiago, and Gouda contain vitamin K2, which, according to Dr. William Li, is anti-cancer and protects arteries from hardening.

## Steamed Baby Bok Choy

2 baby bok choy, halved

Soy sauce

Ultra-thin threads of fresh ginger

**Serves 4**

Calories per serving: 8
Total fat: 0g
Saturated fat: 0g
Calories from fat: 0
Protein: 1g
Carbohydrates: 1g
Dietary fiber: 1g
Sugars: 1g

*Baby bok choy has a very mild flavor, opening itself up to easily take on seasonings. I always steam the baby bok choy whole or halved until the leaves are wilted and there is a little bit of crunch to the stalks, assuring that a good bit of the nutrients aren't lost. Bok choy is one of the anti-angiogenic foods that Dr. William Li recommends to be eaten often to prevent cancer.*

*This bok choy would be excellent to serve with fish and pilaf.*

▼ ▼ ▼

Place the bok choy in a steamer and cook until the stems are crunchy-tender.

Remove from heat and serve on plates, splashed with soy sauce and sprinkled with ginger threads.

*Roasted Brussels Sprouts shown with Grilled Cauliflower Steaks (recipe on page 149) and grilled sweet potatoes (follow same procedure as cauliflower).*

## Warm Fennel Salad

1 tablespoon extra-virgin olive oil

4 Jimmy Nardello peppers or 1 red bell pepper, seeded, thinly sliced

1/4 cup seeded and finely chopped poblano chile

1 medium red onion, halved and sliced

2 garlic cloves, minced

1 teaspoon oregano, crushed to release flavor

2–4 fennel bulbs, halved lengthwise, cored, sliced 1/4-inch thick to yield 4 cups

1/4 cup chopped fennel fronds

1/2 cup minced cilantro, loosely packed

2 tablespoons fresh thyme leaves
or a mix of

1/3 cup minced herbs from garden, such as thyme, rosemary, and oregano

1/2–1 red or green jalapeño chile, seeded and minced

1–2 tablespoons balsamic vinegar

1–2 pinches fine sea salt

Freshly ground pepper

---

**Serves 4**

Calories per serving: 103
Total fat: 4g
Saturated fat: 0g
Calories from fat: 33
Protein: 2g
Carbohydrates: 17g
Dietary fiber: 4g
Sugars: 7g

*This fennel salad complements the flavors of pork and chicken; but my favorite is to use it as a bed for salmon. The contrasting color of the deep orange salmon against a bed of lightly colored fennel is enticing and its mild anise flavor and sweetness harmonized nicely with fish.*

*Note: Simply spray fish with olive oil, splash with lime juice, sprinkle with salt and pepper, and bake at 350 degrees F for 12 minutes for every inch of fish. Pull out of the oven and sprinkle with fennel fronds; then lay on top of Warm Fennel Salad.*

▼ ▼ ▼

In the olive oil, sauté Jimmy Nardellos or red bell pepper, poblano chile, half of the onion, half the garlic, and the oregano in olive oil for a few minutes; then add the sliced fennel, sautéing until crispy but tender. Remove from heat; add the reserved onion and garlic, fennel fronds, cilantro, minced herbs, jalapeño chile, and vinegar, and then toss. Taste, and if needed, season with salt, pepper, and maybe more vinegar and herbs.

## Basil–Lime Quinoa with Squash Blossoms and Black Beans

10 squash blossoms

1 teaspoon extra-virgin olive oil

½ cup medium-chopped sweet yellow onion,

1 garlic clove, run through garlic press

1–2 Jimmy Nardello peppers, thinly sliced, or ¼ cup chopped red bell pepper

1 tablespoon oregano

1 tomato, chopped

1 cup quinoa

1½ cups vegetable broth or chicken broth

½ teaspoon sea salt

1 cup black beans or black tepary beans, rinsed and drained

2 fire-roasted, seeded, peeled, and chopped green chiles (see Fire-Roasting, page 15)

1 cup chiffonade-cut basil

2 tablespoons Key lime juice

Zest from 1 lime

1 teaspoon extra-virgin olive oil

½ avocado, chopped

Lime wedges

**Serves 4–5**

Calories per serving: 294
Total fat: 8g
Saturated fat: 1g
Calories from fat: 69
Protein: 11g
Carbohydrates: 46g
Dietary fiber: 9g
Sugars: 5g

*Squash blossoms add beauty and interest to dishes but are pretty much exclusive to gardeners and farmers' markets. Being extremely perishable, they need to be prepared straight from the garden or almost immediately upon returning home from the farmers' market. They are a good source of calcium, iron, and vitamins A and C. Choose the slender-stemmed male blossoms instead of the females, which have a small bulb at their base.*

▼ ▼ ▼

Remove the stamen inside each blossom and rid them of any ants or such. Rinse the blossoms by gently spraying with water or gently dipping them in water a few times, then shake off water and lay them on clean towel. The water will usually bead off of them.

In a 2-quart saucepan with 1 teaspoon of olive oil, sauté the onion, garlic, squash blossoms, Jimmy Nardello or red bell peppers, and oregano over medium-high heat until the onions are crispy but tender. Add the tomato and sauté for about 2 minutes. Using an ultra-thin strainer, thoroughly rinse the quinoa under cold water; then turn the quinoa into the saucepan, add the broth and salt, and mix thoroughly. Bring to a boil; then reduce heat to low, add the beans, cover, and simmer for about 12 minutes. To save energy, after a couple minutes, turn off the heat. It will continue to cook and will be done in about 30 minutes. Toss with a fork to fluff, add the chopped green chiles, basil, lime juice, zest, and olive oil, then toss again. Top with avocado and splash with lime; serve warm.

### Quinoa

Although quinoa is referred to as a grain, it is not. It's a gluten-free seed that contains more protein than any of the grains and it has all 9 essential amino acids which makes it a complete protein. It also contains phytonutrients, fiber, minerals, and vitamins. These may be the reasons why it was a crop of sustenance for the Incas. It's available in cream, black, purple, and red colors. Quinoa should be rinsed prior to cooking to remove a bitter residue of saponins. I recommend rinsing in an ultra-fine mesh strainer. It is a great convenience food because it cooks in about 15 minutes and can be eaten alone, or turned into a salad or pilaf.

## Cilantro–Lime Quinoa Pilaf

1 cup quinoa (any color), rinsed in ultra-fine strainer

1 ½ cups sodium-free vegetable broth or chicken broth

½ teaspoon sea salt

1 teaspoon oregano, crushed to release flavor

1 cup finely chopped sweet potato or carrot

2 tablespoons finely chopped red onion

½ cup minced fresh cilantro

2 teaspoons Key lime zest

2 tablespoons Key lime juice

1 tablespoon extra-virgin olive oil

**Serves 4**

Calories per serving: 206
Total fat: 6g
Saturated fat: 1g
Calories from fat: 54
Protein: 7g
Carbohydrates: 32g
Dietary fiber: 4g
Sugars: 2g

*For a quick whole-grain pilaf that cooks in one-third the time of whole-grain rice, quinoa pilaf is the answer. It's light and airy and has soaked up a satisfying fusion of flavors and scents that will complement tofu, fish, chicken, or meat.*

▼ ▼ ▼

Combine the quinoa, broth, salt, oregano, sweet potato or carrot, and onion in a saucepan and bring to boil over high heat. Turn to low, stir in the cilantro and zest, and simmer covered for about 12 minutes or until the quinoa has absorbed the water. Fluff the quinoa with a fork and then toss with lime juice and olive oil. Serve warm.

## Stuffed Squash Blossoms

20 squash blossoms

1 cup Mexican Red Rice (page 158)

Extra-virgin olive oil spray

**Serves 4**

Calories per serving: 235
Total fat: 4g
Saturated fat: 1g
Calories from fat: 32
Protein: 5g
Carbohydrates: 46g
Dietary fiber: 3g
Sugars: 6g

*You will enjoy crunching down on crisp squash blossoms filled with tasty Mexican Red Rice. These little roasted bundles are perfect for appetizers, or in place of French fries or chips at a meal. I bought deep orange blossoms from Leo and his son at St. Philips Tucson Farmers' Market. It seems like quite an ordeal for them to bring the delicate blossoms to market; but they do. Each summer squash blossom is still attached to a small squash and individually wrapped.*

▼ ▼ ▼

Preheat the oven to 350 degrees F. Remove the stamen inside each blossom and rid them of any ants or such. Rinse the blossoms by gently spraying them with water or gently dipping them in water few times, then shake off water and lay them on a clean towel. The water will usually bead off of them. Stuff the blossoms with the prepared rice and spray generously with olive oil. Place in the oven for about 10 minutes or until crisp. Remove and serve.

# Beans and Grains

Due to gas-causing enzymes in beans, many people sidestep beans or eliminate them from their diet and miss out on their health-promoting values and great taste. Dan Buettner noted in the *Blue Zones* that beans, grains, and garden vegetables provided cornerstones to healthy centenarians' diets, which they ate pretty much on a daily basis, possibly because animal protein was scarce or too expensive. Beans are a healthy substitute for meat, not only providing protein without the cholesterol but also by providing soluble and insoluble fiber. They also bring to the table a powerhouse of nutrition (they are high in folate, potassium, iron, and magnesium) and disease-preventive compounds, making beans a healthy staple to include in your diet. Since nutrients and antioxidants vary by the type of bean, it's also wise to eat a variety of beans to get the full spectrum of benefits. I admit we usually eat black beans, but we also enjoy Christmas beans, pinto, tepary, adzuki, cannellini, Anasazi, garbanzos, green and yellow split peas, and various types of lentils.

What's astounding is that these healthy centenarians instinctively combined grains and legumes at a meal to form a complete protein. The protein in beans doesn't contain all nine essential amino acids, and neither does the protein in grains such as corn or rice; all nine essential amino acids are needed to produce a complete protein for the body to use. But put the two kinds of foods together, and all the essential amino acids are present to form complete protein. Native Americans not only ate beans and corn together, but they also planted them together, along with squash, to support each other nutritionally and physically in the garden, calling them the "three sisters."

It also must be noted that grains and beans don't have to be eaten at the same meal to form a complete protein, but they should be eaten within a 24-hour period. Also, if meat, eggs, or a dairy product is eaten during the same day as beans or grains, the protein supplied by the beans or grain becomes a complete protein, because any missing essential amino acids are present in the meat. Animal protein contains all essential amino acids.

Dry beans that you buy are never washed because it would rehydrate them, so they come packaged with "bean dust." Therefore, make sure you pick over them to remove any foreign objects such as rocks and twigs, and then thoroughly rinse them.

If you want to reduce the cooking time and reduce intestinal discomfort from gas, soak the beans for eight hours and throw away the soaking water. (Lentils, on the other hand, are quick-cooking and don't need to be soaked to speed up cooking time.) Cooking time and gas prevention aside, there may be little nutritional benefit to soaking beans. There has been conflicting evidence that phytic acid (inherent in beans) binds with minerals and causes mineral deficiencies. Soaking and discarding the water gets rid of some phytic acid. On the other hand, research has shown that phytic acid may have significant health benefits, including anti-cancer properties in the colon.

Other ways to reduce gas from beans is to cook them with epazote (an herb) or a piece of kombu (a type of seaweed or sea vegetable, which is one of Dr. Li's cancer-fighting foods). All beans are cooked in the same manner as in the black or tepary bean recipe on page 156 but require varying amounts of time.

## Seasoned Black or Tepary Beans

2 cups black or tepary beans

6–8 cups water

1 tablespoon oregano or epazote, crushed to release flavor

1–2 whole chipotle chiles, toasted

½ onion

1 bay leaf

8 garlic cloves, crushed with knife blade and chopped

1 piece of kombu

1 teaspoon sea salt

**Serves 4**

Calories per serving: 353
Total fat: 1g
Saturated fat: 0g
Calories from fat: 12
Protein: 22g
Carbohydrates: 66g
Dietary fiber: 15g
Sugars: 4g

*No-refried beans, soup, tamales, enchiladas, and more emerge from this basic black bean recipe. A couple of whole chipotle chiles give it a hint of earthiness and charge it with a mildly spicy smoky flavor. Leave the beans a little soupy for a perfect side of beans in a bowl, topped off with fresh or cooked salsa and avocado. Whether I am cooking black, tepary, or any other dried beans, I use this recipe.*

*Note: Tepary beans may take 3–8 hours to cook depending on age and dryness. I often cook them in a crock pot on high for 8 hours, using the same recipe, but adding at least 8 cups of water.*

▼ ▼ ▼

Pick through the beans to remove any tiny rocks and other foreign objects. Thoroughly rinse the beans and place all ingredients except the kombu and salt in an appropriate size pot, cover the beans with three inches of water, and set over high heat. When the beans start to boil, turn them to low and simmer until done, about 2 hours. Check periodically to make sure they remain covered with water. Add the kombu about 1 hour after starting the beans, and add the salt when the beans are done. Remove and reserve the chipotle. For added heat and chipotle flavor, remove the seeds and stem, and then blend a little chipotle with 1 cup of bean broth in the blender. Return this mixture to the pot of beans and taste; adjust the seasonings by adding more chipotle and salt as needed. They are ready to eat as is, or to turn into No-refried Beans (see below), or to use the whole beans in other dishes.

**Variation: Frijoles de la Olla (Beans from the Pot)** These are just seasoned beans served in a little bowl with some bean broth and a garnish. They will complement practically any meal. A larger serving of the beans, served with a salad and cornbread (like Blue Cornbread with Mesquite Flour), makes a tasty wholesome meal. From the Seasoned Black Beans recipe, transfer ½–⅔ cup of beans with their broth to each of 4 small cups or bowls. Top with Fresh Salsa (page 44) or canned. Or, dress with a little chopped onion and tomatoes, minced Serrano or jalapeño chile, finely chopped cilantro, and ending with avocado pieces and a splash of lime or lemon juice. Serve warm with any meal.

**Variation: No-refried Beans** These beans are as tasty as the traditional refried beans, but without the saturated animal fat. Follow the directions for Seasoned Black or Tepary Beans. After beans are done, remove the lid and simmer until the water level and the level of beans are the same. Remove the bay leaves. Mash the bean mixture with a masher. If the beans are too runny, cook a little longer until they attain the consistency of a thick purée. If they are too thick, add a little water. Taste and adjust seasonings. Remove from the burner and allow to cool for about 5 minutes before serving. Top with Fresh Salsa (page 44) or canned; or dress with a little chopped onion and tomatoes, minced serrano or jalapeño chile, finely chopped cilantro, and ending with avocado pieces and a splash of fresh lime or lemon juice and serve with Mexican rice.

## Heirloom Vegetable Brown Rice Pilaf

1 cup mixed whole-grain heirloom rices
(Forbidden Black Rice, red, and brown)

¼ cup minced onion

1 minced garlic clove

1½ cups unsalted vegetable broth or chicken broth

½ teaspoon sea salt

Freshly ground pepper

2 tablespoons fresh oregano leaves
or 1 teaspoon dry oregano

3 small carrots, grated, about 1½ cups

⅓ cup finely chopped Italian parsley (flat leaf)

**Serves 4**

Calories per serving: 198
Total fat: 1g
Saturated fat: 0g
Calories from fat: 12
Protein: 5g
Carbohydrates: 41g
Dietary fiber: 3g
Sugars: 3g

*Mixing different whole-grain rices is not only appealing to the eye and doesn't just provide pleasing texture and robust flavor, but this strategy also provides a wider spectrum of antioxidants than just one type of rice. They work synergistically to increase their individual antioxidant powers. Organic heirloom mixes are available at Whole Foods and other health-oriented grocery stores, or you can mix your own, which is usually slightly less expensive.*

▼ ▼ ▼

Bring the rice, onions, garlic, salt, a couple grinds of pepper, and broth to a boil. Taste, and if needed, add salt. If you are using dry oregano, add it now and stir. Reduce heat to medium-low, add carrots and two tablespoons parsley, toss with a fork, cover, and simmer for about 30 minutes or until rice is done. When it is done, remove from burner, toss the rice with fresh oregano (if that is being used), and remaining parsley. Taste and adjust seasonings. Keep it covered until ready to serve.

## Tepary Beans

Tepary beans grew wild in the Sonoran Desert and thrived with little moisture—possibly one reason why they were a staple for ancient desert dwellers. A study conducted by Hamama and Bhardwaj in 1997 on tepary beans grown in Virginia showed they had higher contents of protein, calcium, iron, magnesium, zinc, phosphorus, copper, manganese, and potassium as compared to navy, kidney, and pinto beans. They are also easier to digest than most other beans. In addition to being nutritious and supplying plenty of fiber, they have a satisfying, sweet nutty flavor and creamy texture. I have used them in chili, humus, and salads, or served them with rice. I use the same recipe as I do for black beans, see Seasoned Black or Tepary Beans, page 156). However, the tepary beans could take substantially longer to cook. Since they require no more than the normal amount of rainfall in Arizona, they could be a viable bean crop again in the Sonoran Desert, where there is a water shortage. There are a number of varieties, which you can grow in your yard or buy dry from such places as Native Seeds/SEARCH and Tohono O'odham Community Action. They are not available canned.

## Mexican Red Rice

1 cup short-grain brown rice

1 teaspoon extra-virgin olive oil or canola oil

2 garlic cloves, run through garlic press

3/4–1 cup finely chopped sweet yellow onion

1 medium tomato, finely chopped

1 rounded teaspoon tomato paste

1/4–1 jalapeño, seeded and finely chopped

3 1/4 cups chicken broth or vegetable broth

Sea salt

Freshly ground pepper

—

**Serves 4**

Calories per serving: 225
Total fat: 3g
Saturated fat: 0g
Calories from fat: 22
Protein: 5g
Carbohydrates: 46g
Dietary fiber: 3g
Sugars: 6g

*My husband is in charge of the Mexican Red Rice recipe. He used to fry the rice in a little oil just as his grandmother did (she used real lard); but wanting a more heart-healthy version, he has perfected the dish without oil. Health-promoting whole-grain rice is used because it has not been stripped of fiber, nutrients, and antioxidant power.*

▼ ▼ ▼

In a 10-inch dry skillet, stir the rice over medium–high heat until it is golden and there is a scent of toasted rice. Transfer the rice temporarily to a bowl. Put the oil in the skillet and sauté the garlic, onion, tomato, tomato paste, and jalapeño until the onions are translucent. Then, combine the vegetable mixture and the rice together in the skillet and add the broth. Bring to a boil, then reduce heat to low, and simmer. After it cooks a bit, taste, add salt and pepper to taste, and cover until the rice is done and the liquid has been absorbed into the popped-open rice, about 30 minutes. If liquid remains after 30 minutes, remove the lid and continue to cook until there is no liquid. Do not stir the rice!

## Forbidden Black Rice

1 3/4 cups water

1 cup Forbidden Black Rice
(available at gourmet and health-oriented grocers)

Sea salt

—

**Serves 4**

Calories per serving: 160
Total fat: 1g
Saturated fat: 0g
Calories from fat: 13
Protein: 0g
Carbohydrates: 34g
Dietary fiber: 2g
Sugars: 0g

*The deep blackish-purple color of "Forbidden Black Rice" creates a beautiful canvas for fish, chicken, or tofu. Lotus Foods explains that, according to legend, this heirloom rice was eaten exclusively by emperors of the Ming Dynasty to ensure good health and longevity. It is a deliciously nutty, soft-textured grain loaded with health-promoting anthocyanin antioxidants, which are what give it its color (and are also found in blueberries). Anthocyanin antioxidants are believed to reduce the inflammation responsible for many chronic diseases such as cancer, heart disease, and Alzheimer's.*

▼ ▼ ▼

In a 1-quart saucepan, bring the water, rice, and salt to a boil; then reduce the heat to low and simmer, covered, for about 40 minutes or until rice is tender.

## Brown Rice Salad, Chef Elizabeth Mikesell

2 cups cooked brown rice

1 bunch green onions

¼ cup fresh basil

¼ cup fresh mint

¼ cup chopped fresh parsley

1 jalapeno

Zest of 1 lemon

1 tomato

1 orange or can of mandarin oranges

**Lemon dressing**

¼ cup olive oil

1 ounce lemon juice

2 teaspoons honey

**Serves 4**

Calories per serving: 295
Total fat: 15g
Saturated fat: 2g
Calories from fat: 129
Protein: 4g
Carbohydrates: 39g
Dietary fiber: 4g
Sugars: 13g

*Chef Elizabeth Mikesell of Pima Community College, Tucson, Arizona, offers this simple and tasty recipe.*

*Chef's tip: Eating white rice increases the risk of type 2 diabetes; however, eating brown rice reduces the risk of the disease.*

▼ ▼ ▼

Prepare lemon dressing. Mix thoroughly and set aside. Cook brown rice according to package and set aside to cool. Dice up green onions, tomato, orange, basil, mint and parsley. Mince jalapeno. Mix all ingredients together. Add a zest of lemon. Mix in lemon dressing. Salt and pepper to taste.

## Gloria's Tortilla Soup

**Soup**

2 cups quartered tomatoes, or use canned tomatoes

½ sweet yellow onion, coarsely cut

4 garlic cloves, cut into pieces

½ cup roughly cut cilantro leaves and stems

¼–1 serrano chile, cut into tiny pieces (optional)

1 tablespoon extra-virgin olive oil

1 teaspoon oregano, crushed to release flavor

4–6 cups chicken broth

Sea salt

Freshly ground pepper

**Garnish**

3 corn tortillas

Olive oil to rub on tortillas

½ ripe Haas avocado, sliced, peeled, and chopped

4-6 pinches of goat feta cheese, or 2–3 tablespoons of goat cheddar cheese, finely shredded, for each serving

**Serves 4–6**

Calories per serving: 171
Total fat: 9g
Saturated fat: 2g
Calories from fat: 82
Protein: 8g
Carbohydrates: 17g
Dietary fiber: 3g
Sugars: 5g

*In the early 1950s, my husband and his two sisters lived with their grandparents in Jalisco, Mexico, and they have memories of wonderful aromas and flavorful comfort food. They said everyone always ate together at all three meals and that each meal was a ritual. For the main meal, la comida, served around one o'clock, Gloria recounts: "There was always a sopa aguada (watery soup) such as tortilla soup, to open our appetites. Then the maid would remove the empty soup bowl and bring a small bowl of rice mixed with maybe red or green pepper slices or peas. After that was eaten came the main plate, which was chicken, fish, or some type of meat with onions and tomatoes fried in a little* manteca *(lard). There was no oil. When a pig was butchered, the lard was rendered, and we would have lard for months for frying and baking." My husband interjected, "We always had beans, a salad with tomatoes and radishes, and another side vegetable from the garden. And the tortillas for the soup were always freshly made, cooked on a* comal *(griddle) and then cut into strips and fried in lard."*

▼ ▼ ▼

Preheat the oven to 350 degrees F (for the tortilla strips, which you will prepare while the soup is cooking).

For the soup: Using a food processor with the "S" blade in place, process the tomatoes, onion, garlic, cilantro, and serrano by pressing the pulse button a couple times to assure even chopping; then hold down the button and release a couple times until the tomatoes and onions are finely chopped or almost minced. If using chopped canned tomatoes, don't process them with the other ingredients.

In a 4-quart saucepan, heat the olive oil over medium heat. Carefully scrape the tomato mixture into the hot oil; sauté it for a few minutes, add the oregano, and stir to combine. Continue sautéing, stirring occasionally, for about 8 minutes.

Meanwhile, start preparing the tortilla strips (still keeping an eye on the mixture on the stove). Either spray the tortillas with olive oil or put some oil in the palm of one hand, rub your palms together, and then rub the tortillas. Cut the tortillas into thin strips and place the strips, without touching each other, on a cookie sheet; bake until crisp, about 5 minutes. Remove from the oven and reserve for garnish.

Back to the soup: stir in the chicken broth and bring the soup mixture to a boil; taste, adding salt and pepper as needed. Turn heat to low and simmer for 3–4 minutes.

Ladle into individual bowls and top with tortilla strips, avocado pieces, and a tiny pinch of feta cheese or about ½ tablespoon of shredded cheddar.

## Heirloom Lemon Cucumber Salad

4 cups thinly sliced lemon cucumbers

2 Jimmy Nardello peppers, stem and seeds removed, thinly sliced into open rounds

1/4–1/2 cup finely chopped red onion

1 tablespoon chopped fresh dill

2 tablespoons or more cider vinegar

Sea salt

Freshly ground multi-colored pepper

_____

**Serves 4**

Calories per serving: 35
Total fat: 0g
Saturated fat: 0g
Calories from fat: 2
Protein: 1g
Carbohydrates: 8g
Dietary fiber: 1g
Sugars: 4g

*Cute, little, and ever-so-destructive ground squirrels have feasted in my garden for the past two years. They literally pick the eggplants and tomatoes and snip off the cucumber and watermelon vines. Ah, the desert garden! So, I bought beautiful heirloom lemon cucumbers (they look like a lemon, without the lemon flavor) and Jimmy Nardello's red fruity-sweet Italian heirloom peppers from Sleeping Frog Farms to prepare this lovely and ever so refreshing salad—next year, the garden will be encased in wire! Lemon cucumber slices are a colorful change from regular cucumbers, with a delightful non-bitter flavor and a crunchy texture.*

*Note: When seed saver Jimmy Nardello immigrated to the United States in the late 1800s, he brought this pepper's seeds with him from Italy.*

▼ ▼ ▼

Mix all ingredients together, taste, and adjust seasoning. Chill for a couple of hours, and serve.

Variation: Add chopped tomatoes, basil, a little mint, and a light sprinkling of goat feta cheese.

## Eating Wild

Wild plants have always been part of traditional healthy diets. The centenarians of Ikaria included over 150 antioxidant-rich wild greens and herbs gathered from the hillsides nearby, providing variety and a broad range of nutrients and antioxidants, which played a role in keeping them healthy throughout their lives. And since the time of the Aztec and Hohokam civilizations, edible desert plants have provided sustenance for the natives of the arid Sonoran Desert. They harvested food from cacti, agave, yucca, ocotillo, mesquite, and palo verde trees. Wild asparagus, amaranth, purslane, and many other plants provided them with a powerhouse of nutrition and phytochemicals.

We, too, can add nutritious variety to our diet by including wild plants. However, prior to hunting for wild plants, make sure that you can correctly identify them. Take a course or have a knowledgeable person guide you. Books are not a good option, because there might only be a slight difference in appearance between a toxic plant and one that isn't. Also, make sure that the harvesting area has not been sprayed with chemicals, and don't pick near a road due to car exhaust, which can contaminate plants with toxins. Also, there are legal considerations about where you are allowed to pick, such as public lands but not national forest etc. Check regulations in your area.

Regardless of where you live, there are wild plants that will add flavor, variety, and health-promoting compounds to your diet. Every summer in Illinois, we would pick delicious wild blackberries, dandelion greens, mushrooms, and giant white puffball mushrooms.

## Marinated Nopalitos

¼ cup lime or lemon juice

1 teaspoon garlic powder or 2 garlic cloves, run through garlic press

1 tablespoon extra-virgin olive oil

Sea salt

Couple grinds of pepper

4 nopalitos (paddles about 6–7 inches long), see Cleaning and Preparation, page 164

---

**Serves 4**

Calories per serving: 45
Total fat: 3g
Saturated fat: 0g
Calories from fat: 30
Protein: 1g
Carbohydrates: 4g
Dietary fiber: 1g
Sugars: 0g

*Almost everyone likes marinated nopales (cactus paddles). A little bit of the mucilage is sacrificed for the garlicky lemon or lime flavor. You can quickly marinate them for 30 minutes or up to 24 hours. Even if marinated for a short period of time, the lemon and garlic add some flavor. After they are marinated, use them raw or cooked in various dishes. Fresh, raw nopalitos can be stored in a plastic bag or a covered glass container in the refrigerator for about 10 days. Marinate up to 24 hours before using.*

▼ ▼ ▼

Mix together the lemon or lime juice, garlic, olive oil, salt, and pepper. With a knife, lightly score each side of the cactus paddles a few times. Place them in a non-reactive pan and toss in the marinade. Cover and refrigerate a few hours before using. (A tightly lidded glass storage container works nicely because the nopalitos can be tumbled in the container.) Remove, drain, and either eat raw or cook. Drained marinated paddles can be kept for 4 or 5 days in the refrigerator; however, they will continue to release mucilage.

**Variation: Grilled Nopalitos** Use either raw or marinated nopalitos. If using marinated nopalitos, follow the marinating instructions above, then remove from the marinade and drain. Grill the whole nopalitos until they are crunchy-tender. Slice or chop them, and serve as a vegetable dish, or mix with other grilled vegetables, or serve over meats or in salads. For a side of nopalitos, marinated and grilled is probably our family's favorite way to prepare them.

## Purslane

Purslane or *verdolaga*, in Spanish, was an important plant food for Native Americans and also is a traditional food in the Mexican culture that is still enjoyed today. It grows across the United States, so regardless of where you live, it's probably available for the picking or at farmers' markets. Even though it is classified as a weed, it is really a juicy, succulent herb with a delightful crunch and lemony flavor. When lettuce isn't available, purslane can be a tasty substitute. It's also great in stir-fries, soups, sautéed vegetable dishes, pesto, sandwiches, or quesadillas, making it more versatile and nutritious than many vegetables.

It's chock-full of antioxidants and nutrients, especially vitamins C and A. It also provides a hefty dose of alpha-linolenic acid (ALA), the omega-3 fatty acid of plant foods. So, if you are a vegetarian or don't like the oily fish that provide omega-3—eicosapentaenoic acid (EPA) and docosahexaenoic acid (DHA)—purslane is a good option. The body partially converts ALA to EPA and DHA, which supply you with DHA omega-3. Omega-3 reduces inflammation and thus may reduce the risk of heart disease, cancer, arthritis, and Alzheimer's.

Purslane is usually available at farmers' markets; but ask where it was harvested. Add some to your yard, which will allow you to pick it wild, making it a free food source just a step or two from your kitchen.

# Prickly Pear Cactus Paddles

The prickly pear cactus plant bears both vegetables (paddles or *nopales*) and fruit ("pears" or *tunas*). Both parts hold health-promoting compounds of nutritional and phytochemical value. The paddles are an excellent source of a full range of amino acids, which are considered the building blocks of protein. Unlike with most plants, these paddles include all nine essential amino acids, making them a high-quality source of protein. They are also full of soluble and insoluble fiber, which play a part in preventing conditions such as heart disease, cancer, diabetes, obesity, and constipation. The high amount of mucilage in the paddles may have greater digestive benefits than other low-viscosity dietary fibers in slowing down digestion and making you feel full, promoting a healthy weight; in keeping sugar from rapidly entering the bloodstream, which could help control type 2 diabetes; and possibly in binding excess cholesterol and carrying it out as waste. Thus, for the early inhabitants of the desert who relied only on what they could catch or pick, the paddles were a high-quality source of food.

## Harvesting the Paddles

For you desert dwellers, it takes longer to go to the store and pick up vegetables than to harvest nopales from your yard and immediately turn them into a meal. Besides, they are free and health promoting! We harvest wild nopalitos (small tender paddles) from our yard or Indian fig (*Opuntia ficus-indica*) from our neighbor's yard. When picking elsewhere, take caution to make sure that they have not been exposed to pesticides. Toxic sprays may have been used around them to kill weeds. The fruit is available during the summer and the paddles year-round. However, the young bright green nopalitos picked during the spring have the best texture and taste. Once they are harvested and the prickles are conquered, the nopalitos are edible.

To harvest, I hold the paddles with sturdy tongs and then twist off by stabbing and twisting the base of the paddle with a fork (see picture). Never pick up the pads with your fingers, or you will have tiny little stickers imbedded in your skin. Once they are picked the fun begins.

## Cleaning the Nopalitos

Some people wear heavy latex gloves while cleaning the paddles. Lay a paddle flat on the cutting board, securing it with a fork. With a 10-inch knife, remove about ½ inch completely around the paddle, then scrape the thorns and stickers from each side of the paddle. (Scrape against the growth pattern of the stickers.) Holding the paddle with a gloved hand or tongs or a fork, rinse the paddle under water, wiping down the pad with either the knife or a gloved hand.

## Preparing Nopalitos

Nopalitos are tasty either raw or cooked. The type of recipe or personal taste will determine whether to cook or not. Some people don't like the mucilage or "goo" that oozes from the pads; but that may be where many of the benefits are stored, such as the soluble fiber. To get rid of the mucilage, they boil the paddles, and in the process boil away most of the mucilage and nutritional value of the vegetable. If cooking is desired, steam or grill them until they are crispy-tender. and then slice or chop and use as a side dish or add to sautés, soups, salsas, enchiladas, quesadillas, fajitas, and scrambled eggs. Freeze cooked nopalitos so they can be enjoyed year-round.

## Summer Tepary Bean Desert Sauté with Purslane

1 tablespoon extra-virgin olive oil

1 medium or large sweet yellow onion, medium chopped

4 garlic cloves, run through garlic press or mashed with knife blade and chopped

4 Jimmy Nardello pepper, seeded and sliced into open rings, or 1 red bell pepper, cut into strips or chopped

2 cups chopped tomatoes

2 cups frozen or home-canned nopalitos, cut into 1/4 x 1-inch strips (see Cleaning the Nopalitos and Preparing Nopalitos, page 164), optional

1 teaspoon oregano, crushed to release flavor

1/2 teaspoon ground cumin

1/2 teaspoon ground chipotle, optional

1 1/2 cups drained cooked tepary beans, or 1 can cannellini beans, drained

1 tablespoon balsamic vinegar

1 tablespoon lemon juice

1 serrano chile, seeded and minced

1 crookneck squash or other summer squash, finely chopped

1–2 cups chopped purslane, stems coarsely chopped, with leaves intact

Sea salt

Freshly ground pepper

1–2 cups fresh basil or lemon basil leaves, stacked, rolled, and thinly sliced

### Serves 4

Calories per serving: 224
Total fat: 4g
Saturated fat: 1g
Calories from fat: 37
Protein: 11g
Carbohydrates: 39g
Dietary fiber: 11g
Sugars: 9g

*The composition of this sauté is dependent upon the assortment of herbs and vegetables available from the garden and the desert, so it changes with the seasons. Canned tomatoes and home-canned or frozen cactus can be used in place of the fresh ones during their off season. I have more than once picked nopalitos from our yard as a substitute for a more common vegetable in this sauté or for another recipe—after all, they are free and health-promoting! When in season, crunchy, lemony purslane may be substituted for the nopalitos. The sauté is also a tasty way of adding at least 1/2 cup of health-promoting tepary beans to your diet. Beans, by the way, are considered one of the healthy aspects of the Mediterranean diet. Serve with a little meat or for a vegetarian meal, add a side of quinoa or rice.*

*Note: Due to the health-promoting "goo" or mucilage that oozes from cactus paddles, some people refuse to eat them. To reduce the mucilage, marinate from 4 to 24 hours (see Marinated Nopalitos, page 163) before adding them to the sauté. If you don't mind the mucilage, you can skip the marinating step. If you are okay with the slickness of okra, you'll survive cactus "goo" in the sauté.*

▼ ▼ ▼

In the olive oil, sauté the onion, garlic, and Jimmy Nardello or red bell peppers over medium-high heat until the onion is crispy-tender. Add the tomatoes, nopalitos, oregano, cumin, chipotle (optional), tepary or cannellini beans, vinegar, lemon juice, and serrano chile. Simmer on medium-low for about 5 minutes or until the tomatoes are somewhat broken down. Stir in the squash and purslane, season with salt and pepper, and simmer a few minutes; remove from heat, toss in the basil, and stir. Taste and adjust seasonings as needed. Serve warm.

**Variation: Spring Tepary Bean Desert Sauté with Nopalitos** Make the following changes: eliminate red peppers, fresh tomatoes, squash, serrano, purslane, and basil. Add two thinly sliced carrots and 1/2 cup of chopped parsley (include a few stems) and sauté with onions. When onions are crunchy tender, toss in 2 cups of nopalitos, 1 cup or so canned tomatoes, and all other ingredients, simmer for about 5 minutes. Remove from heat, stir in 1 1/2 cups of chopped cilantro (include some stems.) Herbs such as fresh thyme and oregano add enjoyable flavors. If you have them in your yard, toss in a couple tablespoons of each with the cilantro.

## Desert Tepary Bean Salad with Nopalitos

½ cup finely chopped red onion

2 garlic cloves, run through garlic press or minced

2–3 tablespoons Key lime juice (reserve the zest from 1 lime)

½ cup sun-dried tomatoes, rehydrated in hot water until tender, and cooled, or 2 cups chopped fresh tomatoes

1 teaspoon oregano, crushed to release flavor or 2 tablespoons chopped fresh oregano leaves

1 tablespoon extra-virgin olive oil

1½–2 cups cooked and rinsed tepary beans, cooled (see page 156), or canned and rinsed cannellini beans

1–1½ cups chiffonade-cut basil or lemon basil or cilantro (whatever is in season)

2 tablespoons thyme or lemon thyme leaves

1–1½ cups chopped marinated and grilled nopalitos (see pages 163–164)

1 serrano chile, seeded and minced

½–1 teaspoon sea salt

Freshly ground pepper

¼ cup feta goat cheese

½ Haas avocado, chopped

2 tablespoons pine nuts

### Serves 4

Calories per serving: 467
Total fat: 10g
Saturated fat: 3g
Calories from fat: 86
Protein: 25g
Carbohydrates: 74g
Dietary fiber: 19g
Sugars: 8g

*Whether it is spring or summer, our arid desert offers up a plateful of nutritionally dense palate-pleasing options. Different colors of tepary beans are always in my pantry. I use whatever I have on hand—white, brown, black, or a mix of all three. If you don't have access to tepary beans, use cannellini beans. During spring, tender young prickly pear cactus paddles are perfect for the picking and add interesting flavor and crunch to this salad. Summer arrives, and lemony crunchy purslane takes the place of the paddles. Herbs also change as the seasons change, cilantro in the cool weather and basil or lemon basil during warm weather.*

*Note: Since tepary beans are not available canned, allow 3–8 hours cooking time, depending on the age of the bean.*

▼ ▼ ▼

Soak the onions and garlic in the lime juice for a few minutes to tame possibly strong flavors. Toss the rehydrated tomatoes and crushed or fresh oregano in the olive oil. Toss together the tepary beans, lime zest, basil or cilantro, thyme, nopalitos, serrano chile, salt and pepper, the onion/garlic mixture, and the rehydrated tomato mixture; taste and adjust seasonings as needed. Sprinkle with cheese, avocado, and pine nuts. Splash a little lime juice over the avocado and serve at room temperature.

Variation: **Desert Tepary Bean Salad with Purslane** Substitute 1 cup of purslane petals and a few chopped stems for the nopalitos, and substitute 2 cups of chopped fresh tomatoes for the sun-dried tomatoes. Add 1 cup of chopped and seeded Jimmy Nardello or red bell pepper, and 1–2 roasted, peeled, seeded, and chopped green chiles.

## Blue Cornbread with Mesquite Flour

1 cup blue corn meal

½ cup mesquite flour

2 teaspoons baking powder

½ teaspoon salt

1 tablespoon minced fresh rosemary leaves

1 egg

3 tablespoons maple syrup

2 teaspoon olive oil

1 cup unsweetened soy beverage

1 teaspoon vanilla

Butter for pan

**Serves 6**

Calories per serving: 191
Total fat: 5g
Saturated fat: 1g
Calories from fat: 36
Protein: 9g
Carbohydrates: 73g
Dietary fiber: 26g
Sugars: 29g

*This non-gluten cornbread makes a tasty pairing with tepary beans.*

▼ ▼ ▼

With a fork, mix together dry ingredients. Add rosemary and toss. Beat egg with fork until fluffy, stir in maple syrup, olive oil, soy beverage, and vanilla; and then add dry ingredients and mix until combined. Pour into an 8-inch square buttered baking pan. Bake approximately 15 minutes in preheated 425-degree-F oven or until lightly browned on top and when a knife comes out clean.

### Mesquite

Mesquite beans are high in fiber, a good source of protein, and add wonderful sweet cinnamon flavor to dishes. In baked goods, I usually substitute ¼ or ⅓ of the flour with mesquite flower. Go to desertharvesters.org for information on harvesting, grinding into flour, among other interesting facts.

## Brenda's Multi-grain Bread, Queen Creek Olive Mill

**Multi-grain Mix**

Steel-cut oats

Cornmeal

Cracked wheat

Flax seed

Pumpkin seeds, toasted

Sunflower seeds, toasted

Cracked buckwheat, toasted

Sesame seeds, toasted

Millet

Barley flakes

**Bread**

2 tablespoons active dry yeast

½ cup lukewarm water

1 teaspoon evaporated cane juice

2 cups boiling water

3 cups multi-grain mix (as described in the recipe instructions)

⅓ cup molasses or honey

2 teaspoons sea salt

2 tablespoons evaporated cane juice

⅓ cup extra-virgin olive oil

1 cup cold water

2 cups whole-wheat flour

2–3 cups bread flour

More flour for kneading

**Makes 2 large loaves**

Calories per serving: 274
Total fat: 10g
Saturated fat: 1g
Calories from fat: 84
Protein: 8g
Carbohydrates: 40g
Dietary fiber: 4g
Sugars: 3g

*This dense, richly flavored loaf makes great breakfast toast (try it with butter and honey) as well as sandwiches, and it's delicious alongside soup. Brenda always keeps a stash of multi-grain mix in the pantry or freezer for making bread.*

▼ ▼ ▼

To make the multi-grain mix: Combine equal parts of all (or any combination) of the grains and seeds listed (for example, 1 cup of each). You can mix up more than is needed for a recipe of bread and store it in the freezer for future loaves.

To make the bread: Dissolve the yeast in the lukewarm water with the evaporated cane juice. Set aside till it's foamy, about 10 minutes.

In a separate large bowl, pour the 2 cups of boiling water over the multi-grain mix. Add molasses or honey, salt, evaporated cane juice, olive oil, and cold water. When cooled to lukewarm, stir in the whole-wheat and bread flours and the yeast mixture. Keep stirring the dough until it is well blended.

Turn onto a well-floured surface and knead for a few minutes. Let the dough rise in a covered bowl in a warm place until the dough rises to double. (Or let it rise for several hours or overnight in the refrigerator. Bring to room temperature before shaping.) Divide it in two and shape into loaves. Place the loaves on a well-greased baking sheet or loaf pans, and let it rise again until double.

Bake on convection at 400 degrees F, or in a conventional oven at 425 degrees F, for about 40 minutes. Remove from pans immediately to cool.

# Queen Creek Olive Mill

Perry Rea jokes about selling his father's automotive business in Detroit and going from motor oil to olive oil in Queen Creek, Arizona. On a visit to Arizona, he recalls looking at all the olive trees dotting the valley's landscape, which sparked an idea of making extra-virgin olive oil (EVOO). After returning to Detroit, he and his wife Brenda still had olive oil on their minds. Perry learned that no one was making the oil in Arizona, and the viability of producing it looked good. So he planted trees, bought a machine, and started making EVOO for himself.

Iron Chef Beau MacMillan (executive chef of Elements and an advocate of buying local) tasted the oil, loved it, and wanted it for his restaurant; but Perry wasn't set up yet. The following year, he was finally harvesting some olives and doing a little processing. Then, unbeknownst to Perry, Beau took it on the *Sonoran Living* morning show, and people came knocking on the mill's doors. From that point on, the Rea family was planting more trees, developing products, expanding their facility, and adding a café.

Perry doesn't see himself as a farmer and will quickly tell you that his business is agri-tourism, built on boutique expeller-pressed EVOO. Around 200,000 people visit his olive oil mill each year, which is a huge boost for the local economy. Many buy gourmet olive-based products from the shop—85 to 90 percent of all his product sales are out of his store. He sells to a few specialty stores such as Whole Foods and locally owned AJs, but is not interested in supplying a large market. Herbs and vegetables grown in the Mill's organic garden and seasonal produce from local organic farmers and pork from a nearby hog farm are served in their Tuscan inspired cafe, Del Piero.

His 2,500-tree grove is sustainably grown with water-conserving irrigation methods and without the use of pesticides, chemical fertilizers, or genetic modification. Olive trees are a good fit for the desert because, as general manager Rob Holmes puts it, "They don't like to get their feet wet and there are no natural predators."

Perry believes from 30 to 35 percent of the quality of the oil flavor and taste—the oil profile—is attributed to the timing of the harvest (that is, the ripeness of the olives). "I can take mission olives from the same tree, and if they are all green, I am going to get rocket fuel—bitter, herbaceous, peppery, just wonderful drizzling oil; but I can take those same olives and let them go purple ripe and that olive oil will be bland and buttery, great for sautéing or baking." Consequently, during the harvesting season (September–December), olives are picked at various times dictated by their stage of ripeness. To achieve a perfect harmony of flavors, some will be picked green ripe, purple ripe, and some in between, assuring a variety of distinctive tastes achieving a fine aromatic blended oil.

Also, for exceptional quality EVOO, the olives are gently picked from the trees (none off the ground) and cold pressed within 24 hours using a two-step process. Since the oil is not filtered, Perry says, more flavor, polyphenols, and the chemical makeup of the oil are retained. The oil carries a buttery taste and a distinct pepper-like finish. *Zone Diet* author Dr. Barry Sears suggests that this peppery finish is an indication of hydroxytyrosol, a phytochemical (only available in olive oil) that inhibits inflammation, which is a cause of many diseases, including heart, cancer, and Alzheimer's diseases. He also suggests that it is not found in most olive oils produced in the US. According to my taste test, there is a fairly strong presence of hydroxytyrosol in the Queen Creek EVOO. It's also at least half the cost and almost zero the carbon miles of EVOO brands imported from Italy that are known to have the highest amounts of hydroxytyrosol. Also, 75 percent of the olive spews from the press as pomace, which is used as compost in the garden, grove, and on roads to cut dust.

To retain its fresh-pressed flavor, the oil is immediately stored in vats from Italy, specifically designed for olive oil storage, and then blended and bottled only as needed. Perry commented, "All the oils are separated, and then I'll be like a mad scientist with four or five beakers in front of me, and I blend with this ratio to this ratio and this harvest to this harvest. By growing and processing, I have an advantage." To be classified as EVOO in North American, the oleic acid content must be a maximum of 0.8 percent. Oleic acid is a freshness index, and the lower the number, the fresher the oil. Queen Creek prides itself with a value typically around 0.3 percent.

Queen Creek Olive Oil Mill is the Rea's family business, and Perry, Brenda, and their five children all take part in it. They have written a cookbook, *The Queen Creek Olive Mill Cookbook*, which is full of their family's Italian recipes. They have shared with me three of their delightful recipes for you to enjoy.

## Garbanzo Salad, Queen Creek Olive Mill

2 cans (16 ounces each) garbanzo beans, drained and well rinsed, or approximately 4 cups home-cooked garbanzos, drained

2 garlic cloves, chopped

½ cup chopped red onion

½ cup chopped celery

4 tablespoons extra-virgin olive oil

4 tablespoons white balsamic vinegar

3 sprigs Italian parsley, chopped

¼ teaspoon red chile flakes

1 teaspoon sea salt

---

### Serves 6

Calories per serving: 275
Total fat: 11g
Saturated fat: 1g
Calories from fat: 94
Protein: 8g
Carbohydrates: 38g
Dietary fiber: 7g
Sugars: 3g

*Meaty, healthy garbanzos give this marinated salad lots of body and tender crunch. Queen Creek Olive Mill white balsamic vinegar is a good choice for its acid–sweet balance.*

▼ ▼ ▼

Combine all ingredients in a bowl and refrigerate for 1 hour before serving to combine flavors.

*Queen Creek Olive Mill's extra-virgin olive oil.*

# DESSERTS

**Does your palate** ever signal that something settling and sweet is needed at the end of a meal? Maybe this is the reason why ripe, seasonally fresh fruit is the sweet ending note to the traditional, health-promoting Cretan Mediterranean diet. Fruit is also full of antioxidants and provides fiber that will help you feel fuller longer. So if dessert is usually part of your family's daily dining ritual, join the Cretans in enjoying fruit as your dessert most of the time and reserving the sweeter, richer delicacies for special occasions—and served in small portions. The first delicious bite overwhelms your taste buds with excitement, but after two or three bites, the excitement is drastically diminished. So why eat more? Commit to making homemade desserts instead of buying boxed cookies full of dreadful ingredients or a store-bought cake made with shortening.

Whether the dessert is decadent or not, accent it with seasonally fresh, juicy fruit, emitting sweet perfumes that will bring delightful, satisfying flavors to your palate. Unfortunately, supermarkets usually can't deliver such pleasurable fruits. Thus, whenever possible, I buy locally grown fruits from farmers' markets, grocery stores who buy locally, orchards, or pick from our backyard to assure nutrient-dense, top-quality fruit. I also try to find heirloom varieties, not only for beauty and flavor, but to eat for the sake of biodiversity.

My desserts are sweetened with organic evaporated cane juice or raw local honey bought from Freddie, Terry, and Marie at the farmers' market. Nutritionally, there are minute differences between them and white sugar. Both affect blood sugar levels, and too much can make you fat and cause health problems. I use them because their processing is not as destructive to the environment as with white sugar. Since honey is sweeter than sugar, the amount used can be cut by a quarter to a half. It is also more satiating than sugar, so you will wind up eating less to be satisfied. ▶

*Dark Chocolate Lava Cake (recipe on page 174).*

## Dark Chocolate Lava Cake

Butter for ramekins

6 ounces dark chocolate (70 percent cacao), broken into small pieces

8 tablespoons butter (room temperature, cut into pieces)

⅓ cup whole-grain spelt flour, whole-grain wheat pastry flour, or unbleached flour

Pinch of finely ground sea salt

3 eggs, at room temperature

½ cup evaporated cane juice

1 teaspoon pure vanilla extract

1 tablespoon lavender flowers, crushed to release perfume (optional, usually available at Whole Foods and spice shops)

¼ cup macadamia oil or butter

_____

**Serves 12**

Calories per serving: 341
Total fat: 24g
Saturated fat: 13g
Calories from fat: 210
Protein: 10g
Carbohydrates: 23g
Dietary fiber: 3g
Sugars: 13g

*Indulge and blow some calories on warm, decadent lava cake that is baked in small ramekins as a hint that only a little is needed to satisfy. Accenting the small cakes with berries bursting with juicy freshness brings together a duo of intriguing flavors and textures that are simply irresistible. Leftover cakes may be frozen, transforming them into dense brownie-like treats. If you're in a pinch to come up with a last-minute dessert, these little jewels can be whipped up in about 20 minutes and then baked for 10 minutes and served immediately.*

▼ ▼ ▼

Preheat the oven to 375 degrees F. Generously butter, from the bottom to top, 12 ramekins (⅓-cup or ½-cup size), which encourage the cakes to easily rise up the sides.

In a double boiler, melt the chocolate over medium heat and stir to thoroughly melt. When it's melted, remove the chocolate from the burner. Mix in the butter, and stir until completely blended with the chocolate; set aside.

Mix together the flour and salt; set aside. In a small mixing bowl, beat the eggs and evaporated cane juice on high for about 5 minutes, or until smooth and pale. Add the vanilla, lavender, and macadamia oil or butter, and beat for about 1 minute. Set the beater speed to medium, slowly add the chocolate mixture, and then beat until blended. Turn the mixer speed to low and add the flour, mixing to blend—but don't over-mix.

Divide the batter among the 12 ramekins, and place them on a baking sheet on the center rack of the oven. To achieve a liquid or gooey center, bake for 10–12 minutes. The top will have a smooth surface with a slight indention in the middle. If liquid centers are not preferred, bake a little longer for an exceptional moist cake. Allow the cakes to rest for a few minutes out of the oven, then turn the ramekins upside-down onto individual dessert plates. The cake should drop onto the plate. Serve warm. When in season, serve with fresh berries on the side. The batter may be prepared hours earlier, refrigerated, and then poured into the ramekins just before baking.

**Variation: Dark Chocolate Espresso Lava Cake** Pour half the batter into the ramekins, sprinkle ¼ teaspoon of freeze dried coffee or fine-grind (espresso grind) dark French roast over the batter for each cake, add the remaining batter, and bake as directed.

**Variation: Kahlua Chocolate Lava Cake** Pour the batter into the ramekins, top each one off with a scant teaspoon of Kahlua and gently swirl it into the batter; bake as directed.

## Whole-grain and Mesquite Chocolate Chip Cookies

1 cup whole-grain spelt or wheat flour

$1/2$ cup mesquite flour, or substitute another $1/2$ cup spelt or wheat flour

$3/4$ teaspoon baking soda

$1/2$ teaspoon baking powder

2 teaspoons ground cinnamon

$1/2$ teaspoon fine sea salt

$1/2$ cup toasted wheat germ

1 cup firmly packed pitted dates

$1/4$ cup macadamia oil or mild extra virgin olive oil

$1/4$ cup unsweetened soy beverage or nonfat milk

2 eggs

2 tablespoons butter

1 teaspoon grated fresh ginger (use microplane)

$1/4$ cup local honey

1 teaspoon pure vanilla extract

6 ounces dark chocolate, finely grated with microplane (minimum 70 percent cocoa)

1 cup bittersweet chocolate chips

$1/2$ cup toasted buckwheat groats

1 cup old-fashioned rolled oats

1 cup chopped walnuts

1–2 tablespoons chopped fresh rosemary leaves

---

**Makes 48 medium-size cookies**

Calories per serving: 162
Total fat: 7g
Saturated fat: 2g
Calories from fat: 58
Protein: 4g
Carbohydrates: 22g
Dietary fiber: 3g
Sugars: 6g

*Packed with irresistible morsels of dark chocolate and infused with ginger and rosemary— these cookies are sweet, savory, and yummy. Our grandchildren Ty and Aaron totally agree! They helped harvest the mesquite beans and turn them into flour. Being involved from picking to baking to eating makes the cookies even more enticing to them. Fiber-rich dates are the main sweetener, providing a little more health value that's lacking in sugar. Be sure to use aluminum-free baking powder. And when you shop for the chocolate chips, keep in mind that SunSpire® chips are 65 percent cacao; Ghirardelli® are 60 percent.*

▼ ▼ ▼

Preheat oven to 350 degrees F. Line 2 cookie sheets with parchment paper.

In a large mixing bowl, sift together the spelt or wheat flour, mesquite flour (if you are using this), baking soda, baking powder, cinnamon, and salt (stir any tiny particles of the whole grain back into the sifted mix), and then stir in the wheat germ; set aside. In the jar of a blender, blend together the dates, oil, soy beverage or nonfat milk, eggs, butter, ginger, honey, and vanilla, until the dates are finely ground. Transfer the wet ingredients to a bowl and stir in the grated chocolate. With a spatula, combine the dry with the wet ingredients, just until mixed. Fold in the chocolate chips, groats, oats, walnuts, and rosemary.

Use a heaping teaspoon of dough for each cookie, placing the dough spoonfuls about 2 inches apart on the parchment. Bake for about 15 minutes, switching the cookie sheets from top to bottom and front to back, as needed, to assure even browning. Cookies are done when they spring back when lightly pressed with fingertip. Transfer to a cooling rack, and store the cooled cookies in airtight container.

### Dark Chocolate

Scientific research shows that dark chocolate contains up to three times the antioxidants found in green tea, and antioxidants may reduce the risk of heart disease and cancer. However, green tea does not contain the fat or saturated fat that chocolate does. A little bit of chocolate and a lot of green tea may be a health-promoting duo that will also keep a slim waistline.

## Orange Olive Oil Cake

Butter or olive oil for greasing the pan

¼ cup chia seeds

1 cup unsweetened soy beverage or nonfat milk

1 ½ cups whole-grain spelt flour or unbleached flour

2 ½ teaspoons baking powder

½ teaspoon sea salt

2 eggs, at room temperature

⅔ cup evaporated cane juice

½ cup mild-flavor extra-virgin olive oil

1 teaspoon pure vanilla extract

2 tablespoons grated orange rind (use microplane)

**Topping**

Orange-Infused Greek Yogurt (see next recipe)

1 ½ cups fresh local berries, or sliced strawberries, peaches, figs, or whatever is in season

———

**Serves 12**

Calories per serving: 307

Total fat: 13g

Saturated fat: 2g

Calories from fat: 107

Protein: 7g

Carbohydrates: 42g

Dietary fiber: 6g

Sugars: 19g

*These tasty mini-cakes are topped off with a dollop of slightly sweetened, orange-infused Greek yogurt and juicy pieces of in-season fresh fruit. By using olive oil, the saturated fat from butter or shortening is replaced with monounsaturated fat. The cake is also a little bit healthier due to the inclusion of chia seeds, which might be mistaken for poppy seeds! By using chia seeds, some of the eggs and oil that normally would be included were eliminated. Be sure to use aluminum-free baking soda.*

▼ ▼ ▼

Preheat the oven to 325 degrees F. Grease the cups of a mini muffin pan (12 cups, ¼-cup size) with butter or olive oil, or use small paper baking cups.

To prevent the chia from clumping while gelling, use a fork to mix the seeds in the soy beverage or milk, swirling the seeds until just a few are floating on top; then stir again in about 3 minutes. Stir a couple more times while preparing the batter.

Sift together the flour, baking powder, and salt, and set aside. Beat the eggs on high speed for about 2 minutes or until fluffy, then slowly add the evaporated cane juice, and continue beating for 3–4 minutes. Slowly pour in the oil, add the vanilla, and beat for 1 minute.

Vigorously stir the chia seed, making sure there are no clumps. Add the chia seed gel to the wet mixture, and beat until thoroughly mixed; then mix in the orange rind. Fold the wet mixture into the dry ingredients until combined; but don't over-mix. Fill the muffin tins or cupcake papers ⅔ full and bake on the middle rack of the oven for 15–20 minutes, or until the cake is golden and separating from the edge of the tins, and a thin-blade knife comes out clean. Cool on a rack. Serve each little cake on a plate, capped with a dollop of Greek yogurt, with fresh fruit cascading from the topping to the plate.

**Variation: Savory Nutty Rosemary Lemon Cake** Substitute lemon zest for the orange zest in both the cake and the yogurt topping. Add in ¼ cup fresh chopped rosemary leaves and ⅔ cup roughly chopped pecans or pistachios when the zest is added.

## Orange-infused Greek Yogurt Topping

1 cup nonfat Greek yogurt, whey or liquid poured off

4 teaspoons evaporated cane juice

1/2 teaspoon pure vanilla extract

1 teaspoon orange zest without white pith (use microplane)

___

**Makes about 1 cup**

Calories per serving (1 cup): 197
Total fat: 0g
Saturated fat: 0g
Calories from fat: 4
Protein: 14g
Carbohydrates: 34g
Dietary fiber: 0g
Sugars: 33g

*This is a wonderful alternative to store-bought flavored yogurt. You can add any fruit or flavoring while having control over the amount of sugar. Serve as a dessert or add a dollop atop pancakes covered with fruit.*

▼ ▼ ▼

Mix together all ingredients. Refrigerate for a couple of hours to infuse the yogurt with flavors.

## Mexican Lime–Ginger Pudding Parfait

2 cups raspberries and/or blackberries

1 tablespoon evaporated cane juice

1 package (12.3 ounces) Mori Nu Silken Tofu, soft (any firmness)

1/2–3/4 cup local raw mild honey

1/2 cup Key lime juice

1 teaspoon umeboshi plum paste (available in the Asian section of most grocery stores)

1 tablespoon freshly grated ginger

3 teaspoons powdered arrowroot or cornstarch

1 tablespoon lime zest, plus more zest for garnish

1 tablespoon pure vanilla extract

Mint leaves

___

**Serves 6**

Calories per serving: 203
Total fat: 1g
Saturated fat: 0g
Calories from fat: 12
Protein: 5g
Carbohydrates: 46g
Dietary fiber: 3g
Sugars: 40g

*There's no comparison in flavor and juiciness to tree-ripened Mexican limes fresh from our tree. So when it hits 110 degrees in Tucson, we turn them into a refreshing, tangy lime pudding. Puddings are sometimes made with cream and often butter and eggs. Eliminating these is good for your waistline and your heart! Try using as little honey as possible for sweetening. It's still sugar and should not be used excessively. You can also substitute fresh chopped figs for the berries.*

▼ ▼ ▼

Using a mesh strainer, rinse and drain the berries or figs. Sprinkle them with evaporated cane juice, toss, and set aside. Place the tofu, honey, lime juice, plum paste, and ginger in a blender and blend until smooth, about 3 minutes. Add the arrowroot and blend for about 1 more minute. Taste and adjust for sweetness. Place the mixture in the top of a double boiler. Bring the water to a boil and reduce to simmer. Frequently stir the pudding until somewhat thick, about 7 minutes. Remove the pan from the boiler. Stir in the tablespoon of lime zest and the vanilla. As it cools, the pudding will thicken. Using an 8-ounce wine glass or parfait glass, place a few berries in the bottom, cover with pudding, add a more few berries, and cover with pudding. Top it with lime zest, mint leaves, and more berries. Cover with plastic wrap and refrigerate for at least 1 hour.

Note: A heavy saucepan may be used in lieu of a double boiler. Set the saucepan over medium heat, pour the pudding mixture in the pan, and bring to just under boiling, stirring continuously. Don't boil! Turn heat to low; continue cooking and stirring until the pudding thickens. Remove from heat and stir in the vanilla and tablespoon of lime zest.

## Vanilla Chia "Tapioca" Pudding

2 cups unsweetened soy beverage or nonfat milk

¼ cup local honey

1–2 teaspoons ground cinnamon

2 teaspoons pure vanilla extract

2 dashes of ground nutmeg

1 dash sea salt

⅓ cup chia seeds, white or black
(white looks more like tapioca)

Fresh fruit for layered-fruit parfait, or topping

_____

**Serves 6**

Calories per serving: 180
Total fat: 6g
Saturated fat: 1g
Calories from fat: 39
Protein: 6g
Carbohydrates: 27g
Dietary fiber: 10g
Sugars: 16g

*Tapioca pudding is a favorite for many, but here is a healthier option—chia pudding. The magic of the expanding chia thickens into a pudding resembling tapioca, infused with wonderful cinnamon and vanilla flavors, but without the eggs. It has a few more health benefits than regular pudding, too. Chia is an excellent source of omega-3 EFA and has almost a 1:1 ratio of omega-3 to omega-6, is high in fiber, slows converting carbohydrate calories into simple sugars, is high in protein, and is filling. As an added plus, it does not have to be cooked. Our grandchildren Ty and Aaron and their friend Calissa were the testers, and they loved it! Ty and Aaron's dad enjoyed it, too. They also enjoy fresh fruit-layered parfait chia pudding.*

*Note: Chia is available from health food stores, health-oriented grocers, and the Internet. Chia ranges in price from $5 to $21 a pound. Don't be fooled into believing that white chia or Salba brand chia is healthier than black chia and wind up paying $21 a pound for it; leading chia researcher Dr. Wayne Coates, professor emeritus for the Office of Arid Lands Studies, University of Arizona, confirms it's not. It is simply white chia, and white is no different than black. Dr. Coates told me, "The chia is never sprayed with pesticides, so there is no chance of residues. Some growers use pre-plant herbicide or fertilizer. There is certified organic available, but in my mind it is not worth the extra expense. Really the concern with foods is pesticide residues." Both white and black chia are available for about the same price from Dr. Coates' company, AZchia.com.*

▼ ▼ ▼

If the milk is heated—not boiled—the pudding sets faster and the cinnamon blends in more quickly. If the honey has become solid, slightly heat it to thin for easier mixing. Then mix together the soy beverage or milk, honey, cinnamon, vanilla, nutmeg, and salt. Add the chia and mix thoroughly with a fork. Allow it to set for about 2 minutes and mix again. Let it set for about 5 minutes and briskly stir. After another 5 minutes, stir again. (When the chia is mixed with the liquid, the seeds become gelatinous and gluey; thus, frequent stirring within the first 10 minutes is important, or the seeds will stick together.)

Pour the batter into ½-cup ramekins or small glass dessert cups, or alternate layers of fruit with the pudding in a parfait glass. Whatever your choice, top with fruit!

Cover with plastic wrap and refrigerate for a couple hours. For a thicker pudding, refrigerate for at least 12 hours to allow the seeds to totally soften and the flavors to blend.

## Chocolate-dipped Strawberries

1 pound ripe strawberries, washed and dried (leave stems intact)

6 ounces 73 percent super-dark chocolate (or dark chocolate with at least 70 percent dry cocoa solids, not chocolate chips)

**Serves 20 (1 each)**

Calories per serving: 57
Total fat: 4g
Saturated fat: 2g
Calories from fat: 33
Protein: 1g
Carbohydrates: 6g
Dietary fiber: 1g
Sugars: 3g

*Strawberries enrobed in luscious dark chocolate are the dessert of choice at our traditional Easter gathering at Burr and Alice Udall's home.*

*Note: Select fragrant, bright red berries with fresh green leaves. Since water will cause chocolate to become chunky—and if the strawberries are wet, the chocolate won't stick—make sure that the strawberries are completely dry prior to dipping.*

▼ ▼ ▼

Line a cookie sheet with parchment paper.

Melting the chocolate, double boiler method: Pour a small amount of water into the bottom pot of a double boiler, making sure the water does not touch the upper pot. Break the chocolate bar into small pieces and toss them into the top pot. Bring the water to a boil and then reduce to medium-low heat. Melt the chocolate until smooth, stirring as it melts. Since there is more control with this method of melting chocolate than melting it in a microwave, I prefer a double boiler. Turn off the heat and start dipping as explained below. If the chocolate starts to thicken, return the pot to the boiler and heat it again.

Melting chocolate, microwave method: Select a bowl that will not get hot in the microwave (or the chocolate will scorch). Place the chocolate in the bowl, melt for 20 seconds on high, then remove and stir. Repeat. Then repeat in 15-second intervals, stirring thoroughly each time, until the chocolate is about 80 percent melted. When stirred, it will completely melt. Careful—if the chocolate gets too hot, it will be ruined. During dipping, stir the chocolate a few times. If the chocolate cools too much to dip, put it back in the microwave and heat for about 10 seconds; then stir.

To dip the berries, tilt the pot or bowl to pool the chocolate in one area. Holding the stem or leaves, dip about half of the berry into the chocolate. With a twisting motion, bring it out of the chocolate. Allow the excess chocolate to drip off. Place the dipped strawberry on the parchment paper. Repeat with the rest of the strawberries. To use every last bit of chocolate, scrape the chocolate with a spatula from the bottom to pool on the side. If there are no more strawberries, stick a toothpick into each of a few banana slices and dip each of these into the chocolate. Place the cookie sheet in the refrigerator for about 30 minutes; then remove and serve. The chocolate will harden and will stay firm for hours in a comfortable temperature away from direct sunlight. Undipped fresh strawberries with green tops can be mixed in with the chocolate-dipped berries.

**Variation: Chocolate-Chile Dipped Strawberries** To impart a zesty hot-sweet flavor, sprinkle a little bit of New Mexico red chile on a few of the dipped berries before placing them in the refrigerator.

## Kick-the-Can Ice Cream

1½ cups nonfat, lowfat, or whole milk

¼ cup half-and-half or whipping cream (or substitute with milk)

⅓ cup evaporated cane juice (better results if ground fine in a blender)

Pinch of stevia (if needed for sweetness)

1 teaspoon pure vanilla extract

Scant pinch of sea salt

1 cup mashed or puréed in blender fresh strawberries, blueberries, or figs—or whatever is in season

**Serves 4**

Calories per serving: 222
Total fat: 7g
Saturated fat: 4g
Calories from fat: 59
Protein: 4g
Carbohydrates: 38g
Dietary fiber: 1g
Sugars: 31g

*Save on energy and give the kids (and yourself) some exercise by making "kick-the-can" ice cream; then enjoy a small portion of this scrumptious homemade treat. Any type of fruit or flavoring can be added. Use your own favorite recipe that you would make in an ice cream maker. It's fun to kick it around outside, but sometimes it may have to be made indoors. If rolling the can on a hardwood floor, wrap the can in a towel and secure with duct tape to avoid scratching the floor!*

*You will need one 3-pound metal coffee can with plastic lid, one 1-pound metal coffee can with plastic lid, 1 small roll of duct tape, about 4 cups of ice cubes (not crushed) and ½–¾ cup rock salt. When storing cans for future use, make sure they are completely dry or they will rust.*

*Note: Fresh fruit that is puréed will give more fruit flavor.*

▼ ▼ ▼

Toss all the ingredients into the small coffee can and stir until thoroughly mixed. Snap the lid on and secure it with duct tape by wrapping the tape around the can and lid; then place it in the large can. Fill the void between the cans half-full with ice, then evenly sprinkle ¼ cup of rock salt over the ice. Finish filling the can with ice, and evenly sprinkle with another ¼ cup of salt. Snap on the bigger can's lid and secure tightly with duct tape. Play Kick-the-Can for 15 minutes. Open the cans. Scrape the ice cream from the sides into the rest of the batch. If you want it thicker, add some more ice and ¼ cup salt, reseal, and kick for 5 or so minutes more.

## Kick-the-Can Frozen Yogurt with Fruit

2 cups plain lowfat yogurt

½ nectarine, chopped

5 medium strawberries, chopped

2 tablespoons honey

½ teaspoon pure vanilla extract

**Serves 4**

Calories per serving: 123
Total fat: 2g
Saturated fat: 1g
Calories from fat: 18
Protein: 7g
Carbohydrates: 20g
Dietary fiber: 1g
Sugars: 19g

*Our daughter Elicia and her sons Ty and Aaron came up with this tasty, tart alternative to ice cream.*

▼ ▼ ▼

Follow the same directions as for Kick-the-Can Ice Cream.

## Lemon Bars, Chef Scott Uehlein

½ cup and 3 tablespoons unsalted butter, room temperature

⅓ cup plus 1 ½ cup evaporated cane juice

4 tablespoons minced lemon zest

1⅔ cups plus ¼ cup all-purpose flour

½ teaspoon aluminum free baking powder

5 large eggs

⅔ cup fresh lemon juice (approximately 4 lemons)

1 ½ teaspoons pure vanilla extract

_____

**Makes 32 bars**

Calories per serving: 120
Total fat: 5g
Saturated fat: 2g
Calories from fat: 39
Protein: 2g
Carbohydrates: 18g
Dietary fiber: 0g
Sugars: 9g

*Corporate Chef Scott Uehlein of Canyon Ranch, Tucson, Arizona, shares this sweet and tart dessert.*

▼ ▼ ▼

Preheat oven to 350 degrees F. In a food processor, blend together butter and ⅓ cup of the evaporated cane juice and 1 tablespoon of the lemon rind. Gradually add in 1⅔ cups of the flour to form soft crumbs. In a 9 x 13-inch baking pan, evenly press crumbs to form a crust. Bake for 15 minutes.

In a small bowl, stir together 1½ cups of the evaporated cane juice, ¼ cup of the flour, and baking powder.

In a large mixing bowl, with a hand held mixer, beat eggs well. Gradually add evaporated cane juice/flour mixture to beaten eggs. Stir in lemon peel, lemon juice and vanilla extract. Pour lemon mixture over baked crust. Return to oven and bake for 20 minutes or until top and sides are light brown in color.

Allow to bars cool. Cut into 32 squares, about 2 x 1½ inches.

## Totally Awesome Fruit Crumble, Chef Elizabeth Mikesell

1½ cups fresh or IQF frozen blueberries

1½ cups fresh or IQF frozen sliced peaches

1 tablespoon honey

3 tablespoons whole-wheat flour

1 tablespoon orange juice

1 teaspoon orange zest

½ cup rolled oats

¼ cup almonds or pecans (optional)

3 tablespoons brown sugar

¼ teaspoon ground cinnamon

⅛ teaspoon ground ginger

2 tablespoons canola oil

_____

**Serves 4**

Calories per serving: 336
Total fat: 14g
Saturated fat: 1g
Calories from fat: 118
Protein: 6g
Carbohydrates: 51g
Dietary fiber: 5g
Sugars: 6g

*A fun dish to make with kids from Chef Elizabeth Mikesell of Pima Community College, Tucson, Arizona.*

▼ ▼ ▼

Preheat oven to 400 degrees F. Combine fruit and honey, flour, orange zest and orange juice. Divide among four 6-ounce ovenproof ramekins.

Combine oats, nuts, brown sugar, the remaining 2 tablespoons flour, cinnamon, and ginger. Drizzle over fruit mixture.

Place the ramekins on a baking sheet and bake until fruit bubbles and topping is golden—20 to 25 minutes.

Let stand 10 to 15 minutes and serve.

*Lemon Bars.*

## Acknowledgments

I am so grateful to the following amazing people whose input was invaluable in creating this book. At the top of my list is Linda Luft who eagerly tested 95% of the recipes and had friends and family critique them. With much gratitude, I thank my family: my husband Agustin for his recipes and cultural insights, my daughters Elicia Kniffin and Amanda Dashwood for their testing and retesting and discussions about food with me; their husbands Bobby and Ben respectively for reviews, grandsons Ty and Aaron who helped prepare and taste-teste numerous dishes, always giving an honest review, and their friends' (ages 6–8) opinions, whom my daughter Elicia invited for taste-testing events; my daughter-in-law Kim Taylor and my son Alex for their honest and thorough reviews, and her parents Ben and Mary Dong for Chinese cooking lessons, and grandparents Buck and Mable Dong who provided me with ingredients from their garden and instructions on how to prepare them; my sister-in-law Gloria Taylor, who shared family recipes, techniques, wonderful stories, and culture with me. Also a big thanks to other testers: joyful 7-year-old Calissa Perry who joined me in my kitchen to prepare and taste-test recipes, Jackie Ludwig, Toby Parks, Brad Kilburn, Carol Starr, Barbara Earling, Lloyd and Carol Smith, Chris Snodgrass, Alice and Burr Udall and the Sunday night diners. A huge thanks to Meg Beer who helped me through writer's block and provided me with current articles about food, and to Victor Beer, MD who discussed research studies with me and accompanied me on farm and market trips and provided a photo journal of the trips. Thank you, Judith Mattson for being a wonderful local food information resource. Words can't express my appreciation for local farmers Adam and Debbie Valdivia, C. J. Marks, Clay Smith, Jim McManus and Tina Bartsch, Joshua Koehn, and Nathan Watkins, Chris Duggan, and ranchers Dennis Moroney and Gregg Vinson, and olive oil producer Perry Rea, and the Food Bank's dedicated young farmers Franchesca Arevalos, Marianna Hauglie, Anthony Gallegos, and Trisha Gallegos all of whom spent their valuable time with me. I also want to thank gifted chefs Ryan Clark, Scott Uehlein, Elizabeth Mikesell, and Julio Hildago for giving of their time and sharing their delicious recipes. Thanks to Dominic Wallen who encouraged me to share my healthy recipes and backed my first book's publication, and John Heider who continues to promote my books. Special thanks also goes to Caroline Cook, not only for her editing skills, but testing recipes and providing valuable critiques; editor Lisa Anderson's voice of clarity; and my publisher Ross Humphreys and Susan Lowell Humphreys who put my family before my deadline when my brother Paul passed away.

## Anti-angiogenic Foods

Eat to Defeat Cancer™, an arm of the Angiogenesis Foundation, is a global campaign to crush the cancer epidemic by encouraging people to eat foods that starve cancer. Eattodefeat.org contains up-to-date research information, which guides you in choosing the most health-protective foods and how to prepare them.

### Fish
Flounder (sole)
Haddock
Halibut
Herring
Mackerel
Salmon
Sardines
Tuna

### Fruits
Apples
Blackberries
Blueberries
Cherries
Clementines
Cranberries
Grapefruit
Lemon
Nectarines
Oranges
Peaches
Pomegranate
Raspberries
Red grapes
Strawberries

### Herbs & Spices
Basil
Black pepper
Cinnamon
Flax seed
Garlic
Ginger
Ginseng
Lavender
Licorice root
Nutmeg
Oregano
Rosemary
Sesame seed
Tarragon
Turmeric

### Legumes
Lentils
Lima beans
Soybeans
Sword jackbeans
Tofu (soft, firm, dried, fried), miso, natto

### Mushrooms
Enoki mushrooms
King oyster mushrooms
Maitake mushrooms
Matsutake mushrooms
Oyster mushrooms
Reishi mushrooms
Shiitake mushrooms

### Nuts and Seeds
Cashews
Chestnuts
Pine nuts
Sesame
Walnuts

### Seaweed
Arame
Dulse
Kombu
Mozuku
Nori
Wakame

### Shellfish
Cuttlefish
Oysters
Sea cucumber
Shrimp and prawn
Squid and squid ink

### Vegetables
Artichokes
Beets
Bok choy
Broccoli
Brussels sprouts
Cabbage (red, savoy, white)
Carrots
Cauliflower
Chard
Endives
Kale
Mustard greens
Olives and olive oil
Onions
Parsley
Parsnip
Peppers
Pumpkin
Radishes
Salsify
Scallions
Shallots
Soybean sprouts
Spinach
String beans
Sweet potatoes and yams
Thistle
Tomatoes
Turnip and their tops
Watercress
Winter squashes

### Other
Dark chocolate
Green tea
Maple syrup

## For More Information

Ayerza, Ricardo, and Wayne Coates. *Chia: Rediscovering a Forgotten Crop of the Aztecs.* Tucson: University of Arizona Press, 2005.
www.azchia.com

Buettner, Dan. *The Blue Zones: Lessons for Living Longer from the People Who've Lived the Longest.* Des Moines: National Geographic, 2010.

Andrew Weil, MD
www.drweil.com

Angiogenesis Foundation
Eat to Defeat Cancer Campaign
William Li, MD
www.eattodefeat.org

Baja Arizona Sustainable Agriculture
PO Box 40935, Tucson, AZ 85717
(520) 331-9821, Bajaaz.org

Community Food Bank of Southern Arizona
3003 South Country Club Road, Tucson, AZ 85713
(520) 622-0525, communityfoodbank.com

Community Food Connections
www.foodconnect.org

Community Gardens of Tucson
www.communitygardensoftucson.org

Cornucopia Institute
www.cornucopia.org

Desert Harvesters
www.desertharvesters.org

Eat Wild
eatwild.com

Edible Communities
(800) 652-4217, ediblecommunities.com

Environmental Working Group
www.ewg.org

Gary Nabhan, father of the local food movement
garynabhan.com

The Heart Series
Charles Katzenberg, MD FACC, Edna Silva, RN
(520) 544-3720, www.heartseries.org

Local Harvest
www.localharvest.org

Locavores
www.locavores.com

Marine Stewardship Council
www.msc.org

Monterey Bay Aquarium Seafood Watch
www.montereybayaquarium.org/cr/seafoodwatch.aspx

Okinawa Centenarian Study, Okinawa Diet Plan
Makoto Suzuki MD PhD, Bradley Willcox MD, MS, Craig Willcox, PhD
okicent.org

Native Seeds/SEARCH
3061 North Campbell Avenue, Tucson, AZ 85719
(866) 622-5561, www.nativeseeds.org

Prevent and Reverse Heart Disease
Caldwell B. Esselstyn, Jr., MD
www.heartattackproof.com

Preventive Medicine Research Institute
Dean Ornish, MD
www.pmri.org

Slow Food USA
www.slowfoodusa.org

Sustainable Tucson
www.sustainabletucson.org

Tucson Organic Gardeners
(520) 670-9158, www.tucsonorganicgardeners.org

USDA Complete Guide to Home Canning, 2009
revisionnchfp.uga.edu/publications/publications_usda.html

# Index

## About the Author

JANET TAYLOR has spent over 30 years designing good food for her family, based on major research studies linking nutrition and good health. She is the author of the bestselling cookbook, *The Healthy Southwest Table.* Taylor and her husband live in Tucson, Arizona, where she prepares frequent meals for her children, grandchildren, and family friends—who taste-test all her recipes.